POLYHYMNIA

THE RHETORIC OF HORATIAN LYRIC DISCOURSE

GREGSON DAVIS

University of California Press
Berkeley · Los Angeles · Oxford

University of California Press
Berkeley and Los Angeles, California

University of California Press, Ltd.
Oxford, England

© 1991 by
The Regents of the University of California

Library of Congress Cataloging-in-Publication Data

Davis, Gregson.
  Polyhymnia : the rhetoric of Horatian lyric discourse /
Gregson Davis.
    p. cm.
  Includes bibliographical references and index.
  ISBN 0-520-07077-1 (cloth)
    1. Horace. Carmina.   2. Horace—Technique.
3. Odes—History and criticism.   4. Rhetoric,
Ancient.   I. Title.
PA6411.D34   1991
874'.01—dc20   90–49630
                                                          CIP

Printed in the United States of America

9 8 7 6 5 4 3 2 1

The paper used in this publication meets the minimum requirements of American National Standard for Information
Sciences—Permanence of Paper for Printed Library Materi-
als, ANSI Z39.48-1984. ♾

Contents

Preface

I have composed this account of the rhetorical dimension of Horatian lyric not merely for the initiated, but also for a broader audience of literary scholars. Within the narrower circle of specialists in classical philology I hope especially to speak to those who view the subdiscipline of literary studies as contributory, rather than tangential, to the ongoing critical discourses of our time. For the general community of literary scholars and critics, I hope to re-present a canonic lyric *corpus* in ways that attend closely to its rhetorical sophistication and argumentative subtlety.

The intellectual roots of my own hermeneutic practice lie both within and without the precincts of classical scholarship. On the one side, my basic approach to Horace's lyric oeuvre has been profoundly shaped by the pioneering researches of the late Elroy Bundy into the rhetoric of the Pindaric *epinikion*. Those of us who were privileged to attend his seminars at the University of California at Berkeley have universally been nourished by his peerless grasp of the workings of such rhetorical devices as the *priamel* and the *recusatio* within the European literary tradition. To a limited extent, *Polyhymnia* may be seen as carrying forward aspects of his seminal explorations in Greek poetry to the work of a major Latin bard. On the other side, I am no less indebted to modern linguistic theory—especially structuralism and pragmatics—for certain analytic concepts and methods. In my view, there is more common ground than is usually conceded between Bundy's systematic horizontal analyses of Pindaric motifs and the "synchronic" axes promoted by some practitioners of structuralism and semiotics; and the former's effort to ground rhetorical conventions in a covenant between encomiast and audience can be shown to intersect, at a certain level, with the notion of an implied contract between speaker and addressee in some accounts of pragmatics. I have conscientiously striven to acknowledge significant smaller debts to the formidable host of Horatian scholars at pertinent places in the text and notes. Given the gargantuan proportions of the secondary literature on Horace, however, I cannot claim to have done so in a fashion that is exhaustive.

Like most devoted teachers of the *Odes,* especially those whose hair is turning gray, I freely admit to an increasing appreciation of both the craft of the *Carmina* and what I take to be their philosophical substratum. The effect of translucency created by the former often belies the complexity and depth of the latter. In attempting to bring to the surface and expose aspects of both, I have had occasional recourse, in a somewhat eclectic manner, to technical jargon; but I have done so only where I have deemed it indispensable for precise exposition. The English "translations" that I have made of the copious Greek and Latin quotations embedded in the text are uniquely intended to make the non-specialist reader's task palpably easier. Horace, if anyone, has made me poignantly aware of the truth of the witty definition of poetry as "that which is lost in translation."

Tempus erat. . . . I wish to express my special thanks to the following: to the Stanford Humanities Center for an Internal Fellowship that enabled me to devote an entire year to the early stages of this book; to the many Stanford students in my Horace classes who have been the captive audience of my interpretations as they have been forged and refined over the years; to the late Jack Winkler, my former colleague, for his intellectual presence and encouragement, and for having made the fruitful suggestion that I should submit my completed opus to the University of California Press; to William S. Anderson, who made helpful observations, as well as timely and acute comments on the penultimate draft of the typescript; to the anonymous readers of the University of California Press for their constructive suggestions; and last, but by no means least, to my wife, Daphne, and to the children, Anika, Stephen, Julian, Oliver, and Sophia, to whom the final product is dedicated with love and appreciation.

Abbreviations

Bentley Richard Bentley, ed., *Q. Horatius Flaccus,*
vol. 1, 3d ed. (Amsterdam, 1728)

Brink Charles O. Brink, ed., *Horace on Poetry*, vol. 2,
The Ars Poetica (Cambridge, 1971); vol. 3,
Epistles Book 2 (Cambridge, 1982)

Bundy Elroy L. Bundy, *Studia Pindarica*, UC Publ
Class Phil 18, nos. 1 and 2 (Berkeley, 1962;
combined ed. Berkeley and Los Angeles,
1986)

Commager Steele Commager, *The Odes of Horace:
A Critical Study* (New Haven, 1962)

Ernout-Meillet Alfred Ernout and Antoine Meillet, *Diction-
naire étymologique de la langue latine*, 4th ed.
(Paris, 1959)

Fränkel Herman Fränkel, *Early Greek Poetry and Philosophy*, tr. M. Hadas and J. Willis (New
York, 1973)

Fraenkel Eduard Fraenkel, *Horace* (Oxford, 1957)

Gentili Bruno Gentili, ed., *Anacreon* (Rome, 1958)

Gow-Page Andrew S. F. Gow and Denys L. Page, eds.,
The Greek Anthology: Hellenistic Epigrams
(2 vols., Cambridge, 1965 [cited as *HE*]);
*The Greek Anthology: The Garland of Philip and
Some Contemporary Epigrams* (2 vols., Cam-
bridge, 1968 [cited as *GP*])

Housman James Diggle and Francis R. D. Goodyear,
eds., *The Classical Papers of A. E. Housman*
(3 vols., Cambridge, 1972)

Keller-Holder	Otto Keller and Alfred Holder, eds., *Q. Horati Flacci opera*, vol. 1, 2d ed. (Leipzig, 1899)
Kiessling-Heinze	Adolf Kiessling and Richard Heinze, eds., *Q. Horatius Flaccus Oden und Epoden*, 9th ed. (Berlin, 1958)
LP	Edgar Lobel and Denys Page, eds., *Poetarum Lesbiorum fragmenta* (Oxford, 1963)
L&S	Charlton T. Lewis and Charles Short, *A Latin Dictionary* (Oxford, 1879).
LSJ	Henry G. Liddell and Robert Scott, *A Greek-English Lexicon*, 9th ed., rev. H. Jones and R. McKenzie (Oxford, 1940)
Mitscherlich	Christoph W. Mitscherlich, *Q. Horati Flacci opera*, vol. 2 (Leipzig, 1800)
Morel-Buechner	Willy Morel and Carl Buechner, eds., *Fragmenta poetarum Latinorum epicorum et lyricorum praeter Ennium et Lucilium*, 2d ed. (Leipzig, 1982)
Nauck	Carl Wilhelm Nauck, ed., *Q. Horatius Flaccus: Oden und Epoden*, 14th ed. (Leipzig, 1894)
Nisbet-Hubbard	Robin G. M. Nisbet and Margaret Hubbard, *A Commentary on Horace: Odes Book 1* (Oxford, 1970) and *A Commentary on Horace: Odes Book 2* (Oxford, 1978)
OLD	P. G. W. Glare, ed., *Oxford Latin Dictionary* (Oxford, 1982)
Orelli	Johann K. von Orelli, ed., *Q. Horatius Flaccus*, vol. 1, 4th ed., rev. J. Baiter and W. Hirschfelder (Berlin, 1886)
Page	Thomas E. Page, ed., *Q. Horatii Flacci Carminum libri IV; Epodon liber* (Basingstoke and London, 1895)
Pasquali	Giorgio Pasquali, *Orazio lirico* (Florence, 1920)

Pfeiffer	Rudolph Pfeiffer, ed., *Callimachus*, vol. 1 (Oxford, 1949)
PMG	Denys L. Page, ed., *Poetae melici Graeci* (Oxford, 1962)
Porphyrio	Alfred Holder, ed., *Pomponi Porfyrionis commentum in Horatium Flaccum* (Innsbruck, 1894)
Powell	John U. Powell, ed., *Collectanea Alexandrina* (Oxford, 1925)
Ps.-Acro	Otto Keller, ed., *Pseudoacron: Scholia in Horatium vetustiora*, vol. 1 (Leipzig, 1902)
Schanz-Hosius	Martin von Schanz and Carl Hosius, *Geschichte der römischen Literatur* (Munich, 1914–35)
Snell	Bruno Snell, ed., *Pindari carmina cum fragmentis, pars 1: Epinikia*, 5th ed., rev. H. Maehler (Leipzig, 1971)
Snell-Maehler	Bruno Snell and H. Maehler, eds., *Bacchylidis carmina cum fragmentis* (Leipzig, 1970)
Syndikus	Hans Peter Syndikus, *Die Lyrik des Horaz: Eine Interpretation der Oden* (2 vols., Darmstadt, 1972–73)
W	Martin L. West, ed., *Iambi et elegi Graeci ante Alexandrum Cantati*, vol. 1 (Oxford, 1971)
Warmington	Eric H. Warmington, ed., *Remains of Old Latin*, vol. 2 (Cambridge, Mass., and London, 1936)
Wickham	Edward C. Wickham, ed., *Horace: The Odes, Carmen seculare and Epodes*, vol. 1, 3d ed. (Oxford, 1896)
Wickham-Garrod	Edward C. Wickham and H. W. Garrod, eds., *Q. Horati Flacci opera*, 2d ed. (Oxford, 1901)

Prologue

What I have said also makes it clear that the poet's task is saying not what happened but the kind of thing that might happen. . . . That is why poetry is at once more philosophical and more worthwhile [*spoudaioteron*] than history, since poetry tends to make universal statements, whereas those of history are particular.

Aristotle *Poetics* 1451b

The view of Horatian lyric discourse developed in this study derives from critical premises that are best enunciated at the outset, since they often run counter to prevalent assumptions about the poet's modes of organization. The Horatian ode has been so seminal, both in form and content, to the historical evolution of European lyric that it has been relatively easy even for erudite readers to take its organizational principles for granted and to yield to a kind of interpretative inertia born, in part, of unexamined assumptions. Where my proposed readings conflict substantially with some time-honored preconceptions enshrined in the exegetical literature, I have sought to clarify the ramifications of competing interpretations in a manner at once specific and non-polemical. A general overview of my guiding principles and procedures is, however, a necessary preliminary to the specific analyses that constitute the core of this book.

The *Horatius lyricus* who emerges in these essays may be characterized most aptly as a philosophical poet in the widest sense. The epithet *philosophical* may be misleading if it conjures up images of versified ratiocination or jejune argumentation adapted to metrical constraints. As a first approximation to my view of the poet as philosopher, I do not shrink from espousing the well-known Aristotelian judgment (cited as the epigraph to this Prologue) that draws a rudimentary distinction between historical and poetic discourse. Such a conception of the nature of the poetic task does not erase or

1

downgrade the importance of vivid and concrete representation. Thanks to Horace's superb pictorial gifts, Mount Soracte stands out sharply in our minds, as do the limpid waters of the Fons Bandusiae or the antics of the coquettish Licymnia. Graphic description, however, may function as a powerful vehicle of ideas in a poet who is deeply concerned with ethical values and for whom the particular exists, in the phraseology of the *Poetics*, "for the sake of the universal" rather than vice versa. Whether we are dealing with sympotic "foil" (a winter scene in the Soracte ode), an emblem of poetic inspiration (the fountain of Bandusia) or an incarnation of erotic lyric (Licymnia), the composer of the *Odes* is primarily engaged—so at least I hope to sustain—in conveying ideas and philosophical insights in a manner that is rhetorically persuasive.

A major predicate of these investigations, therefore, is that the *Odes* embody what I may refer to without fear of oxymoron as "lyric argument"—with a glance at the etymological sense of the Latin *argumentum* ("proof"). To see a poem as "proving" a point appears to go against the grain of entrenched neoromantic assumptions about the genesis and nature of lyric, but anyone who has looked at a facsimile of Keats's autograph of "Ode to a Nightingale" and observed the meticulous revisions and corrections inscribed therein would do well to ponder the paradoxical implications of Wordsworth's characterization of poetry as the "spontaneous overflow of powerful feelings." Whatever the emotional fountainheads of particular romantic texts may prove to be, it is clear that the feelings described in Keats's "Ode on a Grecian Urn"—to follow up my English lyric exemplar—are demonstrably supportive of the thought, and such gnomic utterances as "Heard melodies are sweet, but those unheard / Are sweeter" are, not merely digressions into the abstract, but pivotal stages in an ongoing argument. The New Critics and formalists of a generation or more ago rightly insisted on the inseparability of "form" and "content," not to mention the famous "heresy of paraphrase," but it would be a regrettable distortion of their critical legacy if we allowed these sound axioms to sponsor a devaluation of the ideational element in lyric poetry.

The poet of the *Carmina*, we may safely posit, desires to persuade. The discursive routes to persuasion are, however, manifold. Rather than proceeding by the more austere methods of syllogism,

Horatian lyric discourse typically "argues" a coherent nexus of ideas through nuanced variations in form and presentation. The building-blocks of these arguments consist of motifs, topoi, recurrent metaphors, and rhetorical conventions that, for the most part, are set forth paratactically. When one of Horace's major models, Sappho, abandons parataxis and introduces an illustrative exemplum with the words "It is easy to make this clear to all," she is merely bringing to the surface a discursive goal of "proving" her insightful proposition that "whatever one loves is the most beautiful" (16 LP, lines 3–6). Both Sappho and Horace frequently elide such overt delineation of the logical links between motifs in their poems. A paramount task of interpretation, therefore, is to unearth and reconstruct the underlying connections as well as the main lines of unfolding lyric arguments.

The enterprise I have adumbrated is fraught with hermeneutic perils, not the least of which is the justly notorious "intentional fallacy." My conception of the "lyric argument" obviously presupposes some form of intentionality: the lyrist is assumed to be interested in persuading the reader to accept a particular way of looking at the world. Though didactic intentions in an author's mind may be irretrievable, there is an important sense in which an intrinsic *rhetorical goal* may be said to be partly accessible in the text, and it is the latter kind of formally determined *telos* that is the primary focus of my analyses (cf. Geoffrey Leech 1983, 13). To illustrate tersely the difference between a limited, textually immanent rhetorical goal and an unverifiable authorial intention extrinsic to the text, let us briefly consider the case of the now well-described device that goes by the name of *priamel*.[1] No one who is familiar with the most common and easily recognizable form of this device ("some like X, others Y, I like Z") would balk at the inference that a stated preference on the part of the speaker is its ulterior goal. The device, in brief, contains its own internal logic—a logic manifest in a clear rhetorical sequence of foil and climax. Of course, poets may and do manipulate our patterned expectations by altering, postponing, and even deleting the climactic term; nevertheless the sense of "goal-directedness" inherent in the array of alternative choices persists despite truncations and radical abbreviations. Robert Frost's playfully perverse variations on the "cap" of the priamel are a succinct case in point:

> Some say the world will end in fire,
> Some say in ice.
> From what I've tasted of desire
> I hold with those who favor fire.
> But if it had to perish twice,
> I think I know enough of hate
> To say that for destruction ice
> Is also great
> And would suffice.
>
> (Frost 1969, 220)

In Horace's programmatic poem dedicated to Maecenas (*Odes* 1.1), an element of the foil foreshadows, by its content, the eventual preference stated in the final lines (19–22):

> est qui nec veteris pocula Massici
> nec partem solido demere de die
> spernit, nunc viridi membra sub arbuto
> stratus, nunc ad aquae lene caput sacrae.

There is the man who neither refuses cups of aged Massic wine nor shrinks from taking away a portion from the compact day, now lying with limbs stretched out beneath the green arbutus, now [reclining] near the gentle source of a sacred fountain.

This sophisticated insertion, which breaks the mainly pejorative tone of the surrounding foil,[2] imparts even greater emphasis to the poet's ultimate election of his elite "society" (to use Emily Dickinson's term) composed of nymphs, satyrs and fellow-poets in the Dionysian grove (28–34):

> me doctarum hederae praemia frontium
> dis miscent superis, me gelidum nemus
> nympharumque leves cum Satyris chori
> secernunt populo, si neque tibias
> Euterpe cohibet nec Polyhymnia
> Lesboum refugit tendere barbiton.

Ivy wreaths, recompense for learned brows, allow me to mingle with the gods above; the cool grove and the light songs of nymphs as they dance with Satyrs set me apart from the crowd, so long as neither Euterpe restrains the flutes nor Polyhymnia shuns from tuning the lyre of Lesbos.

Not all rhetorical goals are as overt as that encoded in even the most complex variations of the priamel form. A rhetorical ploy as superficially transparent as the so-called *recusatio*, for instance, can admit of disparate interpretations with regard to its presumed end. As I shall argue at length in chapter 1, the supposed aim of "refusal" probably masks an intent to *incorporate*, rather than utterly repudiate, matter traditionally regarded as alien to a particular literary orientation. Throughout the ensuing chapters of this book, the terms *aim, goal,* and *intent* invariably refer, not to the extraneous intentions of the historical author, but to the rhetorical goals inherent in a given formal device. My deliberate bracketing of the author carries far from trivial implications for the approach to the Horatian corpus I have adopted here. Lyric arguments are communicated, however obliquely, by "fictional delegates" (to borrow a narratological term) whose ideas and attitudes may or may not coincide with those of the actual historical personage. Other critics may feel confident that they know precisely what Q. Horatius Flaccus, as distinct from the artistic personality, thought and felt on a variety of topics. For my part, the paucity of verifiable and *autonomous* biographical information about ancient authors leads me to a radically agnostic stance in regard to such speculations.[3] Thus whenever in this study a first-person lyric voice is under discussion, I refer exclusively to an internal speaker. In my critical lexicon, such terms as *the poet, the lyrist,* and even, on occasion, *Horace* are all synonyms for this lyric speaker. In a word, the *persona* who is represented as singing his songs to the accompaniment of the lyre is the true focus of my interpretative attention.

The speaker of the *Carmina* has an identifiable "character" (*ethos* in Aristotelian terminology) that is rhetorically germane to the ideas he promulgates in various lyric contexts. The degree to which this *ethos* is consistently maintained in the universe of the *Odes* and *Epodes* is one of the more intriguing questions I hope to explore in what follows. The reader should be forewarned, however, that none of the assertions I make about the speaker's *ethos*, underlying philosophy, or sentiments are in any way to be confused with attempts at biographical reconstruction. Even (or especially) when it is most tempting to assume that a particular autobiographical incident (say, the poet's participation in the battle of Philippi) was transcribed without distortion from historical reality to the writing tablet, I shall adhere to a critical perspective that treats all such episodes as mediated by rhetorical dictates (chapter 2 discusses a number of such mediated experiences). My purpose in maintaining such analytic discrimination is not to deny the reality of such episodes, but rather to separate biographical experience (which may or may not be recuperable) from its representation in art. We may never know (nor would it be necessarily illuminating if we did) whether Horace actually discarded a shield during the rout at Philippi. We do know, however, that the lyric composer of *C.* 2.7 verbally aligns himself, through the topos of the discarded shield, with a tradition of early Greek lyrists who make virtually identical claims of battlefield conduct. An intertextual agenda designed to sponsor certain "lyric" as opposed to "heroic" values seems to be more pertinent to the shape and meaning of Horace's self-presentation than the brute historical data. The telescoping, omission, condensation, and, in general, deliberate distortion of events in the battle of Actium and its Alexandrian sequel in the Cleopatra ode (*C.* 1.37) provide another telling instance of poetic norms restructuring or even replacing historical "reality." It is worth repeating, however, what is surely a truism that dogs all positivist enterprises: historiography cannot arrogate to itself a superior order of objectivity polar to the subjectivity of poetic narration.

As with the speaker, the addressee in the *Odes* is most usefully regarded, in the first instance, as providing a context for lyric utterance. It is part of the necessary fiction of this dyadic lyric model of communication that the poet "sings" to a "hearer," single or multiple. In addition to contextualizing the performance, the formal naming of an addressee has a clearly dedicatory function. The proper name in the vocative case that punctuates the ode, usually in the opening strophe, ipso facto selects and compliments an *amicus*, while effectively serving to define that person as a worthy member of a lyric audience.

The fact that almost all Horace's designated "hearers" have proper names has tended to thicken the critical smoke that billows in the commentaries around the historical recipients of individual *carmina*. Attempts to interpret the *Odes* based on the assumption that documentable circumstances in the careers of particular addressees are a key to enigmatic passages have generally failed to win assent.[4] The typical structure of the *carpe diem* poem, for example, is manifestly independent of the peculiar biography of the named addressee. This is not to allege, however, that proper names in the *Odes* are always semantically inert. It is undeniable, for instance, that a few addressees have names that operate as part of a symbolic infrastructure ("Postumus" and "Grosphus" are instances of persons whose names are exploited for their etymological meaning in the text of odes addressed to them).[5] Comparative analysis of lyric arguments, however, supports the conclusion that the naming of the addressee does not substantially affect the organization of ideas in the *Odes*.

The complex topic of "intertextuality"—in the ordinary, rather than rigorously technical sense[6]—will be a dominant thread in the interpretations I undertake of individual passages and poems. As a recently translated work by Gian Biagio Conte (1986) has brought to the fore in relation to some major classical texts, the sophisticated set of practices variously referred to as "allusion" and "imitation" (not to mention "citation") pose serious theoretical problems for the criticism of poetic discourse. In my handling of such problems in Horace's *Odes*, I shall pay close attention to the *generic* implications of literary allusion. A working hypothesis that has proven fruitful to my investigations in this area is that, more often than not, the lyrist's references to previous poems and poets in the Greco-Roman tradition tend to promote issues of generic decorum. "Homer," for example, is likely to be invoked in contexts in which *epos* is represented as generic foil to *melos*. Thus when the speaker of the *recusatio* in *C.* 1.6 flatteringly dubs a contemporary poet, Varius, a "bird of Homeric flight," it would be a mistake for the reader to conclude that Horace regarded the actual poems of the historical Varius as equal to those of the poet of the *Iliad* (cf. Davis 1987b). Rhetorically, however, the hyperbolic linkage of Varius with Homer promotes the immediate goal of praise of the ruler. Though not every example of intertextuality is reducible to "arguments" about generic boundaries, I hope to establish that the discourse of the *Carmina* is often preoccupied, to a greater extent than is usually imagined, with a concern for such issues as stylistic propriety and thematic choice.

Each of the four substantive chapters that follow this Prologue is devoted to a major rhetorical strategy in the *Odes* and *Epodes*. I have designated these broad strategies "Modes," and my adjunct rubrics indicate what I regard as predominant rhetorical goals. Thus chapter 1 ("Modes of Assimilation") puts forth a radical reinterpretation of the *recusatio* that is the inverse of the conventional interpretation, which considers "refusal" as a sincere goal of the form. Chapter 2 ("Modes of Authentication") explores and analyzes typical ways in which the lyrist seeks to validate his utterances by constructing an *ethos* that is both credible and persuasive. Chapter 3 ("Modes of Consolation") investigates, within the framework of consolatory discourse, the shared infrastructure of odes that are commonly referred to as "sympotic" or "convivial." Chapter 4 ("Modes of Praise and Dispraise") examines some of the more indirect means by which Horace manipulates conventions of encomium and invective, primarily in terms of rhetorical categories discussed in the previous chapters. The remarkable versatility of convivial motifs, for example, in furthering both praise and blame is a principal target of my interpretation of such famous exemplars as the Cleopatra ode.

The chapter divisions of this study are by no means intended to suggest watertight typologies; rather, they point to strictly analytical categories. In practice, no less than in theory, the categories are inseparable and overlapping. Their separation is a purely heuristic device that bows to the exigencies of synchronic analysis. The ode to Teucer (C. 1.7), for instance, is simultaneously "assimilative" (it incorporates heroic figures and episodes into lyric discourse) and "convivial" (it consoles Teucer for his misfortunes through the instrumentality of *carpe diem* argument). On more than one occasion (e.g., *Ep.* 13; the aforementioned "Teucer" ode), my systematic postponement of a diachronic account is highly visible: a segment of the poem is first analyzed under one category, then later "revisited" under a different strategic modality. My long-term desire to present the poems as organic wholes is occasionally in methodological tension with the demands of synchronic analysis. I have striven throughout, however, to acknowledge and confront the claims of both critical axes of interpretation ("paradigmatic" and "syntagmatic" in semiotic jargon) in my account of the arguments of individual odes. The question of the historical order of composition of the poems is partly suspended in the analysis for the obvious reason that the semantic reconstruction of recurrent motifs does not crucially depend on inferences about chronological sequence.[7]

From what I have said above about the centrality of ideas in Horatian lyric, it follows that my approach to the age-old problem of "unity" is to posit an internal consistency at the rhetorical and ideational levels. This is not by any means a trivial issue, since Horatian scholars as eminent as Fraenkel and Pasquali have on occasion sought and demanded unity at other levels of lyric discourse, such as unity of "situation." The former has gone so far as to reprove the poet, in his well-known discussion of the Soracte ode, for violating a proclaimed allegiance to the canons of homogeneity (Fraenkel, 177). A crucial tenet of my own investigation, by contrast, is that the "situation" or "occasion" constructed by the lyrist in specific odes is itself one more counter in a larger argument. Adopting the metaphor of the "scaffolding" from some psychologists of language acquisition, I have instead espoused the view that such fictionalized situations are aids to the construction of an ideational building, which it is part of the business of the critic to reconstruct. Implicit in my borrowed metaphor is the observation that parts of the cognitive "scaffolding" may be abandoned in the course of the poem once their rhetorical raison d'être has been fulfilled—as is the case with the opening scene of the Soracte ode (see pp. 150–51 below). "Unity of place," from this vantage point, is an anachronistic yardstick (perhaps imported into Horatian criticism from neoclassical theories of dramatic composition based on misreadings of Aristotle's *Poetics*) that has engendered many pseudo-problems in the exegesis of the *Carmina*.

The stricter practitioners of deconstruction and related poststructuralist movements in contemporary criticism, who regard all forms of discourse as innately self-subversive, will, of course, be somewhat skeptical about the impression of solidity implied in this preliminary account of Horatian lyric discourse and will seek to uncover unsuspected cracks (unconscious "slippage" and ineluctable "supplements") in the ideological foundations of these lyric "arguments." It is no part of my overall purpose to insist on an unassailable logical solidity reposing on a univocal text. I shall, however, maintain the somewhat outmoded position that there is far greater coherence ("unity") at the ideational level in Horace's *Odes* than is usually conceded by the scalpels of most modern commentators and literary critics. In this comprehensive sense, this study should

go some way towards vindicating the hypothesis of organic composition against those formidable critics who have argued for het-
erogeneity and lax organization in many Horatian poems.

The grave charge of impulsive meandering that has been intermittently laid at Horace's door over the centuries bears a striking
resemblance to similar strictures leveled at Pindar in the critical tradition of the *epinikia*.[8] The defense of Pindaric poetry meticulously
mounted by the late Elroy Bundy can, in my judgment, be profitably applied, in respect to several of its main assumptions, to the
vexed question of "unity" in the Horatian *carmen*. An essential first
step in restoring credibility to Horace's muse, Polyhymnia, is to
reconstitute "from the inside out"[9] the basic rhetorical conventions
and strategies that contribute to the motif parsimony of these
splendidly compact lyric monuments.

Modes of Assimilation

My primary objective in this opening chapter is to offer a radical revision of the standard understanding of the *recusatio* and to redefine it as a rhetorical "mode of assimilation"—a device by which the speaker disingenuously seeks to *include* material and styles that he ostensibly precludes. By way of establishing the usefulness and validity of this reconceptualization, I shall discuss the so-called *recusatio* as part of a dialectical process in which "generic disavowals" (as I prefer to call them) appear as opening gambits in a wider strategy. My detailed investigation of the substructure of such disavowals will take place against the background of a preliminary analysis of other, less paradoxical, forms of assimilation, such as imitation and parody. I hope to show that generic disavowals are best elucidated within the general perspective of a poet's efforts to forge a distinct identity by *both* differentiating himself from *and* incorporating crucial facets of a prestigious Greek tradition.

GENERIC REMODELING

One of the more sophisticated modes of assimilation in Horatian lyric may be termed "generic remodeling." In this rhetorical ploy, the lyrist eschews overt "disavowal" of a rival genre; instead he employs the clever subterfuge of appropriating select features of the opposing genre within his lyric orbit. By remodeling these features in a radical way, he succeeds in integrating otherwise alien motifs and figures. As a point of departure for my investigation of this central mode, let us briefly examine an early example from the *Epodes*.

CHEIRON TO ACHILLES (*Ep.* 13)

Horrida tempestas caelum contraxit et imbres
nivesque deducunt Iovem; nunc mare, nunc silvae

Threicio Aquilone sonant: rapiamus, amici,
  occasionem de die, dumque virent genua
et decet, obducta solvatur fronte senectus.   5
  tu vina Torquato move consule pressa meo:
cetera mitte loqui: deus haec fortasse benigna
  reducet in sedem vice. nunc et Achaemenio
perfundi nardo iuvat et fide Cyllenea
  levare diris pectora sollicitudinibus;   10
nobilis ut grandi cecinit Centaurus alumno:
  "invicte, mortalis dea nate puer Thetide,
te manet Assarici tellus, quam frigida parvi
  findunt Scamandri flumina lubricus et Simois;
unde tibi reditum certo subtemine Parcae   15
  rupere, nec mater domum caerula te revehet.
illic omne malum vino cantuque levato,
  deformis aegrimoniae dulcibus alloquiis."

A horrible storm has contracted the sky, and rain and snow bring
down Jupiter; now the sea, now the woods resound with the North
Wind from Thrace: let us snatch, my friends, the opportunity from
the day, and while our knees are still in bloom and it is appropriate,
let old age be loosened from the contracted brow. You [my friend]
bring in the wine pressed in the consulship of my Torquatus. Leave
off speaking of other matters: a god perchance will restore this all to
stable calm with a benevolent change. Now it is pleasing to be
anointed with Persian nard and to lighten the heart of dreadful anxieties by means of the Cyllenean lyre-string; as the noble Centaur
once sang to his great ward: "O unconquered one, mortal child
though born from the goddess Thetis, the land of Assaracus [Troy]
awaits you, a land cleaved by the cool waters of the small Scamander
and the slippery Simois; your return from this place has been cut off
by the Fates with their unerring threads, nor will your azure mother
bear you back home. While there, be sure to lighten all your misfortune with wine and song, sweet consolations for bitter distress.

In its thematic layout, *Ep.* 13 conforms quite strictly to the binary
movement of the convivial ode (see chapter 3 below). In the first
segment of the poem, the awareness of human vicissitude justifies
the admonition to indulge in the symposium (1–10). In the re-
capitulatory second half (11–18), however, the poet introduces a
distinctly unorthodox comparison between the advice just given to
his companions, on the one hand, and that given once upon a time
by the centaur Cheiron to his heroic ward, Achilles.

Cheiron is, to say the least, an incongruous advocate of the
charms of lyric discourse. In making his paradoxical move, Horace

was, of course, thoroughly cognizant of the grandiose aura that enveloped the literary tradition of the "Precepts of Cheiron." In Pindar's *Pythian* 6.19–27 (Snell), to choose an example from a text very familiar to Horace, we find a specimen of the Centaur's verbatim advice to his illustrious pupil:[1]

> σύ τοι σχεθών νιν ἐπὶ δεξιὰ χειρός, ὀρθὰν
>   ἄγεις ἐφημοσύναν,
> τά ποτ' ἐν οὔρεσι φαντὶ μεγαλοσθενεῖ
> Φιλύρας υἱὸν ὀρφανιζομένῳ·
> Πηλεΐδᾳ παραινεῖν· μάλιστα μὲν Κρονίδαν,
> βαρύοπα στεροπᾶν κεραυνῶν τε πρύτανιν,
> θεῶν σέβεσθαι· ταύτας δὲ μή ποτε τιμὰς
> ἀμείρειν γονέων βίον πεπρωμένον.

Now you, keeping him at your right hand, maintain the order, the advice that, men say, Philyra's son [Cheiron] once imparted on the mountaintops to the great-hearted son of Peleus, when he was separated from his parents: to venerate above all other gods the son of Kronos, the deep-voiced minister of lightnings and thunders; and never to deprive his parents of such honors throughout their ordained life-span.

This Pindaric excerpt, in which an epinikian victor receives praise for emulating his father, may be taken as a model of the kind of grandiloquence and seriousness that surrounded the exhortations of Cheiron (see line 23, παραινεῖν: advise). It is with a certain mischievous tongue in cheek, therefore, that the poet of the *Epodes* conscripts the pedagogic centaur into his convivial service.

Far from deemphasizing, at the outset, the noble allure of his mythical exemplum, Horace ushers in his comparison by harping on the generic "otherness" of the characters (line 11): "*Nobilis* ut *grandi* cecinit Centaurus alumno" ("as the *noble* Centaur once sang to his *great* ward"). The two epithets I have italicized mark off the preceptor and pupil respectively as belonging to the domain of elevated discourse. Brusquely inserted into the light-hearted ambiance of the banquet scene, this collocation of noble personages momentarily strikes the reader as a startling intrusion from a foreign sphere. The conjunction *ut*, sandwiched between the two adjectives, promises an analogy between two seemingly disparate worlds. If the analogy is to attain credibility, the words of Cheiron must, we feel, assume an iconoclastic aspect.

As is to be expected, the content of Cheiron's prophetic chant (*cecinit*) turns out to be anything but the grandiloquent utterance promised by the resounding epithets that preface it. On the contrary, we are treated to a methodical *diminution* of the heroic environment that is the essence of "generic remodeling" as it occurs in the *Odes* and *Epodes*. A careful perusal of the centaur's speech reveals how thoroughly the poet of *Ep.* 13 has accomplished the task of whittling down the heroic figures to the modest proportions of a convivial set piece. In the first line of his quoted song, Cheiron addresses Achilles as *puer*—a designation that, however precise in narrative terms, has the effect of diminishing a hero who has been introduced as *grandis*, by the poet, and *invictus* by the embedded speaker himself. A similar lessening of status is discernible in the ironic juxtaposition of *mortalis* and *dea* (line 12).[2] Achilles' dual heritage of a divine and mortal nature is, of course, a grand Homeric theme and, as Whitman has notably argued, imparts depth and urgency to the hero's effort to give meaning to his existence during his abdication from the war (Whitman 1958, 181–220). The transposition of this grave theme to a sympotic setting, however, has the effect of giving a new meaning to Achilles' mortality. For if the mortal is destined to prevail over the immortal component of his heritage, then Cheiron's precepts can plausibly be slanted towards a powerful reformulation of the basic lyric premise that a meaningful engagement in life depends upon an enhanced consciousness of one's mortality. In expatiating on the mortality of his pupil, the master circuitously mentions a ruptured "homecoming" (*reditus* in line 15 renders the standard term for the coveted epic *nostos*); but the diction of the disclosure (with its echoes of Catullus 64) has a distinctly Alexandrian color.[3] As Cheiron's speech progresses, it becomes more and more evident through the permutations of tone and message that he has been brought into the poem as a proxy for the lyrist. The interchangeability of the two voices ("Horace's" and "Cheiron's") is marked in the text by the imperative future *levato* (17), which chimes, in a manner typical of Horace, with *levare* in line 10.

The centaur's adroitly worded forecast contains a *reductio* of epic so audacious as to cause bewilderment to commentators inattentive to the extensive remodeling that is taking place in the epode. In sketching the topography of Troy for his ward, Cheiron scandalously applies the epithet "small" (*parvi*) to the river Scamander (line 14). The resulting clash with the epic canon is so blatant (Homer, indeed, had used the epithet "great" to characterize the river, as, e.g., at *Il.* 20.73) that several philologists, including the redoubtable Housman, have been prompted to emend the received text (Housman, 104–5).[4] Housman's literary judgment failed, in this particular case, to apprehend that the *contradiction* of Homer—the deliberate inversion of scale from "great" to "small"—is precisely what the anomalous "citation" of Cheiron seeks to accomplish. Homer's *megas potamos* is a victim of generic assimilation: it must pay a heavy toll in order to accommodate to the dimensions of a lyric landscape. Gone is the mighty river that, when swollen to awesome proportions, presents a formidable adversary to the cosmic hero of *Iliad* 21. Shrunken in size, it can more readily take its place alongside that other "lyricized" stream, the "slippery" (*lubricus*) Simois (line 14). As with the Scamander, there is a transformation in the description of the companion river. Whereas Virgil, in stricter fidelity to the Homeric conception, was to describe the Simois as "violent" (cf. *Aen.* 5.261, *rapidum Simoenta*), that strange mouthpiece of the lyric muse, Horace's Cheiron, substitutes the image of a gentle rivulet.[5] The profusion of *u* and *i* vowels in the words depicting the diminished Homeric rivers makes the line mellifluous and enhances the impression of a pleasing, innocuous miniature. The overriding effect of these transformations of topography and manipulations of sound is to conjure up the vision, not of an imposing epic terrain, but of a typical *locus amoenus* of lyric discourse. The "cool streams" (*frigida flumina*) of a scaled-down Scamander that cleave (*findunt*) the Trojan land evoke a setting more suitable to pastoral than to heroic striving.

The rationale for such a complete redrawing of the Trojan environment is patent: in its scaled-down contours, it becomes the *locus* of a convivial celebration, comparable, say, to the banks of Tibur. It is in such an appropriately reduced context that Horace's Cheiron abandons his Polonius-like role, as we know it from Pindar's odes, and proceeds to enunciate the *carpe diem* injunction to imbibe wine as an antidote to human vicissitude. In performing this volte-face, the surrogate lyrist, Cheiron, does not omit the crucial element in an Horatian symposium—that is, poetry (*cantu*, 16). This adjunct to wine is material to the generic recasting of the centaur's precepts, since Achilles is being urged to become a total convert to the lyric way of life; in fine, to embody the paradigm, not of the epic hero, but of the composer of "sweet" discourse (*dulcibus alloquiis*, 18).

Horace's assimilation of grand matter into the *genus tenue* of *Ep.* 13 is all the more effective inasmuch as it brings into focus (and into question) the whole ethos of heroic endeavor—an ethos that Homer's Achilles himself had put to a drastic test when he withdrew from the fray and sought solace in the lyre and the feast with his companion Patroclus. What in Homer had been an aberrant and temporary gesture on the part of an aggrieved hero is transmuted, in Horace's subversive text, into a general principle of conduct, a prescription for a life-style made meaningful through "lyric" values (wine and song). The direct speech of Cheiron, then, is a masterstroke of generic remodeling, by which the poet contracts heroic themes and landscape in order to assimilate them, at a deeper level, to the argument of sympotic verse.[6]

Teucer to His Comrades (C. 1.7)

The consummate craft with which Horace reinterprets the experience of an archetypal epic hero in *Ep.* 13 bears a significant resemblance to the process by which another Homeric figure, Teucer, is unceremoniously appropriated into the texture of *C.* 1.7. In this complex convivial ode, which I shall analyze from a different perspective in chapter 3, an exemplum from heroic saga is also drafted into the argument to subserve the ends of a purely lyric consolation:

> Teucer Salamina patremque
>   cum fugeret, tamen uda Lyaeo
> tempora populea fertur vinxisse corona,
>   sic tristis adfatus amicos:
> "quo nos cumque feret melior fortuna parente,   25
>   ibimus, o socii comitesque.
> nil desperandum Teucro duce et auspice: Teucri
>   certus enim promisit Apollo
> ambiguam tellure nova Salamina futuram.
>   o fortes peioraque passi   30
> mecum saepe viri, nunc vino pellite curas;
>   cras ingens iterabimus aequor."

Teucer, though in flight from Salamis and his father, nonetheless bound, they say, his wine-soaked temples with a poplar wreath, and with these words addressed his sad friends: "Wheresoever fortune, better than a father, shall take us, let us go, O comrades and allies. You need not despair with Teucer as your leader and your prophet! For infallible Apollo has promised that there shall be a namesake Salamis founded by Teucer in a new land. O men of courage, who have often endured worse circumstances with me, now drive away your anxieties with wine; tomorrow we shall resume our journey over the vast sea."

As in his culminating "citation" of Cheiron, Horace here attributes to an epic figure words and values that are the hallmark of the convivial posture adumbrated earlier in the ode (15–21) with the words:

> albus ut obscuro deterget nubila caelo
>   saepe Notus neque parturit imbris
> perpetuo, sic tu sapiens finire memento
>   tristitiam vitaeque labores
> molli, Plance, mero, seu te fulgentia signis
>   castra tenent seu densa tenebit
> Tiburis umbra tui.

As Notus often turns to white and wipes away the clouds from a dark sky, nor brings forth rain showers continuously, so you in your wisdom remember to put an end to the sadness and the toils of life, Plancus, with a mellow unmixed wine, whether you are detained by the camp, gleaming with standards, or by the dense shade of your beloved Tibur.

In his exhortation, Teucer begins with an unconditional acceptance of vicissitude (*fortuna*, 25), which he is prepared to confront without despair. Unlike the Achilles of *Ep.* 13, he has been emboldened by a prophecy of Apollo that ensures him a new home, despite an originally abortive *nostos*. His essential strategy of consolation, however, is, like Cheiron's, to promote the symposium as a present and compelling panacea for past and future misfortune. The fact that his diction parallels the epic consolation of Aeneas to his storm-tossed companions (*Aen.* 1.199) serves to highlight the glaring appropriation, for the garlanded and wine-soaked hero (22–23) utters sentiments that closely echo those of the lyric speaker (cf. Santirocco 1986, 36–38).

Horace's generic remodeling of Teucer would have seemed especially subversive to a contemporary audience acquainted with Roman tragic drama, in which the story of the hero's disastrous return and expulsion by his father was a well-worn theme.[7] Epic and dramatic discourse are traditionally seen as affiliated in terms of stylistic elevation and subject matter. In this regard, the repetition of the name in line 27 may indicate more than the "proud self-confidence" of the speaker (Page *ad loc.*); for "Teucer," we recall, was not merely the proper name of an individual hero: in its plural form, the appellation refers generically to the "Trojans."[8] The speaker bears a name that calls attention to the "Trojan" legend itself, and his employment of the third person in reference to himself places that nomenclature on center stage. The speaker does not let us forget who "Teucer" is; on the contrary, he drums the name into our ears. The discrepancy between his heroic identity, loudly reiterated in the name, and the lyric attitudes expressed in his speech of consolation is therefore all the more scandalous. This image of Teucer as a prototypical symposiast is perfectly at home in the poetic ambiance created by Horace's version of the convivium.

Despite its stilted diction, Teucer's set speech has a lyricized aura, not least because he pronounces it while wearing a banqueter's wreath: *populea . . . corona* (23). The floral content of the *corona* in Horace's sympotic verse is more often than not thematically germane. The poplar was especially associated with the figure of Hercules, "to whom as a wanderer Teucer would offer sacrifice" (Wickham *ad loc.*). There is, however, an additional, important nuance in the association. Hercules had a legendary reputation for a more than hearty indulgence in food and drink—a proclivity that makes the choice of wreath especially apt. Like his devotion to the Bacchic source of inspiration (cf. *uda Lyaeo / tempora*), Teucer's moistened appearance attests to his novel role as ambassador of the realm of lyric. In terms of the underlying argument of the ode, the climactic "citation" of Teucer performs a function analogous to that of Cheiron in *Ep.* 13.

HORACE TO XANTHIAS (C. 2.4)

I have presented two illustrations of Horace's technique of "lyricizing" epic figures as a means of assimilating them into the disparate universe of convivial poetry. Cheiron, in addressing Achilles, and Teucer, in haranguing his comrades, articulate the fundamental outlook of the seasoned banqueter. To appreciate how extensively the technique is employed in the *Odes*, let us briefly compare an instance of partial generic assimilation in a short erotic poem, *Ne sit ancillae*.[9]

In a typically cogent discussion, Pasquali drew attention to the jocular tone of the ode as a whole, and persuasively demonstrated both its indebtedness to, and its departure from, kindred motifs in Hellenistic epigram (Pasquali, 489–95). While I acknowledge these important roots in conventional topoi, my main concern in the present inquiry is the peremptory manner in which the light love-lyric appropriates such intractable worthies as Telamonian Ajax and Agamemnon, in addition to Achilles. Though the reworking of weighty matter from epos is not as complete as in the foregoing examples, it is no less instructive for our purposes.

The first half of the ode (stanzas 1–3) contains a gentle admonishment of the addressee, buttressed by heroic paradigms:

> Ne sit ancillae tibi amor pudori,
> Xanthia Phoceu, prius insolentem
> serva Briseis niveo colore
>   movit Achillem;
> movit Aiacem Telamone natum   5
> forma captivae dominum Tecmessae;
> arsit Atrides medio in triumpho
>   virgine rapta,
> barbarae postquam cecidere turmae
> Thessalo victore et ademptus Hector   10
> tradidit fessis leviora tolli
>   Pergama Grais.

Do not be ashamed of your passion for a servant girl, Xanthias of Phocis; in days gone by the slave girl Briseis with her snow white complexion excited the passion of haughty Achilles; Ajax, son of Telamon, was excited by the beauty of the captive Tecmessa; the son of Atreus [Agamemnon] burned with love for a captured maiden at the very moment of his triumph, once the foreign troops had fallen at the hands of the Thessalian victor and Hector's death had rendered Troy an easier target for destruction by the war-weary Greeks.

By adorning the addressee with a pompous title ("Xanthias of Phocis"), the speaker sets the stage for the hyperbolic allure of the comparisons to follow. In supporting his advice not to be ashamed of one's passion for a slave girl, Horace marshals a trio of epic warriors notorious, at first blush, for their unyielding personalities, Achilles, Ajax, and Agamemnon.[10] All three of these formidable personages, Horace asserts, succumbed to an overwhelming passion for slave women. As if to underscore their subjugation to *amor*, the poet employs such powerful devices as anaphora, alliteration, and symmetrical word placing (cf. *movit Achillem*, 4; *movit Aiacem*, 5; *arsit Atrides*, 7). Thanks to the synthesizing talents of Pasquali, we are alerted to the fact that Horace was by no means original in borrowing epic figures for erotic-lyric precedents. Some of the details of the borrowing, as well as the subtle alterations, are relevant to our topic of generic remodeling.

The case of Briseis is particularly salient. Horace fleshes out the sparse Homeric portrayal with the precise information that Achilles' famous female captive was blond (*niveo colore*, 3). This demonstrably non-Homeric, Alexandrian import onto the scene neatly suits Horace's generic sleight of hand, which here takes on the external manifestation of a harmonizing of colors among the main dramatis personae: Xanthias (whose very name, derived from the adjective *xanthos*, signifies blondness); his sweetheart Phyllis (whom we learn in line 14 is *flava*—a Latin equivalent of the Greek *leukē*); and last, but not least, Achilles himself, who is specifically portrayed as blond (*xanthos*) by Homer, though this well-known feature is elided in the ode.[11]

The romanticization of Achilles' attachment to Briseis is an extrapolation from the rather discreet Homeric depiction of the relationship. Whether or not we concur with Whitman's opinion that Achilles was deeply enamoured of his concubine, it is fairly certain that honor (*timē*) was at least equally important as a factor motivating the Achilles of the *Iliad* to hold on to his female prize, whatever her physical attractions (Whitman 1958, 186–87). In the Horatian account, however, Achilles' former *insolentia*—the arrogance of the non-lover—gives way comprehensively before the superior force of erotic desire.[12] Thus both of the principals in Horace's first analogy, Achilles and Briseis, have been refashioned so as to be consistent with the atmosphere of "Alexandrian" erotic epigram.

The second example of an amorous warrior is Telamonian Ajax (lines 5–6), who was captivated by the beautiful Tecmessa. With

the anaphora of *movit*, Horace links the doughty Ajax to the senti-
mentalized Achilles of the opening stanza (the acoustic aspect of
the linkage being further emphasized by the jingling syllable *mo* in
the line: "*mo*vit Aiacem Tela*mo*ne natum"). The ponderous patronymic expression *Telamone natum* accomplishes more, in my view,
than a mark of identification, distinguishing this Ajax from the son
of Oileus; it also subtends an etymological play on "Telamon," a
name denoting "strap" and derived from a verb meaning "to hold
out," "endure." [13] Even that legend of immovability, Ajax, (so the
pun suggests) was ultimately "moved" by the beauty (*forma*) of his
captive. Since Ajax was notorious for stubbornness as well as for
staying power, his novel role as *amator* involves a total transformation—a point the poet intimates by juxtaposing the words *captivae
dominum*. In the erotic *servitium*, as it is conventionally treated in
Roman amatory verse, the roles of captor and captive are metaphorically inverted, with the result that Tecmessa has become *do-
mina* and Ajax her *captivus*.

The homogenization of Homeric heroes into mundane lovers
reaches a climax with the most outrageous example of all, that of
Agamemnon, the haughty leader of the Greek host. In a shocking
jeu de mots that would have delighted Ovid, the son of Atreus, who
set fire to Troy, is himself said to be "inflamed" with love (*arsit*).
Equally shocking, from the point of view of the dialectical opposition between love and war, is the circumstance that Agamemnon's
internal fires were lit at the very moment of his military victory (*me-
dio in triumpho*). Horace indulges in a similar play on the literal and
metaphorical senses of *ignis* in *Ep.* 14.13–14: "quodsi non pulchrior
ignis / accendit obsessam Ilion" ("but if the 'flame' that burnt besieged Troy was no more gorgeous"). [14] The speaker's resounding
roster of outstanding soldiers (Achilles, Ajax, Agamemnon) has
been converted, partly through the perverse fire metaphors, into a
parade of infatuated *amatores* in the banal "Alexandrian" mold.

The process of assimilation I have been discussing takes place
under the aegis of a mock-solemn style that becomes even more
elevated in the succeeding strophe (lines 9–12), in which a trailing
temporal clause (introduced by *postquam*) renarrates episodes from
the fall of Troy (cf. Nisbet-Hubbard *ad loc.*). In the course of the
selective renarration, we learn that the victory of the Greeks was
rendered considerably easier by the prior removal of Hector. To be

sure, the speaker's sarcastic detraction is not in itself an invention
of Horace; rather, he follows the venerable lead of his model, who
attributes the same sentiment to Priam at the point where he up-
braids those Trojans who attempt to dissuade him from the expedi-
tion to ransom Hector's body (*Il.* 24.239–46):

> "ἔρρετε, λωβητῆρες ἐλεγχέες· οὔ νυ καὶ ὑμῖν
> οἴκοι ἔνεστι γόος, ὅτι μ' ἤλθετε κηδήσοντες;
> ἦ ὀνόσασθ' ὅτι μοι Κρονίδης Ζεὺς ἄλγε' ἔδωκε,
> παῖδ' ὀλέσαι τὸν ἄριστον; ἀτὰρ γνώσεσθε καὶ ὔμμες·
> ῥηΐτεροι γὰρ μᾶλλον Ἀχαιοῖσιν δὴ ἔσεσθε
> κείνου τεθνηῶτος ἐναιρέμεν. αὐτὰρ ἔγωγε
> πρὶν ἀλαπαζομένην τε πόλιν κεραϊζομένην τε
> ὀφθαλμοῖσιν ἰδεῖν, βαίην δόμον Ἄϊδος εἴσω."

"Away with you, cowardly wretches. Do you not have grief at your
own home, so that you come to bother me here? Or are you dissatis-
fied that Zeus, son of Kronos, has given me the pain of losing my
best son? Yet you also will come to know the same; for you will be far
easier for the Achaeans to slay now that he is dead. But for my part,
may I go down to the house of Hades before I set my eyes upon the
city sacked and pillaged."

The lyric appropriation of Priam's remonstrance is most arresting
in a single detail: the choice of the comparative *leviora* (lighter) in
reference to the weakened citadel of Troy. The charge that the war-
weary Greeks (*fessis . . . Grais*) needed only to deliver a final coup
de grace to take the city clearly diminishes their glorious achievement. What is more, the pejorative *leviora* is marvellously consonant with the "lighter" generic constraints to which the entire
climactic episode has been artfully assimilated. In sum, the pedagogic speaker of the "light" love-lyric has built his humorous argument on the ruins of epic enterprise, having undermined military achievement and, conversely, glorified erotic submission. The
assimilative process, then, takes place mainly in the direction of
erotic lyric;[15] for if Xanthias of Phocis is indeed heroized, he pays
the same price that Achilles and the other worthies do—that is, he
is reduced by *amor* for his slave girl to a subordinate role as defined
by an "Alexandrian" erotic catalogue. The apparent upgrading is
laden, in retrospect, with irony and ultimately leads to a downgrading of all the heroic characters in the erotic scenario.

GENERIC PSEUDO-IMITATION

Generic remodeling, as I have delineated it in the previous section, entails a certain deformation of epic matter in the direction of lyric norms. A less radical mode of assimilation in the *Odes* is the selective renarration of heroic episodes with only minor alterations in treatment and stylistic level. This kind of pseudo-imitation, by its very nature, occurs when the episodes in question already have a common thematic denominator with canonic lyric concerns. By selecting for imitation epic motifs in which the heroic ethos is challenged from within the genre itself, the lyric poet can exploit his model by re-presenting those motifs with novel, self-serving emphases. One benefit of such an ingenious stratagem is to provoke the reader to reflect upon the critical differences between genres of narration in terms, not so much of style (which is, within limits, partially assimilated), as of worldview.

NEREUS TO PARIS (C. 1.15)

By way of illustration, let us consider that unique piece of unaddressed narration, C. 1.15:[16]

> Pastor cum traheret per freta navibus
> Idaeis Helenen perfidus hospitam,
> ingrato celeres obruit otio
>   ventos, ut caneret fera
> Nereus fata: mala ducis avi domum,   5
> quam multo repetet Graecia milite,
> coniurata tuas rumpere nuptias
>   et regnum Priami vetus.
> heu heu, quantus equis, quantus adest viris
> sudor! quanta moves funera Dardanae   10
> genti! iam galeam Pallas et aegida
>   currusque et rabiem parat.
> nequiquam Veneris praesidio ferox
> pectes caesariem grataque feminis
> imbelli cithara carmina divides,   15
>   nequiquam thalamo gravis
> hastas et calami spicula Gnosii
> vitabis strepitumque et celerem sequi

Aiacem; tamen heu serus adulteros
    cultus pulvere collines.   20

Non Laertiaden, exitium tuae
gentis, non Pylium Nestora respicis?
urgent impavidi te Salaminius
    Teucer, te Sthenelus sciens

pugnae, sive opus est imperitare equis,   25
non auriga piger. Merionen quoque
nosces. ecce furit te reperire atrox
    Tydides melior patre

quem tu, cervus uti vallis in altera
visum parte lupum graminis immemor,   30
sublimi fugies mollis anhelitu,
    non hoc pollicitus tuae.

iracunda diem proferet Ilio
matronisque Phrygum classis Achillei;
post certas hiemes uret Achaicus   35
    ignis Iliacas domos.

While the faithless shepherd was carrying off his hostess, Helen, over the seas in his Trojan ships, Nereus subverted the swift winds with an unwelcome calm, so that he might pronounce a savage doom: "Under an evil omen you are leading home a spouse whom Greece will seek to win back with a huge force bound and determined to shatter your nuptials as well as the ancient kingdom of Priam. Alas, alas, what sweat is in the offing for horses, what sweat for men! What destruction are you bringing on the Trojan race! Already Pallas [Athene] is preparing her helmet, her aegis, her chariot, and her wrath. In vain will you comb your locks, formidable by virtue of Venus's protection, and on your unwarlike lyre share songs that are welcome to women; in vain in your bedchamber will you avoid heavy spears, the darts of the Cretan reed, the battle-din, and Ajax, swift in pursuit; you will yet begrime with dust (alas, too late) your adulterous coiffure. Do you not heed the son of Laertes, who will cause your race to be destroyed, not heed Nestor of Pylos? Pressing upon you fearlessly are Teucer of Salamis and Sthenelus, who knows his battlecraft, and is no slouch, if ever as charioteer he has to govern a team of horses. You shall also get to know Meriones. See, the fierce son of Tydeus, more valiant even than his father, is madly seeking to find you. Delicate, your uplifted head gasping for air, you shall flee from him, like a deer forgetful of the pasture, when once it has seen the wolf in a separate part of the valley—you who promised your beloved a far different showing. Achilles' wrathful squadron shall postpone the day of reckoning for Ilium and for

Phrygian mothers; but after the predestined term of winters a Greek
fire shall burn down Trojan homes."

As renarrated in the Nereus "citation," the consequences of the ab-
duction of Helen reflect Horace's skill in exploiting generic expectations. Despite its complex "subtext," which I hope shortly to explore, the ode has suffered from unfavorable evaluations by many
leading Horatian scholars. According to the conventional wisdom,
Pastor cum traheret is an impoverished (and generically inappropriate) effort at narration in the grand manner, betraying signs of
immaturity and lack of polish.[17] Yet few poets are as openly self-
conscious about generic decorum as Horace; so we ought, as cau-
tious readers, to assume a more sophisticated rationale for the imitation. As long as the poem continues to be read as a naive attempt
to reproduce epic themes *tout court*, it cannot fail to come across as
superficial and ill-conceived. If, on the other hand, one pays close
attention to the generic implications of such motifs as Paris's devotion to the lyre (line 15), it becomes clear that C. 1.15 poses chal-
lenging questions about the true nature of a lyric, as opposed to an
epic, program.

To begin our more detailed analysis, it is important to stress,
with Wickham, that "the imagery of Horace's ode is really Homer's
rather than that of the Greek lyrists" (Wickham *ad loc.*). In terms
of a demonstrable pattern of imitation, the dominant frame of reference is Homeric epic. To be precise, there are no fewer than eight
unequivocal reminiscences of Homeric diction, most of them trace-
able to famous scenes in the *Iliad*.[18] From the point of view of "assimilation," then, the primary issue on our agenda is: what rhetorical gain does the poet of the *Carmina* derive from such a renarration,
conducted, as it is, within the channels of an unmistakably epic
diction? Since the ode is stylistically parasitic on epic norms, the
lyric transfusion here achieved is very different from the deliberate
reductions we have discerned above in connection with *Horrida
tempestas* and *Ne sit ancillae*. In place of systematic diminution (as
with the remodeling of Achilles to fit the scale of lyric enterprise),
we have the diametric contrary—amplification of the lyric horizon
to accommodate such grand motifs as the "wrath" of Achilles (cf.
iracunda . . . classis Achillei from the poem's final strophe). A com-

parison between the rehandling of the fall of Troy in *C.* 2.4 and *Pastor cum traheret* brings the difference sharply into focus: whereas the tired Agamemnon of the former text is "lyricized" by virtue of his untimely desire for the captive Cassandra, the awe-inspiring Greeks of the latter burn the citadel with vengeful (and decidedly non-figurative!) flames. Horace's rapprochement to heroic norms in this instance is all the more remarkable in view of the well-established bias in the lyric tradition towards treating the episode from the perspective of Helen, rather than that of her abductor (cf. Nisbet-Hubbard *ad loc.*).

It is against an undimmed and firmly drawn contour of epic grandeur that the portrayal of Paris in this ode takes on its special, ironic meaning. Nereus's credentials for such a rhetorical role are impeccable: he was an ancestor of Achilles (whose mother Thetis was a Nereid)—a point that Horace makes in *Ep.* 17.8 when he calls Achilles by the patronymic "Nereius." Although Horace's Nereus proceeds to purloin his damning critique of the Trojan seducer from the pages of the *Iliad*, he does so in a manner that underlines the paradox of that anti-hero's "lyric" life-style. The development of this supreme paradox repays a closer inspection, since it contains, in my view, the crux of the poem's argument.

The basis of Nereus's vehement vilification of Paris is the conventional "opposition," in the dialectical sense, between "love" and "war." The antinomy is brilliantly highlighted in the oxymoron *Veneris praesidio ferox* ("formidable by virtue of Venus's protection," 13); for what Paris manages to achieve with the help of the love-goddess is merely to comb his locks and thereby augment his physical appeal (*pectes caesariem*, 14). The martial epithet *ferox* thus acquires a set of inverted commas, rhetorically speaking—a point that becomes brutally manifest by hindsight when Paris is later likened to a "soft" (*mollis*) stag (32). By contrast, the truly formidable soldier is his superior adversary, Diomedes, who is allocated a non-ironic synonym of *ferox*—that is, *atrox* (line 27).

Thus far Horace's character portrayals as filtered through the surrogate voice of the sea-god are largely in keeping with the norms of Homeric narration. When, however, the speaker represents Paris as playing songs on his "unwarlike lyre" (*imbelli cithara*, 15), he introduces a note of complexity to the account. In addition to the opposition love/war, we now have the familiar disjunction lyric/war, which is dear to the composer of the *Odes*. We may recall that in his formal *recusatio* of epic in *C.* 1.6, Horace ostensibly declines to write an encomium of Agrippa's military exploits on the grounds that his "unwarlike" (*imbellis*) Muse prohibits such a generic impropriety (line 10): "*imbellisque lyrae* Musa potens vetat . . ." ("The Muse who controls my *unwarlike lyre* forbids . . ."). At first blush, the delinquent Paris appears to have something in common with the standard *persona* of the lyrist, insofar as he has chosen to compose *carmina* on the premier instrument that repudiates *bellum* in favor of erotic themes. Thus the line "imbelli cithara carmina divides" ("You will share songs on the lyre opposed to war")[19] resonates, with cunning irony, in a collection of *carmina* in which the author defines his lyric vocation by insisting on its "soft," antimilitaristic character (cf. *mollibus . . . citharae modis* in *C.* 2.12.3–4). An attribution that, throughout the text of the *Carmina*, is part of a positive, self-defining distinction between lyric, on the one hand, and epic, on the other, here receives a negative coloration in the context of an imitated epic scene. In this permutation, Paris represents the *perversion* of lyric discourse: a lover who mimics the lyric stance with his non-belligerent *cithara*, but whose resemblance to the authentic love-lyrist remains external and contingent. By such subtle means, Horace is able to exploit the Homeric original by renarrating a nodal episode in terms that differentiate the true from the false, the genuine lyric poet from the opportunist *poseur* who performs his *carmina* in the service of seduction.

The critique of Paris *qua* lyrist is taken a step further in the following stanza (lines 16–19) where the embedded speaker, Nereus, deploys a theme that is endemic to Horace's lyric: the futility of trying to avoid death:

> nequiquam thalamo gravis
> hastas et calami spicula Gnosii
> vitabis strepitumque et celerem sequi
> Aiacem . . .

in vain in your bedchamber will you avoid heavy spears, the darts of the Cretan reed, the battle-din, and Ajax, swift in pursuit . . .

The thought, which is reinforced by the repetition of the adverb *nequiquam* in asyndeton, may be paralleled from such gnomic statements as *C.* 2.13.13–20 and 2.14.13–16. By abandoning the arena of battle, Paris behaves in a way antithetical, at bottom, to both the Horatian (lyric) and the Homeric (epic) hero; for the former is under no illusion that death can be postponed or circumvented by shifting one's theater of operations from battlefield to bedchamber, while the latter is, in principle, willing to face death in pursuit of *aretē*. At a deeper level, therefore, the Paris of C. 1.15 turns out to be the antitype, not merely of Teucer and Diomedes, but of the philosophically grounded lyrist, whose *carmina* are rooted in an acceptance of mortality.

To conclude, the speech of Nereus, like the other examples we have perused of *oratio recta* in mythographic renarration, indirectly broaches issues that are germane to the vocation of "light" lyric. Horace, through the mouthpiece of his marine prophet, absorbs epic discourse into a lyric universe by the witty device of "fore-grounding" normally positive epithets, such as *imbellis* and *mollis*, in a context that imparts a negative allure. Whether or not we judge the poem to be chronologically early,[20] it cannot, on the account given here, be downgraded to a pointless exercise in imitation.

GENERIC DISAVOWAL (*recusatio*)

A complex form of assimilation (not generally recognized under this rubric) is one I propose to call "generic disavowal." The term *generic* here and throughout the remainder of this study signifies "pertaining to genre" and has an exclusively literary reference. The conventional label for this rhetorical strategy is *recusatio* ("refusal")—a modern designation, which, despite its widespread acceptance, is partly misleading.[21] In offering a revised account of a familiar device, I hope to reformulate the underlying principles at work and so provide a more adequate understanding of the Horatian (and, more broadly, Greco-Roman) praxis.

To begin with, the term *refusal* carries a misplaced emphasis. Taken at its literal value, *recusatio* implies an intention to *exclude* and, perhaps for this reason, many students of the form have supposed that the composers of such poems sincerely repudiate rival literary kinds. To assume such sincerity, however, is to confuse means and ends; for an ancillary objective of many proclaimed "refusals" is not to *exclude*, but, paradoxically, the opposite—to *include* generically disparate material while protesting vigorously against it. If inclusion under the guise of exclusion appears grossly illogical, the skeptic may be convinced by considering the closely analogous device of the *praeteritio*. In this familiar gambit, the writer makes the formal claim to "pass over" (exclude) irrelevant matter; but, as is well understood, he disingenuously includes it in the very process of specifying its contents. What is gained by this rhetorical contrivance is parsimony at the expense of literalness: the *praeteritio* is, at bottom, an ironic form of abbreviation. When, for instance, in the encomium of Drusus (*C.* 4.4), the poet parenthetically defers (*distuli*, 21) the topic of the exotic weaponry of enemy forces, he is essentially incorporating it in a brief digression (17–22):

> videre Raetis bella sub Alpibus
> Drusum gerentem Vindelici—quibus
>   mos unde deductus per omne
>   tempus Amazonia securi
> dextras obarmet, quaerere distuli,
> nec scire fas est omnia . . .

The Vindelici saw Drusus waging war beneath the Rhaetian Alps—
the origin of their custom, reaching back to time immemorial, of
arming their right hands with the Amazonian axe, I have refrained
from inquiring into, nor is it proper to know everything . . .

In declining to expatiate on the origin of the custom (*mos*), he has contrived nonetheless to feature it in a way that is not merely economical but also self-promoting; for by claiming to preclude irrelevant topics, he wins for the *laudator* the credentials of thematic decorum and good judgment.[22]

Like the more obvious *praeteritio*, which is common in forensic oratory, the more subtle *recusatio* often functions as a device of parsimonious "inclusion" in poetry that is restricted in length and therefore hospitable to methods of abbreviation. This is tantamount to asserting that "assimilation" constitutes the hidden program of most *recusationes*—an assertion that I hope to substantiate in the following pages. For this reason, I have chosen to promote the more cumbersome term *generic disavowal*, since *disavowal* more readily suggests an act of verbal protestation without regard to the issue of underlying sincerity. *Disavowal* properly emphasizes the discursive aspect of the device and thereby restores its underlying "paradoxical intent." Generic disavowal, in my revised schema, is the preliminary gauntlet in a highly sophisticated dialectical strategy. The speaker begins with a deferral and ends in a synthesis—hence my decision to invert the usual terms of reference and treat the operation under the category of "modes of assimilation." Seen as part of a total gestalt, stylized disavowals may be fruitfully analyzed in terms of the various ingenious ways in which they assimilate foreign motifs, styles, and literary kinds. In the remainder of this section, I shall examine pertinent aspects of the economy of several Horatian "disavowals," some of which have not previously been classified in the literature on the *recusatio*. My discussion will take into account the diversity of disavowed genres (elegy and iambus as well as epic), and will explore the principal methods by which the poet appropriates a differentiated "other." As a point of departure, let us consider some of the ways in which such appropriations are typically engineered.

ASSIMILATION BY TROPE
(C. 2.12 and C. 1.6)

The self-contradictory nature of generic disavowals in poetry is most apparent in an often overlooked stratagem that Horace employs with telling effect in the *Odes:* the climactic use of a key metaphor to rehabilitate, so to speak, a degraded facet of an opposing genre. Two salient instances, which I have discussed more fully elsewhere, may serve to clarify the procedure.[23]

Facili saevitia: Horace to Licymnia (C. 2.12)

In this ode, addressed to Licymnia, the speaker initially excludes, as generically inappropriate to the lyric genus, such proven epic themes as the Punic wars and the Gigantomachia (1–9):

> Nolis longa ferae bella Numantiae
> nec durum Hannibalem nec Siculum mare
> Poeno purpureum sanguine mollibus
>   aptari citharae modis,
>
> nec saevos Lapithas et nimium mero
> Hylaeum domitosque Herculea manu

> Telluris iuvenes, unde periculum
> fulgens contremuit domus
> Saturni veteris . . .

You would not want the long wars of fierce Numantia, nor hard Hannibal, nor the Sicilian sea reddened with Punic blood to be fitted to the soft measures of the lyre; nor the savage Lapiths and the wine-crazed Hylaeus and the sons of Earth subdued by the hand of Hercules, on which occasion the shining home of old Saturn trembled at the danger . . .

The catalogue of excluded types goes on to embrace not only historical and mythological epos, but also prose history on contemporary military achievements (9–12):

> tuque pedestribus
> dices historiis proelia Caesaris,
> Maecenas, melius ductaque per vias
> regum colla minacium.

and you, Maecenas, will tell more appropriately in prose histories of Caesar's battles, and of the necks of threatening monarchs being led through the streets.

The generic foil, which sometimes is restricted to a single rival kind, is here richly differentiated, though it is clearly the very last item in the list—a laudatory historical narrative—that the poet more particularly claims to decline. In graciously deferring to Maecenas, incidentally, Horace has included a radically abbreviated praise of Augustus. The first half of the poem, then, contains the formal disavowal of a pluralized generic "other" whose features are etched in a series of derogatory epithets such as "long" (*longa*), "fierce" (*fera*), "hard" (*durum*), "blood-red" (*Poeno purpureum sanguine*) and "savage" (*saevos*). Grammatically, these terms are applied to persons and places treated in the unnamed epic accounts, but they also carry a stylistic connotation, which is highlighted by the familiar opposition between *durum* (referring to the character of Hannibal) and *mollibus* (referring to the "soft" character of lyric verse).

In the second half of the ode, the poet avows his preference for love-lyric (*dulcis cantus*) and proceeds to laud the charms of his mistress, Licymnia (13–20):[24]

me dulces dominae Musa Licymniae
cantus, me voluit dicere lucidum
fulgentis oculos et bene mutuis
    fidum pectus amoribus,

quam nec ferre pedem dedecuit choris
nec certare ioco nec dare bracchia
ludentem nitidis virginibus sacro
    Dianae celebris die.

the Muse wanted me to tell of the sweet songs of my mistress, Licymnia; me to tell of her brightly shining eyes and her heart faithful
in a fully shared passion—a mistress for whom it is not unbecoming
either to perform in choruses, or to contend in repartee, or to link
arms in dance celebrations with the glowing band of girls on Diana's
festal day.

Not content, however, with unequivocally maintaining his sworn
allegiance in the generic competition, Horace makes a bold "foray"
(to anticipate the trope) into the opposing camp of epic: he recap-
tures the imagery of "savagery" that he had previously derided
(*saevos Lapithas*, 5), civilizing it, in the process, by the adjective *facili*
(21–28):

num tu quae tenuit dives Achaemenes
aut pinguis Phrygiae Mygdonias opes
permutare velis crine Licymniae,
    plenas aut Arabum domos,

cum flagrantia detorquet ad oscula
cervicem aut *facili saevitia* negat,
quae poscente magis gaudeat eripi,
    interdum rapere occupet?

Surely you would not want to exchange the holdings of rich
Achaemenes or the Mygdonian opulence of well-stocked Phrygia or
the Arabs' affluent mansions for a single lock of Licymnia's hair,
when she twists back her neck to receive blazing kisses, or with an
innocuous fierceness denies you kisses, which she takes a greater delight in having snatched from her than given on demand, and sometimes she herself preempts by snatching?

In a demonstrably large number of Horatian odes, as we shall
see throughout this study, the main argument is clinched by the
emphatic repetition of key cognate words. In the case before us,
the attribute "fierce" (*saevus*), which earlier modified the mytho-

logical Lapiths, is transposed, by a bold oxymoron, to an adverbial phrase describing Licymnia's coquetry. Thus two contrasting manifestations of "ferocity" are played off against each other in a surrounding context that appropriates other military metaphors (cf. *detorquet, eripi, rapere, occupet*). One consequence of the metaphorical co-optation of "bellicose" conduct is to reintegrate the more aggressive aspects of the disavowed entity. The manner of the co-optation suggests that the love-lyric, the preferred genre, is in some undefined sense all-inclusive and therefore, by subtle implication, superior. In this respect, the poem's argument may be said to rest upon a "synecdochic" claim—namely, that the part (the small genre) contains, at a figurative level, the whole experience (the larger genres).

Proelia virginum: Horace to Varius (*C. 1.6*)

A closely parallel mode of incorporation occurs in the classic disavowal of *epos* in *C. 1.6*. I shall revert to this ode in the following section when I come to inspect a different side of the assimilative *modus operandi*. For my immediate purpose, it suffices to single out the panache with which the lyrist paradoxically includes warfare in the alien domain of light, convivial themes by metaphorizing it as *proelia virginum* ("maidens' battles"):

> Scriberis Vario fortis et hostium
> victor Maeonii carminis alite,
> quam rem cumque ferox navibus aut equis
>   miles te duce gesserit:
>
> nos, Agrippa, neque haec dicere nec gravem   5
> Pelidae stomachum cedere nescii
> nec cursus duplicis per mare Vlixei
>   nec saevam Pelopis domum
>
> conamur, tenues grandia, dum pudor
> imbellisque lyrae Musa potens vetat   10
> laudes egregii Caesaris et tuas
>   culpa deterere ingeni.
>
> quis Martem tunica tectum adamantina
> digne scripserit aut pulvere Troico
> nigrum Merionen aut ope Palladis   15
>   Tydiden superis parem?

> nos convivia, nos *proelia virginum*
> sectis in iuvenes unguibus acrium
> cantamus vacui, sive quid urimur
> non praeter solitum leves.   20

You will be written about by Varius—a bird-bard of Homeric song—
as valiant and victorious over the foe, whatsoever exploit by ships or
on horseback the savage warrior has waged under your leadership;
we, Agrippa, attempt to tell neither of such matters, nor of the heavy
bile of Peleus's son, ignorant of compromise, nor of the wanderings
of shifty Ulysses over the sea, nor of the fierce house of Pelops—we
being too meager for such grand subjects—so long as modesty and
the Muse who controls the unwarlike lyre forbids me to demean the
praises of eminent Caesar and of yourself through a deficit of talent.
Who could write in terms worthy of the subject about Mars covered
in adamantine tunic, or Meriones blackened with Trojan dust, or
Tydeus's son, made equal to gods through the help of Pallas? We
sing of banquets, we sing the battles of ferocious young women,
their nails sharpened to fight young men, whether we are fancy-
free, or whether we are in some way inflamed, in our customary
light mode.

It is not by accident that the young girls who have sharpened their
fingernails for use as erotic weapons in the arena of love-battles are
assigned the epithet "fierce" (*acrium*); for like *saevus* in reference to
the house of Pelops (line 8) or to the Lapiths in C. 2.12.5, *acer* signifies martial ferocity (cf. *ferox* modifying the soldier in the rejected
themes of stanza 1). In this ode, no less than in the song devoted
to Licymnia, disavowal turns out, in retrospect, to be the opening tack in a sophisticated discourse whose sequel is metaphorical
absorption.

The assimilative technique I have partially dissected is by no
means original with the clever Augustan bard. One of Horace's
major models, Sappho, can be shown to have employed it with an
even greater degree of subtlety. A well-known text of the latter, 16
LP, contains an elegant example of figurative assimilation. In the
opening priamel (lines 1–4), despite the ostensibly neutral list of
others' preferences, there is an implicit disavowal, marked off by
the contrastive particles, of military display in favor of "whatever
one loves":

> ο]ἰ μὲν ἱππήων στρότον οἰ δὲ πέσδων
> οἰ δὲ νάων φαῖς᾽ ἐπ[ὶ] γᾶν μέλαι[ν]αν

ἔ]μμεναι κάλλιστον, ἔγω δὲ κῆν' ὄτ-
τω τις ἔραται·

Some say an array of cavalry, some of foot soldiers, some of warships
is the most beautiful sight on the dark earth, but I say: it is whatever
one loves.

Though Sappho does not explicitly refer to literary kinds, the
mention of an array of cavalry and of foot soldiers is sufficient to
evoke the appropriate heroic foil. The bifurcation into horsemen
and foot soldiers is, of course, a conventional polar "merism" that
serves to denote the whole rejected sphere.[25] The erotic arena is, as
often in love-poetry, dialectically opposed to the military, though
in this instance we view them from the perspective of their visual,
aesthetic appeal (*to kalliston*).

It is in a later stanza (lines 17–20), however, that Sappho reveals
her skill in the art of incorporation:

τὰ]ς ⟨κ⟩ε βολλοίμαν ἔρατόν τε βᾶμα
κἀμάρυχμα λάμπρον ἴδην προσώπω
ἤ τὰ Λύδων ἄρματα †κανοπλοισι
μ]άχεντας.

I would prefer to see her lovely gait and the bright sparkle of her face
than the chariots of the Lydians and [shield-bearing foot soldiers]

The imagery with which she clothes the description of her beloved, Anactoria, has a point of convergence with the martial spec-
tacles preferred by others: as Page has suggested, the *glitter* and
gait of the beloved girl are co-opted, in an elliptical way, from the
sort of glitter and motion that emanate from warriors' accoutrements on parade (Page 1955, 57). By her choice of metaphor, the
poet appropriates facets of the "other," while simultaneously reas-
serting her distance from it. The rhetorical ground of resemblance
to Horace's assimilative technique is far from negligible, though the
obliqueness and tact are vintage Sappho. A fine illustration of the
Roman poet's adoption of the form (and perhaps in this case, also
the content) of a Sapphic "appropriation" occurs in the Licymnia
ode (see above), where the speaker in praising his *puella* conspicuously redeploys the same participle, *fulgens*, that he used earlier to
describe the "disavowed" theme of the Gigantomachy (cf. "*fulgens
contremuit domus / Saturni veteris*" in lines 8–9 with "*fulgentes*

oculos" in line 15). In this regard, Horace is truly the successor to the lyric art (and artifice) of the Lesbian poets.

ASSIMILATION BY PARODY (C. 1.6)

In my analyses of various modes of assimilation, I shall frequently return to poems previously discussed in order to bring to light different, complementary aspects of their economy. Since the modes are structurally interrelated, they commonly overlap in the same poem. My method of investigation, on the other hand, obliges me to unravel separate strands in the tightly woven texture of the Horatian *carmen*. An ulterior objective of my inquiry is to understand poems as coherent wholes; hence it will often be necessary to spell out the relation of the separate strands to each other and to the total fabric. To this end, let us now revert to C. 1.6 (*Scriberis Vario*), which has already provided us, in the foregoing section, with a prime example of assimilation by metaphor.

As I have noted above, generic disavowal constitutes the major framework for metaphorical assimilation. Logically, an attribute must be openly disavowed in the text before it can be reintegrated in the manner I have sought to describe. The readoption of a previously disavowed image, however, may sometimes occur as the culmination of a process that has involved the poet in conscious parody of the foil genre. To elucidate the interaction between parody and figurative appropriation, it is instructive to reexamine the disavowal portion of C. 1.6. In the opening stanza of the ode, in which Horace ceremoniously defers to the epic poet Varius, the ground is prepared for good-humored parody, if not downright travesty, by the stilted appositional phrase that puts the latter on a par with Homer: *Maeonii carminis alite* ("bird-bard of Homeric song").[26] The speaker then goes on to unfurl a triple generic disavowal, marked off by the disjunctives *neque/nec/nec*. He unequivocally excludes (a) encomium on the military exploits of Agrippa, (b) *epos* on the Homeric model, and (c) tragic drama on the house of Pelops. The ostensible exclusion of encomium (a) actually promotes, as we have seen, the unstated purpose of abbreviated praise, since it implies that only a grand poem on an epic scale could match the grand exploits of the addressee. Where, then, does the element of parody enter in, and what does it contribute to the epideictic agenda?

An overtone of unmistakable parody permeates the description of the second generic foil, that of Homeric epic. What the lyric poet has done in disavowing epic discourse is to give a synopsis, bordering on travesty, of the stated themes of both *Iliad* and *Odyssey*. Thus the Iliadic "wrath [*mēnis*] of Peleus's son, Achilleus" is regurgitated as "the heavy bile [*stomachum*] of Peleus's son"—with the unflattering adjunct "ignorant of compromise" (*cedere nescii*); while the Odyssean "man of many resources who wandered much" is rendered irreverently by "the wanderings of shifty Ulysses over the sea." If the reduction of the Homeric *mēnis* to *stomachum* is marginally ludicrous, the stereotyping of the hero as unrelenting is a disparaging half-truth; for Homer's Achilles does indeed finally yield in the magnificent scene of the ransoming of Hector (*Il.* 24).[27] Similarly, by summing up Odysseus's resourcefulness in the pejorative epithet "shifty" (*duplex*), the speaker manages to distort that hero's character not so much by calumny as by omission. Through his parodic rewording of the two famous Homeric prooemia, Horace demonstrates, in an exaggerated way, the point he wishes to make about the effect of generic impropriety. Just as to rehandle the great bard's themes within the paltry confines of the lyric genre would, he argues, belittle those themes, so the composition of high-blown panegyric to Agrippa and Augustus would entail the "demeaning" of their achievements (cf. *deterere*, 12). The point of the parody, then, is one with the argument of the poem: it contains a *specimen* of disavowed matter, so rehandled as to make its generic incongruity grotesquely patent. That argument, no less than the modest stance that advertises it, is, of course, fundamentally duplicitous. As readers of the *Odes* are fully aware, Horace is quite capable in different circumstances of writing lyric encomia to the ruler or his victorious generals. His rhetorical aim in *C.* 1.6, however, requires him to argue for an innate incapacity on his part (*culpa ingeni*) to compose in the grand manner. He thereby circumvents a lengthy encomium while simultaneously bestowing a high compliment on the *laudandi*, Augustus and his general.

It is this ambivalent desire to "have one's cake and eat it too" that lies at the bottom of most Horatian disavowals. A basic misun-

derstanding of this paradoxical intent is the root cause of the per-
plexity that has bedeviled so much of the scholarly debate on the
meaning of the poem's penultimate stanza. The issue has centered
on the proper answer to the rhetorical question posed by the
speaker, "quis Martem . . . *digne* scripserit?" ("Who would do jus-
tice to the subject of Mars, etc.?"). Housman supposed the strictly
logical answer to be "no one" and therefore recommended an awk-
ward transposition of lines where some of his illustrious, though
equally literal-minded, predecessors had proposed radical surgery.
Fraenkel, in criticizing Housman et al., thought that the correct response was, "no ordinary person, and certainly not I." What these
various interpretations of Horace's rhetorical question conspicuously miss, however, is the *generic* dimension in the speaker's argument. As so often in the *Odes,* Horace is posing a question in terms
of representative *types,* where commentators insist on seeing only
particular individuals. In this sense, the appropriate response to
the question (and *a fortiori* the one that accords with the defined
issue of generic impropriety) is "only an *alter Homerus* like Varius"
and, as a corollary, "*no composer of light lyric verse* like myself" (cf.
Davis 1987b). The force of the adverb *digne* is to bring into prominence the issue of stylistic aptitude. The fact that the quoted specimen which the poet proceeds to display mimics Homeric diction
elegantly clinches the analogy between the skills required to compose a fitting panegyric and those required to rival Homer. In other
words, the "specimen" of quasi-Homeric battle scenes, like the earlier parodies in the second stanza, are designed to convey the notion that such grand matter is generically inappropriate. On the
other hand, as we have seen above, "battles" can indeed be accommodated to lyric on condition that they are metaphorized into
"battles of maidens." To lose sight of the generic factor, then, is to
obscure both the explicit terms of the disavowal and their assimilation through parody, imitation, and metaphor.

Parody is, at a certain level, a debased form of imitation. It is
therefore appropriate, at this juncture, to clarify the points of intersection, as well as the divergences, between the two modes of assimilation described here and in the previous section. Both parody
and imitation utilize the device of the *specimen:* a poetic sample of
the kind of poetry that is, on the surface, markedly disparate. But
whereas the imitated specimen seeks to blur, or even obliterate, con-

ventional generic boundaries, the parodied specimen tends to fore-ground generic difference. One lays stress on interchangeability and commonality of theme, the other on stylistic incompatibility. Underlying both stratagems is the will to "contaminate" lyric dis-course through the ruse of denial or artful mimicry.

DISAVOWAL OF ELEGY

So far I have considered techniques of parody and imitation solely in relation to disavowals of the grand manner. Epic poetry does not, however, comprise the unique foil for generic disavowals, de-spite the almost exclusive focus in the secondary literature on the paradigmatic rejection of heroic verse. Equally crucial to the poet-ics of the *Odes,* though less overt, is the devaluation of the elegiac genre through the artifice of the "parodied specimen." In this vari-ety of disavowal, the lyric *persona* distinguishes his own brand of love-poetry from the kind of amatory verse typified by such poets as Tibullus and Propertius. In stigmatizing elegiac discourse, Hor-ace often couches the difference between it and his own *carmina* in terms of inexperience versus emotional maturity, naïveté versus sophistication. Thus the generic confrontation sometimes assumes a non-literary alibi—the deprecation of other composers' values and erotic attachments.

MELIOR VENUS: HORACE TO TIBULLUS
(C. 1.33)

In an ode addressed to his poetic contemporary, Tibullus,[28] (*Albi, ne doleas*), Horace displays remarkable deftness in combining as-similation with disavowal. While dissuading the love-elegist from practicing his chosen genre, he succeeds both in disaffiliating him-self from elegiac discourse and in pretending to an earlier affiliation with it. The economy of the poem is handled through a network of literary allusions, verbal plays, and literary-symbolic nomenclature. Before going on to trace the intricacy of this network, let us cast a brief glance at the main literary stereotypes that dominate the open-ing lines (1–9):

> Albi, ne doleas plus nimio memor
> immitis Glycerae neu miserabilis

> decantes elegos, cur tibi iunior
> laesa praeniteat fide,
> insignem tenui fronte Lycorida
> Cyri torret amor, Cyrus in asperam
> declinat Pholoen; sed prius Apulis
> iungentur capreae lupis,
> quam turpi Pholoe peccet adultero.

Albius, lest you persist in grieving excessively, obsessed with sour Glycera, or in rehearsing your pitiable elegies, complaining that a younger rival outshines you in her eyes and that her fidelity has been impaired, be aware that desire for Cyrus scorches Lycoris, renowned for her petite forehead, while Cyrus, in turn, leans towards callous Pholoe; but surely roe-deer will mate with Apulian wolves sooner than Pholoe will have an adulterous affair with such a disreputable lover.

When the speaker ascribes the epithet "pitiable" (*miserabilis*) to the genre of elegy (*elegos*), he is, by common consent, following the popular etymology that connects it with the expression of doleful emotion. In the *Ars poetica* (line 75), Horace also takes for granted the link between name and nature in the constitution of "elegy"— a link that he seeks to typify by the use of the catchword *querimonia* ("complaint"). Like the epithet *flebilis* ("lugubrious") in C. 2.9, Horace's *miserabilis* purports to tap the very essence of the elegiac source. The play on the name of the genre is curiously silhouetted by the phrase that immediately precedes it, *immitis Glycerae*, which itself depends on an etymological *jeu*. "Glycera," whose name promises "sweetness" (from the Greek *glukus*) is given the epithet *immitis* ("unripe; sour"). The resulting oxymoron has the effect of marking the *contradiction* between name and nature. By contrast, the play on "pitiable elegies" in the same stanza points to a *coincidence* between name and nature. By juxtaposing these two different orders of *figura etymologica* early in the poem, Horace foregrounds the role that symbolic denominators are to perform in the ensuing verses.

The opening exhortations against grief (*ne doleas*) and elegiac song (*neu decantes*) are negative in more than a strictly grammatical sense: they decry a lack of *moderation*.[29] In very explicit terms, the addressee is enjoined not to go beyond proper limits (*plus nimio*) in his mourning; less explicitly, the compound verb *decantare* in line 3

("sing over and over again") may be taken in a disparaging connotation. To cap his dismal presentation of a poetry of self-pity,
Horace cleverly "cites," in an indirect question, the substance of
Tibullus's complaint: he is "outshone" by a younger rival (*cur tibi
iunior . . . praeniteat*). The cited specimen of lamentation functions
as a succinct parody of elegy with its stock refrain of bruised fidelity (*laesa . . . fide*). To judge by its overture, then, the ode assumes a
decidedly literary orientation, as it progresses rapidly from advice
to a love-sick fellow-poet (1–2), to generic devaluation (2–3), to pejorative citation (3–4).

The preponderantly literary dimension of the poem is strikingly
manifest in the names of the chief female figures in the erotic farce
adumbrated in the second stanza. It is hardly a coincidence that the
first woman mentioned in the "chain of love" (Pasquali's *catena di
amore*) bears the name "Lycoris"—the familiar pseudonym adopted
for his *puella* by the influential elegiac poet Cornelius Gallus. Surely
no alert member of Horace's literary coterie would have failed to
catch the generic significance of a notorious appellation like "Lycoris" in a poem whose opening salvo was a critique of *miserabilis
elegos*.[30] The other *puella* in the chain, Pholoe, possesses literary associations that are no less contextually apt (cf. Mitscherlich *ad loc.*).
Her namesake is to be found not merely in other Horatian odes, but,
even more pertinently, in a well-known elegy of the addressee,
Tibullus (1.8), where she is described as taking part in another erotic
"chain" involving the latter poet and a character named Marathus.
In fine, both "Pholoe" and "Lycoris" are appellations that convey
(and would probably have conveyed to a contemporary audience)
paradigmatic meanings in the literary scenarios of "pitiable elegies."

The two prominent literary allusions that circumscribe the motifs
of the second stanza are routinely documented in standard commentaries. The "chain of love," for instance, has been shown to
have a Hellenistic antecedent in Moschus, while the content of the
adunaton, "sooner may roe-deer mate with Apulian wolves" chimes
with a passage in Virgil's *Eclogues*.[31] What has apparently not received attention, however, is the *systematic* aspect of the allusions
and, more particularly, their joint contribution to the ongoing generic dialogue. Common to both references is a provenance in
bucolic *loci*. This generic extension to bucolic can hardly be considered otiose in a poem directed at an elegist who is distinctive,

among other things, precisely for his adaptation of *pastoral* conventions to erotic themes. The coherence of the intertextual frame appears all the more nuanced when we recall that Gallus's "Lycoris," who initiates the chain in line 5, is accorded a central position in Virgil's tenth eclogue—a poem that conspicuously plays the claims of elegy off against those of pastoral. The motival links established between these versions of pastoral (Moschus; Virgil) and elegy (Gallus; Tibullus) would not, in my judgment, have escaped the attention of the sophisticated poet-addressee.

From a formal point of view, the remainder of the ode consists in a gnomic statement concerning the nature of the erotic bond (10–12) and a pseudo-biographical sequel that is supposed to verify the gnome with a concrete instance (13–end):

> sic visum Veneri, cui placet imparis
> formas atque animos sub iuga aenea
>   saevo mittere cum ioco.
> ipsum me melior cum peteret Venus,
> grata detinuit compede Myrtale
> libertina, fretis acrior Hadriae
>   curvantis Calabros sinus.

So Venus would have it: she is fond of placing, with sadistic humor, incompatible bodies and minds under the same bronze yoke. I myself when sought after by a superior love, was detained in pleasant bondage by the freedwoman, Myrtale, a woman more harsh than the waters of the Adriatic where it bends to form the Calabrian gulf.

Unreciprocated love, we learn from the generalization, is caused by Venus's cruel delight (*saevo . . . ioco*) in yoking together disparate personalities and physical types (*impares formas atque animos*). In adducing himself as an example of the benighted lover, the speaker engineers a nimble about-face. Whereas he has hitherto distanced his persona from that of the elegiac *amator* by assuming the avuncular mask of teacher, he now confesses an earlier affinity with the type of the hapless gallant. The final "confession" mitigates the sharpness of the prior disavowal and allows the poet to assimilate an alien Eros in a measured way.

The comparable *Erlebnis* that Horace recollects by way of consoling the pathetic Tibullus is, however, crucially mediated by time: it is definitively in the past. The implication hovering over the reminder is that the wise speaker has now transcended that kind of immature "elegiac" enslavement. The typification of past experience is revealed in the choice of the name "Myrtale," which continues the game of significant nomenclature; for the myrtle plant is especially associated with the love-goddess, Venus, who, as we know from the apposite gnome, is ultimately responsible for the poet's plight. Myrtale, then, is a representation of Venus's penchant for cruel wit, which, in this case, acquires an ironic twist. Like Tibullus's "Glycera" who turns out, paradoxically, to be "sour" in her lack of compliance, Horace's "Myrtale" proves to be the inverse of the amorous female promised by her *nomen:* she is, we are told, "more harsh [*acrior*] than the waters of the Adriatic." As an emblematic counterpart to the ungentle "Glycera," the vehement "Myrtale" signifies the lyrist's closing gesture of assimilation. From a retrospective angle of vision, the gesture has been anticipated earlier in the poem with the concatenation of Greek names, all of which, with the exception of "Lycoris," are documentable in the rest of the *Odes* as lovers' appellations.[32]

If the foregoing line of interpretation is valid, the cryptic locution *melior Venus* in the final strophe acquires a somewhat wider significance than is generally conceded to it. The comparative *melior* has an obvious relevance to social class, since Myrtale is designated as a *libertina*.[33] In addition to her social position, however, the "superior" lover who goes unnamed may be imagined as embodying certain desirable qualities in which the fictive "Myrtale," a stereotyped *hetaira*, may be presumed to be deficient—for example, fidelity and "mildness." In the last analysis, the speaker's confessed failure to follow a "superior love" during his past elegiac *servitium* may buttress the claim of greater maturity on the part of the lyric *amator*.

QUERULA TIBIA: HORACE TO ASTERIE
(C. 3.7)

When he calls upon a leading practitioner of elegy and professes to dissuade him from composing *miserabilis elegos*, Horace appears at his most explicit in confronting lyric with elegiac norms of discourse. He is also capable of utilizing more covert means of making invidious generic comparisons. As H. J. Mette (1961), for instance, has succinctly argued, it is a cardinal, though unstated, principle of Horatian lyric that human *mores* are often represented as indissociable from literary tastes. A presumed correlation between style and moral values undergirds many odes that, on the surface, seem to be founded on trivial or flippant prescriptions of conduct. A conspicuous example is *Persicos odi,* which, though apparently a trivial expression of tastes in wreaths, purveys a compact argument in favor of the plain style (see pp. 118–26 below). Built into several Horatian lyric harangues on matters of erotic behavior is a programmatic discrimination of literary values. A lucid illustration of this double critique is to be seen in that tour de force of elegant wit, *Quid fles, Asterie (C. 3.7).*

> Quid fles, Asterie, quem tibi candidi
> primo restituent vere Favonii
>   Thyna merce beatum,
>   constantis iuvenem fide,
>
> Gygen? ille Notis actus ad Oricum   5
> post insana Caprae sidera frigidas
>   noctes non sine multis
>   insomnis lacrimis agit.
>
> atqui sollicitae nuntius hospitae,
> suspirare Chloen et miseram tuis   10
>   dicens ignibus uri,
>   tentat mille vafer modis.
>
> ut Proetum mulier perfida credulum
> falsis impulerit criminibus nimis
>   casto Bellerophontae   15
>   maturare necem, refert:
>
> narrat paene datum Pelea Tartaro,
> Magnessam Hippolyten dum fugit abstinens;
>   et peccare docentes
>   fallax historias monet.   20
>
> frustra: nam scopulis surdior Icari
> voces audit adhuc integer. at tibi
>   ne vicinus Enipeus
>   plus iusto placeat, cave;
>
> quamvis non alius flectere equum sciens   25
> aeque conspicitur gramine Martio,
>   nec quisquam citus aeque
>   Tusco denatat alveo.

prima nocte domum claude neque in vias
sub cantu querulae despice tibiae, 30
    et te saepe vocanti
    duram difficilis mane.

Why do you lament, Asterie, for Gyges, whom in early Spring the
sky-clearing breezes of Favonius will restore to you, blessed with
Bithynian goods, a young man of constant faith? He, driven off
course to Oricum by south winds after the Goat's mad stars arose,
spends cold nights deprived of sleep and not without copious tears.
And yet the messenger sent by his amorous hostess, reporting that
Chloe sighs and in her wretchedness burns with desire for your
lover, tempts his virtue deviously by countless means. She relates
how a faithless woman drove gullible Proetus by means of false
charges to advance the day of death for the too-chaste Bellerophon:
she tells the story of Peleus who was almost consigned to Tartarus
when in his abstinence he shunned Magnesian Hippolyte; and she
deceitfully recounts cautionary tales that inculcate cheating. To no
avail: for deafer than the crags of Icaros he listens to her words with
his integrity still intact. But for your part, be wary lest your neighbor
Enipeus be more attractive to you than is proper; although no other
youth is generally seen to be as adept at guiding the horse over
the turf of the Campus Martius; nor does anyone swim as quickly
down the Tuscan waterway. In the early evening close up your home
and do not look downwards into the streets at the sound of the
plaintive flute and, though he often calls you "harsh," continue to
be unresponsive.

Thanks to the meticulous spadework of Hans Peter Syndikus,
the full scope of Horace's redeployment of clichés from love-elegy
in this ode has been abundantly disclosed (Syndikus, 98–102). All
the principals in the erotic intrigue exhibit attitudes and conduct
that are typical of the conventional elegiac "situation": Asterie laments (*fles*) the absence of her lover, Gyges; he, for his part, is tear-
ful and spends cold, sleepless nights of anguish ("non sine multis /
insomnis lacrimis"); Chloe, a would-be rival of Asterie, is anxious,
full of sighs and wretched (*sollicitae; suspirare; miseram*); Enipeus, a
potential rival of Gyges, serenades Asterie on the lugubrious flute
(*querula tibia*). This schematic overview of the dramatis personae in
no way exhausts the ramified elegiac texture of the poem. In sum,
the web of conduct that the speaker is at pains to build up is spun
with the worn threads of erotic-elegiac stereotypes.

To observe the proliferation of elegiac topoi is an important and necessary first step in exposition. An adequate rhetorical account of the ode, however, must go beyond the compilation of parallels with *Liebeselegie* so as to unravel the programmatic purport of such a conglomerate of motifs. As a first approximation to unpacking Horace's compressed program, let us examine the terms of the implied critique of elegy in relation to the four main characters in the erotic configuration.

To begin with, Asterie, the addressee of the *carmen*, receives the most extensive portrayal. As I have sketchily noted above, she is initially depicted as indulging in inappropriate grief—inappropriate because inspired by a misapprehension of Gyges' true circumstances. She unnecessarily suspects Gyges of infidelity, while in fact (so the speaker reassuringly asserts) he has remained loyal to her. In the surprise denouement of the poem, which is marked by a resumption of the personal address to Asterie (cf. *at tibi* in line 22 with *quem tibi* in line 1), she is pointedly warned not to be overly attracted to her neighbour Enipeus ("ne *plus iusto* placeat").[34] By intimating that she herself is severely tempted by a persistent suitor, Horace partially undermines her posture of extreme misery over her lover's imagined inconstancy. Asterie, we may cautiously infer, is perhaps guilty of what in modern psychotherapeutic parlance is known as "externalization": she unwittingly masks her own (unacknowledged) attraction to her handsome suitor under the guise of an extreme concern for the absent lover. Horace's delicate critique of her behavior is, from a psychological perspective, penetrating.

Recurrent as a kind of leitmotif in the speaker's portrait is an astrological "code" that is inaugurated with the symbolic name "Asterie." The "stellar" aspect of the lover includes, as Nauck shrewdly saw, her physical glitter (Nauck *ad loc.*). The reader cognizant of Horace's fondness for onomastic games will also bring into play the locution "mad stars of the Goat" (*insana Caprae sidera*)—the meteoric sign of the inclement weather that detains her hapless paramour at Noricum; especially since "sky-clearing breezes of Favonius" (*candidi . . . Favonii*, 1–2) have earlier been prognosticated as harbingers of his return. In the verbal persiflage of the speaker, it is an occasion for sardonic wit that a seafaring lover with eyes firmly fixed on a distant "Asterie" should be led off course by "mad stars" of a more mundane kind. In spite of her symbolic name, then, the glittering and potentially fickle "Asterie" is incapable of interpreting the celestial signs signaling changes in the weather, and by extension, changes in the circumstances of her vagrant sailor-lover. In this light, the poet's injunctions in the final stanza further advance the ludic dimension, for "Asterie," who fittingly opens her elevated window in the early evening (*prima nocte*), is admonished not to cast her eyes downward (*despice*) on the seductive scene below. To complete the sidereal perspective of Asterie vis-à-vis her aspiring lover, there is a hint of quasi-hymnal diction in the reference to *te saepe vocanti* in the penultimate line.[35]

Horace's facetiousness at Asterie's expense is multi-layered and mildly disparaging. In the corresponding case of Gyges, however, there has been some unaccountable myopia in the secondary literature concerning the poet's tone. Despite some counterindications in the text, the portrayal of Asterie's lover is largely perceived as sympathetic. The most significant discrepant note, in my view, pertains to Gyges' supposedly unshakable loyalty in matters amorous. It is true that the omniscient speaker assures us in the second strophe that Gyges is a young man of "constant faith" (*constantis fide*). The conscious archaism of the genitive *fide*, however, adds to the hyperbolic aspect of the declaration; and in adverting for a second time to this trait (*integer*) the speaker cautiously qualifies it with the adverb *adhuc* (line 22).[36] The qualification is disturbing, if not damaging to the image of eternal fidelity. Gyges, it seems, resists powerful temptation, but his vaunted constancy turns out to be contingent after all. The innuendo that limits his resolve to the present seems marginally insidious because it is postponed to the end of an exaggerated declaration of fidelity that conjoins a metaphorical cliché (*scopulis surdior*) with a ludicrously pronounced oxymoron (*surdior audit*). The fact that the same oxymoron occurs in Euripides' *Medea* (line 28) and in *Ep.* 17.54 points in the direction of stylistic affectation and suggests that the speaker may, in Shakespeare's immortal phrase, "protest too much." As against the prevailing opinion about the couple, according to which a virtuous male is contrasted with a frail female, it is my contention that there is no marked asymmetry, in the text, between Asterie and Gyges in respect of constancy; on the contrary, the poet reveals the latent analogy in the two situations of temptation and the erotic vulnerability of both characters.

Gyges' "integrity" is subject to other forms of qualification in the poem, chief among which are his *name* (resoundingly placed at the beginning of a stanza) and his *occupation* (mentioned even before we learn the name). To begin with the latter, it is a truism of the *Odes* that rich merchants fare badly in the array of vocational stereotypes. The *mercator* who braves stormy seas to make a profit is given short shrift in Horace's scale of values (cf. C. 1.1.15–18). To make matters more suspect, the philosophical lyrist consistently denigrates the pursuit of Mammon for its own sake throughout the *Odes*. It is therefore far from accidental, given the speaker's penchant for onomastic conceit, that Asterie's star-crossed lover should be given a name that is virtually synonymous in Greek literature with excessive wealth. In a famous Archilochean fragment, for instance, the *persona* rejects the "super-rich Gyges," as being too distant, in favor of the proximate ("what is before the eyes").[37] Since Archilochus is a seminal model for Horace, it is at least arguable that the dismissal of the distant Gyges in the familiar Greek text is here being brought into play with the sentiment expressed in the adage, "out of sight, out of mind." In addition to the semantic cargo of the notorious name, our "Gyges" is specifically characterized as a highly successful trader ("Thyne merce *beatum*"), so the reader is left wondering whether his true felicity resides more in the possession of profitable wares than in romantic bonds.

As far as "Chloe" is concerned, her name itself (*chloē*: "first shoot") is the signifier of her youth—a factor that, despite her putative matrimonial status, makes her even more threatening as a rival to Asterie.[38] Our view of her amorous disposition is mediated through the reported speech of her messenger (*nuntius*) in stanzas 3–5. Notwithstanding the oblique character of the resulting portrait, the words of the *nuntius* are clearly designed to reflect the profile that the sender of the message (Chloe) wishes to convey. We are ironically encouraged to imagine Chloe in terms of her own (manipulated) self-presentation—that is, as a typical elegiac lover described with such catchwords as *misera; sollicitare; suspirare; tuis ignibus uri* (9–11). The implied critique of love-elegy here reaches a level of refinement that is exquisitely realized in the modality of indirect narration. It is especially pertinent to my interpretation that the messenger's words cunningly involve the technique that I have

been denoting by the rubric "assimilation." What the *nuntius* contrives to do in renarrating the grand temptations of heroic figures is
analogous, on the surface, to the kind of generic appropriation I
have delineated above; for the Bellerophon episode is transposed
from a well-known passage in Homer, while the Peleus-Hippolyta
exemplum is indebted to the Pindaric account in *Nemean* 4.[39] The
tradition of inverting the moral lessons of heroic sagas by reediting
them into pretexts for adulterous conduct is itself an elegiac topos
well attested in Propertius and others.[40] In the present context, the
semantic deformation of the heroic tales acquires a special modulation because it is editorialized by the authorial voice (cf. "peccare
docentes *fallax* historias monet," 19–20; and "perfida credulum,"
13). The internal narrator, then, practices a kind of duplicitous appropriation in the interest of an immoral liaison.

   The lover whose portrayal rounds off the quartet (and the ode)
receives the suggestive river-name "Enipeus."[41] If Nauck's observation is correct, "Enipeus" may be connected in popular etymology
with *enipto* ("upbraid"). His further speculation to the effect that as
a river-name it is suggestive of sound (*crepans: der Rauschende*) is
attractive in view of the young man's persistent and agonizing serenade. Amorous river-gods are often typecast in Greek mythology
as aggressive, if not prone to rape. In the case of Enipeus, as Nicola
Festa has shown, there was in circulation an erotic tale in which the
god Poseidon assumed the form of the Thessalian river in order to
rape the nymph Tyro (Festa 1940, 65–69). The poet's advice to Asterie may therefore contain a diluted hint at the potentially violent
proclivities of her suitor "Enipeus." Whether or not we acknowledge an undercurrent of aggression inhering in the Greek name,
there is no doubt of the persistence, or of the athletic ability, of Asterie's wooer. The second-to-last strophe mischievously advertises,
in a concessive clause, the impressive credentials of Enipeus, but it
does so through the medium of trite amatory topoi of praise.[42] The
amusing finale presents us with perhaps the most hackneyed scenario of all: a mournful serenade intoned by an *exclusus amator.* To
be sure, the shut-out male lover singing querulous songs to the accompaniment of an oboe is not exclusive to love-elegy (cf. Copley
1956), but taken in concert with the other generic tonalities in the
ode, the motif of the *exclusus* provides a suitable closure to Horace's
disavowal of immoderate (elegiac) lament.

The lyric voice of C. 3.7 is detached and clinical. The speaker is mysteriously prescient as well as periscopic: he knows what is happening to the absent lover in Epirus and even forecasts his safe restitution; he is even able to divine the content of Chloe's message to Gyges. His omnipresence is spectacularly evident when he switches the scene from Epirus to the immediate vicinity of Asterie. In consonance with this privileged status, he dispenses lofty advice to the conflicted *puella*. Whereas all the members of the erotic quartet are caught in a net of illusion and frustrated desire, the lyric *praeceptor* is alone capable of separating illusion from reality, and true from false *historiae*. Horace's "warning to a tempted woman" (to borrow a caption of Pasquali) is a minor masterpiece of generic disavowal that refuses to admit elegiac discourse except at an exorbitant price. In contradistinction to the deprecatory ode addressed to Albius Tibullus, there is no mitigating gesture of commiseration; instead the lyrist elects to contemplate the chain of immature (elegiac) patterns of behavior from a superior vantage point (cf. Quinn 1963, 154–58).

FLEBILES MODI: HORACE TO VALGIUS
(C. 2.9)

Non semper imbres nubibus hispidos
manant in agros aut mare Caspium
   vexant inaequales procellae
     usque, nec Armeniis in oris,

amice Valgi, stat glacies iners   5
mensis per omnis aut Aquilonibus
   querceta Gargani laborant
     et foliis viduantur orni:

tu semper urges flebilibus modis
Mysten ademptum, nec tibi Vespero   10
   surgente decedunt amores
     nec rapidum fugiente solem.

at non ter aevo functus amabilem
ploravit omnis Antilochum senex
   annos, nec impubem parentes   15
     Troilon aut Phrygiae sorores

flevere semper. desine mollium
tandem querelarum, et potius nova
   cantemus Augusti tropaea
     Caesaris et rigidum Niphaten,   20

Medumque flumen gentibus additum
victis minores volvere vertices,
    intraque praescriptum Gelonos
    exiguis equitare campis.

Not without cease do the rains drip from the clouds onto shoddy
fields or irregular squalls harass the Caspian sea; nor does the lifeless ice persist, Valgius my friend, on the fringes of Armenia
through all months of the year, or the oak stands of Garganus strain
under blows from the north wind, or ash trees stay bereft of their
leaves. You without cease, however, carry on over the death of
Mystes in mournful measures, nor do your "Love-songs" decline either when Vesper rises or when he flees the rapid sun's approach.
Yet even old [Nestor], who had lived through three generations of
men, did not lament his beloved son, Antilochus, incessantly, nor
did his parents or his Phrygian sisters mourn without cease for
young Troilus. Cease at last your effete complaints, and rather let us
sing together of the new trophies of Augustus Caesar, and of the
snow-packed Niphates, and of the Euphrates river added to the pool
of conquered tribes and rolling in diminished eddies, and the Geloni
riding within circumscribed bounds over reduced plains.

Horace's exhortation to his respected fellow-poet Valgius is distinguished both for the lucidity of its organization and the cohesion of its literary allusions. As a comprehensive disavowal of the
elegiac genus, it is no less remarkable for the diversity of its "foil,"
in which lyric, didactic, and encomiastic paradigms are marshaled
into a countervailing force to *flebiles modi*. For convenience of treatment, I shall follow the quadripartite plan that is staked out by the
poet's well-placed grammatical markers: (a) *non semper* (1); (b) *tu semper* (9); (c) *at non . . . semper* (13; 17); (d) *desine . . . tandem* (17; 18).[43]

The first main segment of the ode, which comprises the two
opening stanzas, brings into play, by way of generic foil to elegy,
several favorite motifs of the lyric *carmen* as practiced by Horace.
The cross-references would, of course, have been recognizable to
Valgius, who was a prominent member of the literary circle around
Augustus and Maecenas that included Virgil and Varius (cf. *S.*
1.10.82). The contrapuntal arrangement of representative lyric motifs is manifest at two levels: the philosophic and the imagistic. To
commence with the latter, Horace interweaves into the second
stanza at least three images borrowed from his own well-known
Soracte ode (*C.* 1.9). the following tabulation makes the correspondence manifest:

stat glacies iners	flumina *constiterint* acuto
querceta . . . *laborant*	silvae *laborantes*
et foliis viduantur *orni*[44]	nec veteres agitantur *orni*

Considered in isolation, the parallels with the imagery of the Soracte ode may be thought to be accidental echoes; taken in concert, however, and in the surrounding ideological cadre, they amount to a systematic pattern of cross-reference.

The lyric speaker is at pains to inculcate a general, philosophical insight that complements the specific self-allusions to C. 1.9. The point of the variegated examples from nature[45] is the master-principle of alternation: no one state prevails for ever (*semper*). Precisely, then, as in the Soracte ode, frozen winter landscapes and storms both on land and sea merely mark unwelcome swings of the pendulum. The ethical conclusion that humans ought to draw from the contemplation of nature's oscillations is that they should adjust their emotional life to its rhythm. To mourn incessantly, the poet contends, is to deny the intrinsic cyclicality of nature and therefore to ignore limit and vicissitude. In a later chapter of this volume, I shall explore the wider implications of this important "vicissitude motif" for Horace's philosophical outlook. In the context of his chastening verses to his friend Valgius, it is sufficient to stress, along with the emphatic textual signpost, *nec semper*, the speaker's grounds for denigrating the immoderate expression of grief. By opting for a kind of "metaphysical revolt," the ceaseless mourner betrays a fundamental defect in worldview—a defect that is responsible for his failure to observe, and respond in a mature way to, change. From this perspective, the two opening strophes clearly expose the epistemological bedrock of all Horace's convivial poetry—that is, the unqualified acceptance of alternation. The same message is also conveyed in the Teucer ode in quite similar language: "albus ut obscuro deterget nubila caelo / saepe Notus neque parturit *imbres* / *perpetuo*" (cf. the phrase *nec semper imbres*). It is clear that Horace is repeating ideas and images that are fundamental to his version of *carpe diem* poetry.

The ethical critique of the addressee's conduct is soon revealed as having a crucial *literary* dimension. As I have already reiterated, life and literature form an indissoluble nexus in the *Odes*, so it comes as no surprise to learn in the next portion (lines 9–11) that Valgius is a composer of love-elegies ("urges *flebilibus modis*"). Syndikus has cogently emphasized the precise focus on Valgius *qua* elegist that emerges from such quasi-technical epithets as *flebilis* and *mollis* (line 17). In addition, it is highly plausible that the plural *amores* (line 11) is meant to denote a conventional title of a collection of love-elegies (cf. Ovid's *Amores*), and not merely the actual "passions" of the historical Valgius. The latter was, indeed, as we glean from assorted sources, a versatile author whose poetic works may have encompassed bucolic as well as elegy.[46] It suits Horace's rhetorical objectives, however, to present his friend as a prototypical *elegiac* mourner—to equate his poetic manner (in a consciously reductionist way) with that of a Tibullus or a Cornelius Gallus. By narrowly focussing on the addressee as a monotonous composer of *flebiles modi* (cf. the kindred expression *miserabilis elegi* in the ode to Tibullus), the clever speaker can suggest a correlation between defective insight, immoderate lament, and literary predilections. An important consequence of the resulting antinomy between (lyric) acceptance and (elegiac) non-acceptance of alternation is the devaluing of elegiac *amores* as being seriously flawed at the core.

The intergeneric badinage is by no means restricted to the upgrading of *carmina* in relation to *amores*. The lyrist adds further complexity to the literary horizon when he introduces the first of several significant allusions in the poem to *loci* in Virgil's *Georgics*. The words Horace deploys to describe Valgius's uninterrupted lament ("nec tibi Vespero / surgente decedunt amores / nec rapidum fugiente solem") are distinctly reminiscent of Virgil's diction (and vowel music!) in the famous Orpheus-Eurydice episode in the fourth book of the *Georgics* (lines 465–66):

> te, dulcis coniunx, te solo in litore secum,
> te veniente die, te decedente canebat.

you, sweet spouse, you he sang by himself on the lonely shore; you as the day began, you as the day declined.

To what end, in terms of the poem's argument, does Horace superimpose Virgilian overtones on the melancholic outpourings of Valgius? To allude to an admired passage in the writings of a mutual

friend and poet in a context that, as we have seen, makes invidious generic comparisons, would seem, on the face of it, counter-
productive, if not in questionable taste. Horace's ulterior motive in
imparting an "Orphic" flavor to Valgius's effusions is both facetious and sophisticated: the Orpheus myth functions as a kind of
Alexandrian coda to *Georgics* 4—a sentimental idyll that shares certain underlying values with elegiac discourse, such as immoderate
grief, a radical negation of change, and a refusal to accept the death
of a beloved person. Thus the transposition of Virgilian colors from
the sentimental context of the Orpheus tale to the elegiac canvas of
Valgius's mourning is richly significant. By this allusive technique,
Valgius's muse is artfully affiliated with a mythological episode that
"digresses" most clearly from the main pseudo-didactic path of the
poem as a whole. The erotic digression, as filtered through the elegiac mode, is later to be played off, in Horace's ode, against other
passages in the *Georgics* that adhere to the norm of didactic, public-
spirited encomium.

   With its deeply etched antithesis, *tu semper* (cf. the opening *non
semper*), the third strophe launches into more corrosive criticism of
flebiles modi. A crucial ingredient in the ensuing blend of literary allusion and philosophical ethos is the patent symbolism of the
nomen fictum, Mystes. Apart from the routine observation that
"Mystes" signifies "initiate," the exegetical literature has been silent, to the best of my knowledge, on the relevance of the ideas
surrounding the concept of "initiation" to the thematic import of
the passage. Modern annotators, in particular, have tended to di-
vert attention away from the name's pertinence into the tangential
byways of a putative affair between Valgius and his slave boy.[47] Yet
the prevalent and often repeated assumption that "Mystes" is the
real name of Valgius's lover contravenes a standard elegiac convention, according to which the beloved who inspires erotic elegy is
usually given a fictive, *literary* name. If Horace is alluding in the
expressions *flebiles modi* and *amores* to the love-elegies of Valgius (a
hypothesis that is highly plausible) then we are bound to read
"Mystes" as an adopted name for the *amatus* (real or invented).
The obvious consequence of this inference is that, as in the case of
all such erotic sobriquets in Latin elegy, the name would have been
selected for its connection with divine (especially Apolline) patrons of song (see note 32). "Mystes," in fact, appears as a cult-

epithet of Apollo, as well as of other deities.[48] In the semiotics of elegiac love-names, it is entirely consonant with convention that "Mystes" should connote the beloved in his aspect as instigator (Muse) of amatory verse.

In extraliterary terms, "Mystes" is a ritual title that has special significance in mystery religions, such as the Orphic and Dionysiac cults. In this respect, the title may be borne by human neophytes as well as divine protagonists. There exists a well-established Greco-Roman tradition that posits a metaphorical affinity between mystery cults, on the one hand, and the poetic vocation, on the other—a tradition to which Horace playfully subscribes in the two "Bacchus" odes (*C.* 2.19; 3.25). Thus we are led by either route (religious cult-name or elegiac convention) to the same conclusion: the appellation "Mystes" is marvellously congruent with the rhetorical context of an *amatus* celebrated in *Amores*.

In redirecting interpretive attention to the literary-symbolic code, we may profitably inquire whether the topic of "initiation" is also coherent, in a non-trivial sense, with the specifics of Horace's argument. The answer to the question is positive, provided we remain alert to the thematic implications of the Virgilian "tag" from *Georgics* 4 mentioned above. Orpheus, as recounted by Virgil, is the mythical archetype of the figure who not only transgresses metaphysical boundaries (life/death), but also comes into head-on conflict with the female initiates of Dionysus, the bacchants.[49] Through the association with the Orpheus myth, Valgius's "mournful songs" for his "lost Mystes" are both apposite to those of the poet-musician for the lost Eurydice and, at the same time, similarly exorbitant. From a philosophical standpoint, however, excessive mourning for a deceased "initiate" (*mystēs*) is deeply paradoxical, in view of the fact that the paramount reward of initiation into the mysteries is to transcend human limits and earthly existence, and to gain privileged entrance into the eternal cycle of death and rebirth. If *nomen* is indeed meant to be *omen* in this case, then to mourn *Mysten ademptum* is singularly out of tune with the metaphysics, though in tune with the immature posture, of Virgil's Orpheus. Thus Horace's continuing critique of the protracted mourner effectively exposes an internal contradiction between poetic denomination (*mystēs*) and incommensurate elegiac emotion (*flebiles modi; mollium querelarum*).[50] At the same time, the addressee's dis-

tance from the lyric stance, which is based on the opposite premise—the philosophical acceptance of death—becomes even more
pronounced.

Horace began the ode by contrasting lyric insight and restraint
with elegiac lack of moderation. In the final segment (13–17),
in which the framing words *non* . . . *semper* are preceded by a
strongly adversative *at*, he extends the generic counterpoint even
further by appropriating cautionary episodes from the realm of
epos. In this deliberately ironic extension to another rival genre, the
act of annexation belongs to the benign category I have discussed
above as "assimilation by imitation." To be sure, consolatory topoi
are notoriously promiscuous and do not respect generic compartments. Homer's Achilles, for instance, who himself learns to master his overwhelming grief for Patroclos, delivers a famous speech
to the mournful Priam in which he adduces the exemplum of
Niobe (*Il.* 24.599–620):

> "υἱὸς μὲν δή τοι λέλυται, γέρον, ὡς ἐκέλευες,
> κεῖται δ᾽ ἐν λεχέεσσ᾽· ἅμα δ᾽ ἠοῖ φαινομένηφιν
> ὄψεαι αὐτὸς ἄγων· νῦν δὲ μνησώμεθα δόρπου.
> καὶ γάρ τ᾽ ἠΰκομος Νιόβη ἐμνήσατο σίτου,
> τῇ περ δώδεκα παῖδες ἐνὶ μεγάροισιν ὄλοντο,
> ἓξ μὲν θυγατέρες, ἓξ δ᾽ υἱέες ἡβώοντες.
> τοὺς μὲν Ἀπόλλων πέφνεν ἀπ᾽ ἀργυρέοιο βιοῖο
> χωόμενος Νιόβῃ, τὰς δ᾽ Ἄρτεμις ἰοχέαιρα,
> οὕνεκ᾽ ἄρα Λητοῖ ἰσάσκετο καλλιπαρῄῳ·
> . . . .
> ἀλλ᾽ ἄγε δὴ καὶ νῶϊ μεδώμεθα, δῖε γεραιέ,
> σίτου· ἔπειτά κεν αὖτε φίλον παῖδα κλαίοισθα,
> Ἴλιον εἰσαγαγών· πολυδάκρυτος δέ τοι ἔσται."

"Your son, elderly sire, has been released as you requested, and lies
upon a bier. As soon as dawn appears, you shall see him yourself as
you bear him away. Now, however, let us attend to supper. For even
the fair-haired Niobe attended to her supper, though twelve of her
children perished in her halls—six daughters and six sons in their
prime. The sons were slain by Apollo, in his anger at Niobe, [with
arrows] from his silver bow; the daughters by Artemis the archer,
because Niobe had compared herself with Leto of the lovely cheek.
. . . But come and let us also, reverend sire, attend to our supper.
After that you shall mourn over your beloved son, once you have
conveyed him into Troy. He shall have his full measure of mourning
from you."

Epic, then, like lyric, also contains (and purveys) a superior ethical insight into the proper circumscription of grief for the dead. Elegy, by an increasingly discriminating set of comparisons, begins to seem like a solipsistic spoilt child in the family of literary kinds.

Horace's trick of subverting elegy by using it against itself was manifest in the third stanza, where the fictional "Mystes" was the inappropriate motive for excessive lamentation. To similar effect, he selects in the fourth stanza an epic exemplar that was favored, though in a disparate context, by Valgius and other neoteric epigoni—namely, the Homeric Nestor. Curiously enough, Nestor had acquired some rhetorical standing in the neoteric-Hellenistic esthetic milieu as a model of eloquence and, in particular, of the "middle" style (Rostagni 1961, 424). In an extant Valgian fragment, for instance, the poet "Codrus," whose historical identity is disputed, but who figures in more than one passage of Virgil's *Bucolics*, is compared in poetic skill to Nestor and Demodocus: [51]

> Codrusque ille canit, quali tu voce canebas,
>   atque solet numeros dicere, Cinna, tuos,
> dulcior ut numquam Pylio profluxerit ore
>   Nestoris aut docto pectore Demodoci . . .

The famous Codrus sings his songs in the same manner as you used to sing, and is wont to intone your verses, Cinna. A sweeter sound never poured forth from the lips of Nestor of Pylos, or from the skilled breast of Demodocus. . . .

Given the scholastic status of Nestor as the embodiment, not merely of eloquence in general, but of a particular rhetorical ideal, it is perhaps not insignificant that Horace adduces him as a prime instance of a heroic mourner who observes a just limit on grieving ("at non . . . ploravit omnis . . . annos"). At the same time, and with a more evident irony, he converts, in a typically Alexandrian appropriation, the youths Antilochus and Troilus into tokens of erotic desire (cf. *amabilem* in line 13, and Nisbet-Hubbard *ad loc.*). Thus even as he utilizes heroic paradigms to convey an anti-elegiac message, Horace, through the subterfuge of the assimilative technique, manages to "Alexandrianize" the narration by adding erotic colors. It is as if he were saying to the modish elegist: "not only epic paradigms (such as Nestor) but even Hellenistic revisions of those paradigms call into question your generic proclivity for *flebiles modi."* At this juncture in the ode's progress, the ongoing critique of elegiac discourse reaches a crescendo, marked by the vowel monotonies of *flevere semper.*

In the concluding section of the ode (17–24), Horace shifts his ground (syntactically and rhetorically) from declaration to frontal exhortation. He climaxes his strictures on elegiac lament with an imperative reinforced by a *tandem:* "desine mollium / tandem querelarum" ("cease at last your effete complaints"). He now openly urges the bereaved poet to disavow elegy (tidily summed up in the catchphrase *molles querelae*) in favor of an encomium of Augustus's military exploits (*et potius . . . Caesaris*). The shift of focus is instructive insofar as it clarifies both the intertextual argument (with reference to the *Georgics* passage) and the generic distinctions that structure the ode.

To pursue the latter point first, it might appear to a superficial observer of *recusatio* strategies that our poet has inverted the terms of the disjunction between the lighter genres and high encomium. If a disavowal on the order of, say, *C.* 1.6 (*Scriberis Vario*) be taken as the norm, then the Valgius ode might appear to be a reversal of values, inasmuch as the praise of military prowess now appears to be the preferred ("hard") genre, as against the "soft" (*molles*) effusions of lyric and elegy. The contradiction seems pronounced at the level of content, but recedes into insignificance at the level of structure; for disavowal and assimilation, as we have seen, are conjoint techniques of privileging the particular genre to which one is currently committed. The genres themselves are, in principle and practice, reversible, because the "disavowals" are essentially tactical. Hence the poet can, on one occasion, claim a fictive "inadequacy" to the panegyric task (as in *C.* 1.6); while on another (the present ode) he eschews modesty, confident in his versatile *ingenium* ("et potius nova / cantemus Augusti tropaea / Caesaris"). Just as encomium may operate as the negative foil for amatory lyric, so amatory poetry itself (in this case, elegy) can function as a demoted "other" to an encomium. On the structural plane, therefore, the technique is one and the same: disavowal becomes the handmaiden of incorporation.

In the closing lines of the Valgius ode, the bold move of enlisting the elegist himself into the encomiastic camp (the underlying motive for the rejection of *molles querelae*) acquires didactic overtones from the unmistakable parallels with the prooemium to *Georgics* 3.[52] As is the case with most such citations in Horace, the reader is meant to do more than register the lexical correspondences. Within the peculiar tonality of his reproof to Valgius, it is of crucial import that a quite disparate passage from the *Georgics*—the Orpheus "digression"—has already been alluded to earlier in the same ode. The second *locus*, the Virgilian panegyric of Augustus from the beginning of *Georgics* 3, constitutes a deliberate contrast to the first, the quasi-elegiac mourning of Orpheus for his lost Eurydice in *Georgics* 4. For his own didactic purposes, Horace is subtly differentiating between two opposed manners at work in the Virgilian texts: a more public-spirited and outer-directed, versus a private, self-absorbed orientation. Valgius, by bewailing his Mystes in the manner of the inconsolable Orpheus, has opted for the inferior, self-pitying mode; the lyric voice of *C.* 2.9, on the other hand, seeks to privilege the other (also Virgilian) mode of public celebration, in which merely private obsessions are thrust aside in the face of compelling communal themes—the achievements of the *princeps*. By his double "citation" of a work known intimately, we are entitled to assume, to the circle of Maecenas, the poet succeeds in elaborating the generic discriminations that form the basis of his denigration of elegy. In this light, the "we" in the hortatory expression *cantemus* ("let us sing") may be intended to embrace not only Horace and Valgius, poet and addressee, but also Virgil, whose very words supply the paradigm for appropriate eulogy. In its final cadences, then, the ode to Valgius incidentally pays graceful tribute to a mutual friend, Virgil, as the supreme poet who understands what is poetically *kairos*.

The separate, complementary allusions to Virgil's great didactic poem advance the related goals of upgrading encomium and downgrading *molles querelae* (both of which are represented in the model text). As an additional sophistication, Horace's annexation of the Virgilian toponymic phraseology also looks back to (and assimilates) Valgius's "wintry" obsessions in order to transcend them. In the second stanza, Horace had reproached his friend for behaving as though he regarded winter (including extreme northern ones) as perpetual: "nec Armeniis in oris . . . stat glacies iners / mensis per omnes." In the corresponding geographical catalogue that frames Augustus's victories (lines 20–24), the wintry Armenian scene resurfaces in the guise of the *rigidum Niphatem* (the Virgilian tag in *rigidum* recalling the picture of inertia in *stat*). The now unanimous encomiasts, Horace and his rehabilitated addressee, are projected as singing (*cantemus*), inter alia, of distant frozen landscapes, but such panegyrical *loci* will have their measured (and ipso facto superior) epiphany within the "prescribed"[53] boundaries of a lyric eulogy.

SUBVERTED DISAVOWALS
OF EROTIC LYRIC

In three odes that are closely connected by explicit cross-references as well as topoi (*C.* 1.19; 3.26; 4.1), Horace exploits the contradictions of the disavowal manqué. In each case the speaker ceremoniously claims to have renounced *amor*, only to find his renunciation subverted. The manner of the subversion varies from poem to poem; basic throughout, however, is the artfully manipulated disjunction between strenuous disavowal, in the first instance, and subsequent acquiescence. Above all, the unsuccessful disavowal, in which the goddess Venus plays a decisive role, serves as a ruse enabling the poet to legitimate his resumption of a type of poetry he has previously abandoned.

FINITI AMORES: DISAVOWAL REVERSED
(C. 1.19)

The ode *Mater saeva Cupidinum* (lines 1–12) will serve as a point of departure for my observations:

> Mater saeva Cupidinum
> Thebanaeque iubet me Semelae puer
>   et lasciva Licentia
> finitis animum reddere amoribus.
>   urit me Glycerae nitor   5
> splendentis Pario marmore purius:
>   urit grata protervitas
> et vultus nimium lubricus aspici.
>   in me tota ruens Venus
> Cyprum deseruit, nec patitur Scythas   10
>   et versis animosum equis
> Parthum dicere nec quae nihil attinent.

The ruthless mother of Desires and the son of Theban Semele and wanton License command me to give myself over once again to loves that were closed. I am inflamed by the radiance of Glycera, whose gleam is purer than Parian marble; inflamed by her pleasing provocative ways, and her face too unsettling to look upon. Venus has abandoned Cyprus to rush upon me without any mercy; nor does she permit me to sing about Scythians and Parthian horsemen, formidable in retreat, or other such irrelevant matters.

In this trenchant example, the speaker does not enlarge upon his failure as *renuntiator*; rather he presents the reversal of his former resolve as brusque and ineluctable. His compliance with the peremptory order of a potent trio of divinities is both speedy and involuntary. As I have noted above in my analysis of the ode to Valgius (*C.* 2.9), the plural *amoribus* may constitute a twofold reference—to amorous experiences and to the love-poems they sponsor. The latter aspect emerges unambiguously in lines 9–12, where a vehement Venus is pictured as restraining the poet from composing (*dicere*) any verses irrelevant to the erotic domain. In view of the control that Venus exercises over the poem's theme, it is by no means otiose that she is accompanied not only by Bacchus but by the personified *Licentia*, whose appearance in the climactic position in the list puts her in the forefront of the ideological scheme. *Licentia*, which is cognate with the verb-form *licet*, helps to authorize the fiction of poetic constraint; for while the abstract noun normally connotes the idea of "excessive freedom," the surrounding context of words denoting control (e.g., *iubet* and *nec patitur*) lends some weight to the etymological play on the root notion of "permission." The lyrist's freedom to compose is circumscribed by a hypostasized principle ("License") that mediates the borders of discourse and decrees what is to be permitted in the present *carmen*.[54] Thus by reneging on his resolve and giving himself over (*animum reddere*) to the imperatives of *Licentia*, Horace paradoxically loses his "license" to write on all subjects indiscriminately (*quae nihil attinent*), but gains, by the same token, a new lease on erotic poetry, which is privileged as uniquely pertinent.[55]

When the poet proceeds to profess his burning passion for Glycera ("Sweet") in lines 5–8, it is noteworthy that his laudatory phraseology is palpably indebted to Pindar's *Nemean 4*, a poem he also alludes to elsewhere in the *Carmina*.[56] Juxtaposition of the two passages will render the correspondences in diction and word-order salient:

Glycerae nitor
splendentis Pario marmore purius

(5–6)

στάλαν θέμεν] Παρίου λίθου λευκοτέραν·

(N. 4.81 [Snell])

to set up a monument whose gleam is a purer white than Parian marble

It is significant that in the Pindaric *paragone* the radiance of the poetic "monument" (*stalan*: cf. *monumentum* at C. 3.30.1) is declared to be superior to Parian stone; whereas in the Horatian transposition, it is the lover's appearance that is deemed more resplendent than *Parium marmor*. The main purpose of the Pindaric tag is to shed lustre (cf. *nitor; splendentis*) on the lyric-erotic theme as such; for Glycera, like other typical *amatae* in the *Odes*, is basically a signifier for the variety of poetry she instigates in the *amator*. The intertextual dimension of the ode is not, incidentally, restricted to the comparison borrowed from Pindar: in the subsequent description of the renewed onset of passion (lines 7–10) there is an unmistakable echo of the erotic diction of a poem by Sappho.[57] In sum, Horace has elected to clothe his relapse into (supposedly) terminated *amores* in the verbal finery of his major lyric models. As if to mark the significance of the resumption in terms of writing no less than *Erlebnis*, the poet pointedly resorts to the conventional language of "generic disavowal" when he specifies the excluded topics ("nec patitur *Scythas* / et versis animosum equis / *Parthum* dicere nec *quae nihil attinent*"). As Mitscherlich pertinently comments *ad loc.*, the proper names "Scythian" and "Parthian" are allegorical, standing for subject matter that is alien, remote, heroic, and, by extension, irrelevant to Eros (*quae nihil attinent;* see pp. 117 and 176 below). The rhetorical onus of the ode, then, is on the triumphant vindication of *amor* as theme—a vindication prepared by the overture of unsuccessful renunciation.

To cap his rededication to Eros, Horace concludes with a set of concrete instructions to his attendants to perform a fitting sacrifice to the goddess (13–16):

> hic vivum mihi caespitem, hic
> verbenas, pueri, ponite turaque
> bimi cum patera meri:
> mactata veniet lenior hostia.

Place the fresh turf for me here, boys; place here the sprigs and the incense along with a bowl of unmixed wine that is two vintages old. The goddess will be more gentle in her approach once we have sacrificed a victim.

Implicit in the closing vignette of a sacrifice is the concomitant feast that will provide the raison d'être for the obligatory *convivium*. The return to *amores*, in short, leads to a re-commitment to erotic-sympotic lyric. At the same time, the closing reference to the pacification of Venus (*veniet lenior*) is contrapuntal to the topic of *saevitia* with which the poem opens; for as I pointed out above in regard to the Licymnia ode (*C.* 2.12), "savagery" may be incorporated into the "gentle" sphere of love at the price of a certain (metaphorical) domestication. In the ode under discussion, the compliant poet-*amator* fervently desires, through the magic of sacrifice and the *carmen* itself, to convert Venus's *saevitia* into *lenitas* in order to accommodate it. *Mater saeva*, therefore, is a verbal counter in a dialectical game, whose rules allow for an anticipated reversal in divine attitude in the direction of an eventual mitigation (*saeva*/*lenior*).

TANGE CHLOEN: DESIRE READMITTED
(*C.* 3.26)

By way of transition to the more elaborate disavowal of *C.* 4.1 (*Intermissa diu Venus*), it will be expedient to glance at a straightforward and concise example of subverted *renuntiatio amoris*—namely, *C.* 3.26:

> Vixi puellis nuper idoneus
> et militavi non sine gloria;
>   nunc arma defunctumque bello
>   barbiton hic paries habebit,
> laevum marinae qui Veneris latus   5
> custodit. hic, hic ponite lucida
>   funalia et vectis et arcus
>   oppositis foribus minaces.

o quae beatam diva tenes Cyprum et
Memphin carentem Sithonia nive,   10
regina, sublimi flagello
tange Chloen semel arrogantem.

In my life thus far I have been eligible for young women, and in the fray I have done not undistinguished service; now my arms and my lyre that have retired from warfare will be kept on this wall, which protects the left flank of Venus, the sea-goddess. Place here, right here, the bright torches and the crowbars and the bows that threaten opposing doors. O queen, who rules over fortunate Cyprus and Memphis, devoid of Thracian snow, touch once with your upraised whip the supercilious Chloe.

The renunciation of desire in the first two strophes is strenuously ostentatious and takes the form of a valediction within the ritual context of a dedication. It is in the metaphorical substructure of the ode, however, that an ironic counterstatement becomes manifest, for the speaker begins by deliberately "contaminating" the two domains of war and love. Commentators routinely point out that warfare is often a trope for love in Latin poetry, but they often fail to note the converse—that *amor* is no less commonly presented as antinomic to *bellum*. When a sophisticated composer of love-lyric couches his amatory experience (in this case, the whole course of his love-life) in terms of a military service, we are thereby alerted to a contradictory subtext in which *amor* and *bellum* (frequently decoupled) are here facetiously "contaminated."[58]

The contradiction between love and war does not remain latent. After an initial flourish of martial imagery (*idoneus; militavi non sine gloria; arma*), there surfaces, in a highly obtrusive fashion, the very emblem of erotic poetry, the Lesbian *barbiton*. In an arresting dissonance, the *barbiton* is described as having ended its war-mongering (*defunctum bello*)! The bold attribution of *bellum* to a lyre that is elsewhere typified as *imbellis* (cf. C. 1.15.15: *imbelli cithara*) is tangible proof, if indeed proof is needed, that love-poetry, rather than love-life, is the primary target of renunciation.[59] The enumerated "instruments" of the poet—the lyre no less than the weapons—are, it appears, to be hung up in the temple of Venus; though it is not yet clear at this juncture in the poem whether we are to imagine the actual instruments or painted representations of them (*hic paries habebit*). The ambiguity is only partially resolved by the command that follows, presumably addressed to slaves, to devote various other emblems to the goddess, since at least two of those emblems, torches (*funalia*) and bows (*arcus*) are equally appropriate to both military and erotic contexts.[60] The overriding aura of mock-solemnity, when taken in concert with the ambiguities and contradictions at the figurative level, constitutes a perfect foil for the *supplementary* gesture of the concluding prayer, in which the brittle facade of the *miles gloriosus* (cf. "militavi non sine gloria") collapses to reveal the soul of the unrequited *amator*: "regina, sublimi flagello / tange Chloen semel arrogantem" ("O queen, touch once with your upraised whip the supercilious Chloe").

The pathetic final request to Venus uttered by the speaker is, at first glance, innocuous enough, and certainly falls within his prerogatives as delimited by the dedicatory *cadre*. Having devoted the instruments of a lifelong service to the love-goddess, he can legitimately claim a favor in return. The content of the request, however, betrays the speaker insofar as it inadvertently discloses his persistent desire to humble the youthful lover who has rejected him (cf. *arrogantem*). Thus the very desire that has been ceremoniously disavowed in the opening lines is subtly readmitted at the close, and the reader is now compelled to revise his perception of the original act of renunciation in the light of a lover's fervent wish. If Horace has revealed an underlying ambivalence about his desire for "Chloe," such ambivalence also reflects a continuing attraction for the suspended *barbiton*.

Intermissa bella: The Return of the Disavowed (*C.* 4.1)

The inaugural ode of the fourth book not only limns the thematic contours of the collection to follow, but also reverts to subjects handled in the earlier *tribiblos*. To be precise, the poetic argument of the kind I have been investigating receives marked prominence in the renewed lyric program. Horace signals the typological continuity of his *carmina* by inserting recognizable allusions to prior odes. In making explicit references both to *C.* 1.19 and to 3.26 (in the former case, through auto-citation; in the latter, through discrete verbal tags), the poet securely locates the ode within the category of the failed renunciation. Thus line 5, *mater saeva Cupidinum*, is a verbatim reproduction of the first line of 1.19, while the words *bella, idoneum,* and *militiae* (lines 2, 12, 16) together recall the pseudo-martial valedictory to love in 3.26.1–3 (cf. *idoneus; militavi; bello*). Moreover, the structural affiliations of the three odes interlinked by cross-references tend to support the notion that the composer of the *Odes* is relying on the reader's perception of a shared rhetorical gambit. It is therefore pertinent to examine 4.1 in relation to the similar movement of ideas in the two cognate odes to which it self-consciously alludes.

We observe, at the outset, that the device of "contaminating" *amor* and *bellum* is conspicuously flaunted in the opening fanfare of the ode (1–2):

> Intermissa, Venus, diu
> rursus bella moves?

O Venus, are you once again stirring up battles that have long been adjourned?

The conceit is carried forward into the eulogy of the youthful Paulus Maximus (15–16):

> et centum puer artium
> late signa feret militiae tuae

and a young man of countless endowments who will carry far and wide the standards of your military service.

As in 3.26, the erotic *renuntiator* seeks a camouflage in the uniform of the opposite province: that of the soldier. One way in which the text registers the latent incorporation is in the characterization of the actions of Venus (4–7):

> desine, *dulcium*
> mater *saeva* Cupidinum,
> circa lustra decem flectere *mollibus*
> iam durum imperiis . . .

Cease, O *ruthless* mother of *sweet* Desires, to bend to your *soft* commands one approaching his fiftieth year and already tough.

The very divinity who is typecast, in the auto-citation, as ruthless (*saeva*) is said, in a harsh oxymoron, to engender "sweet" loves and to issue "soft" commands. The fact that the framing epithets *mollis* and *dulcis* carry erotic connotations does not diminish, but rather reinforces, the clash with the savagery (*saevitia*) of the love-goddess. The effect of the borrowed line in the novel context of 4.1 is to foreground the paradoxical aspects of Desire in a manner calculated to sponsor a brutal sabotage of the speaker's protestations.

As is also common in the generic disavowal, the composer first disqualifies himself for the role at hand ("non sum qualis eram bonae / sub regno Cinarae," 3–4); then proceeds to propose a surrogate who is advertised as more appropriate (9–12):

> *tempestivius* in domum
> Pauli, purpureis ales oloribus
>   comissabere Maximi,
> si torrere iecur quaeris *idoneum*

More appropriately shall you, in a winged chariot drawn by bright-hued swans, join the band of revelers on their way to the home of Paulus Maximus, if you are intent on inflaming a liver that is *eligible*.

The ostensible ground for self-disqualification in this instance is the poet's advanced age (*circa lustra decem*, 6), while the "other" possesses the attribute of youth (*puer*, 15). In the rhetorical protest, Horace attempts to distance his *persona* from the experience of *amor* and, by extension, from the practice of erotic verse. From a formal point of view, he avails himself of the lexicon, not of valediction (as in 3.26), but of the apotropaic hymn.[61] In the course of the poem, the opening gesture of disavowal exfoliates to embrace a lengthy praise of the surrogate (13–19), as well as an enumeration of the honors that the latter will bestow upon the goddess (19–28).

The final extension of the disavowal is so extravagant that it seems most implausible in terms of the Horatian system of values (29–32):

> me nec femina nec puer
> iam nec spes animi credula mutui
>   nec certare iuvat mero
> nec vincire novis tempora floribus.

No longer does love for man or woman bring me pleasure, nor naive hope of reciprocal affection, nor drinking contests with unmixed wine, nor having my temples bound with wreaths of freshly picked flowers.

When, in the former of the above couplets, the speaker abjures all lovers of either sex and, paratactically, appends a jaundiced view of any prospect of reciprocated affection, the disclaimer still retains a modicum of credibility. The following two lines, however, severely tax the audience's gullibility with their blunt denial of any pleasure in that Horatian hallmark, the symposium. If the symposium is, as I shall argue below (chapter 3), an emblem of lyric values, then the sweeping renunciation here comes close to an implied stricture upon the production of new *carmina*. The sudden irruption of desire that renders the disavowal abortive (lines 33–40) rescues both Eros and, by implication, the *convivium* from a scandalous abnegation. The climactic negation (and its sabotage) are Horace's means of announcing that whatever new directions he might be tempted to take in the ensuing *carmina* of book 4, he will not entirely abandon his preferred subgenre of erotic-sympotic lyric. In a word, the "failure" of renunciation is manipulated so as to confirm the poet's predilections in regard to theme and manner.

An adequate analysis of the ode, however selective in focus, should provide a persuasive account of the proper names "Cinara" and "Ligurinus." Despite the efforts of many critics to establish the historical reality of these personages, the agnostic view best accords with the simple, but frequently ignored, circumstance that both names carry a symbolic load related to the poem's argument.[62] On the former, Kiessling and Heinze (*ad loc.*) come fairly close to the mark in raising the possibility that "Cinara," as a symbol of the poet's youth, may actually be interchangeable with "Glycera." It is notorious that "Cinara" as an *amata* is absent from the earlier *tribiblos*. The inference to be drawn from this curious bit of evidence is not unambiguous: since the early erotic lyrics are saturated with female names, some of them recurrent, that fulfill the same role, the onus is on the believers to disprove the hypothesis of the interchangeability of the *puellae*. If 4.1 is, programmatically, a pseudo-reluctant return to an earlier kind of lyric, then "Cinara" is just another increment to the list of youthful *amatae*.

Whether or not "Cinara" existed, it is undeniable that her Greek name signifies a delectable plant, the artichoke, that was a Roman culinary favorite. Given Horace's penchant for exploiting onomastic signifiers, there is a strong prima facie case for interpreting the name as a "place-holder" or symbolic variable in a paradigmatic description. As in the case of "Chloe," for instance, the poet employs the botanical figure to indicate the bloom of youth (cf. C. 1.23). The "regime" of young Chloe may not be readily distinguishable from that of Cinara (cf. C. 3.9.9: "me nunc Thraessa Chloe *regit*" with "sub *regno* Cinarae" in line 4). With the good "Artichoke," the speaker introduces a gastronomic bagatelle that it is difficult to gloss over in view of the later reference to the banquet in 31–32. Moreover, the coupling of the artichoke with wine-drinking has established literary as well as cultural significance. A memorable fragment of Alcaeus that begins "soak your lungs with wine" prominently lists the artichoke in bloom as one of the seasonal cues for a hearty midsummer symposium (Alcaeus 347 LP). On the evidence from a passage in Columella,[63] the taste of the artichoke was popularly thought to be especially enhanced by wine. The Alcaean motif, when considered in conjunction with the popular belief, serves to corroborate Horace's etymological wordplay in regard to the sympotic aptness of "Cinara."

Those who may be inclined to balk at the critical assumption of coherent name-signifiers in this and other odes are entitled to demand that the name "Ligurinus," which emerges into prominence at the end of the poem, be subjected to a similar analysis as a test of my interpretive principle. "Ligurinus," of course, denotes "Ligurian," and could therefore pass for a banal Roman *cognomen* (cf. Kiessling-Heinze *ad loc.*); yet despite the geographical eponym, one does not have to strain the phonemic evidence to hear distinct resonances from the verb, *ligur(r)io*, which evokes, in at least one of its common connotations, *gastronomic* preciosity, if not gourmandism.[64] If we assume an intention to pun, then "Ligurinus," no less than "Cinara," readily yields an association with gustatory appetite and, ipso facto, with the recurrent convivial leitmotif.

To uncover the latent signification of the names is to come face to face with complementary, facetious tokens of the banquet (artichokes and epicures). The complementarity extends to sexual identity as well, the *amata* at the beginning counterbalancing the *amatus* at the end. The polarization is rhetorically all-inclusive—a point that is made explicit in the disjunctive denial "me nec femina nec puer" (line 29). A plausible inference from these points of correspondence is that the intrusion of the *puer* "Ligurinus" in the final apostrophe after a total rejection of *amor* is more than the return of repressed erotic desire. Taken in conjunction with the *puella* "Cinara," and in the context of a strenuous denial of sympotic pleasures, "Ligurinus" is meant also to encode the return of a disavowed attraction for the pleasures of the *convivium.* Read in this way, the ode seeks to redefine the Horatian lyric program in one of its central manifestations after a lengthy "intermission."

The motifs and diction that shape the apostrophe to Ligurinus substantiate this line of interpretation (33–36):

> sed cur heu, Ligurine, cur
> manat rara meas lacrima per genas?
> cur facunda parum decoro
> inter verba cadit lingua silentio?

> But why, oh, why, Ligurinus, does the occasional tear drip down over my cheeks? Why does my tongue, known for its eloquence, lapse, in mid sentence, into an unbecoming silence?

The conventional portrayal of the symptoms of passion in lines 33–34 with its echo of Sappho recollects passages in the youthful *Epodes* as well as book 1 of the *Odes*[65]—a clear signal of an incipient resumption of an earlier style. The resumption, however, is not without its acute anxiety, as we learn from the speaker's claim to failure in eloquence (*facunda . . . inter verba cadit lingua*). By professing to be tongue-tied at the crucial moment (*parum decoro . . . silentio*), Horace authenticates his amatory credentials[66] while simultaneously inscribing his current *aporia* in respect to erotic discourse. The aporetic stance, which is based on the notion of an "indecorous silence" is, of course, contradicted by the eloquent closure of the ode, with its mellifluous and seductive vowel harmonies and assonance (37–40):

> nocturnis ego somniis
> iam captum teneo, iam volucrem sequor
> te per gramina Martii
> Campi, te per aquas, dure, volubilis.

> In my dreams at night I hold you fast at one moment; at another, I chase you as you fly over the sward of the Campus Martius; and you, yet again, O unfeeling one, over the swirling waters.

This final cri de coeur, though cast in a confessional mold with its prominent *ego* and repeated *te,* is nevertheless beholden to a well-worn formula from the earlier *amores:* the *amatus* exercising on the

Campus Martius or swimming in the Tiber (cf. *C.* 3.7.25–28). This far from "silent" passion, then, is mediated through a familiar lexicon that discloses "Ligurinus," not as a novel theme, but as a reformulation of a motif of the early erotic verse. The name of the beloved has changed, but the fictive situation and the rhetorical colors that portray it are deliberately retrogressive.[67]

To summarize: the three poems I have partly dissected above share the motif of the abortive disavowal. They differ from the standard *recusatio* paradigm, as narrowly defined in the standard literature, in that they do not rely on an alien genre as foil; instead they build on the treacherous foundation of a denial of the very genre they sponsor—namely, erotic lyric. That self-denial, in turn, is negated by the poems' surprise denouement—a triumphant return of a banished Eros with redoubled force. Though there is ellipsis of the generic foil, the disavowal is no less effective in terms of the ultimate goal of reaffirmed engagement.

THE DISAVOWAL OF *IAMBI*

Most discussions of the *recusatio* in the Augustan context are misleadingly restricted to poems in which a species of the *genus grande* is denigrated in preference to some exemplar of the *genus tenue*. As I have already observed above, however, the rival genre need not be comparatively elevated for the disavowal to accomplish its basic objective. The choice of foil genre is, in principle no less than in practice, unrestricted. The substantive feature of the disavowal ploy is that the "other" (generically speaking) is endowed with attributes that appear (or are made to appear) incommensurate with those ascribed to the preferred genre. The claim of alienation is to be construed not as an absolute statement of anathema, but as a relative *prise de position*. To corroborate this broadened conception of the *recusatio*, I propose to analyze briefly two poems in which the generic foil is *iambi*—Horace's term for the kind of poem represented by many of his own epodes.[68]

INCEPTOS . . . IAMBOS (*Ep.* 14)

Mollis inertia cur tantam diffuderit imis
    oblivionem sensibus,
pocula Lethaeos ut si ducentia somnos
    arente fauce traxerim,

candide Maecenas, occidis saepe rogando: 5
  deus, deus nam me vetat
inceptos, olim promissum carmen, iambos
  ad umbilicum adducere.
non aliter Samio dicunt arsisse Bathyllo
  Anacreonta Teium,   10
qui persaepe cava testudine flevit amorem
  non elaboratum ad pedem.
ureris ipse miser: quodsi non pulchrior ignis
  accendit obsessam Ilion,
gaude sorte tua; me libertina neque uno   15
  contenta Phryne macerat.

Forthright Maecenas, you are finishing me off by asking so often
why a decadent torpor has spread such profound oblivion throughout my senses, as though I had quaffed with dry throat the cups that
induce Lethaean sleep; for a god, a very god, interdicts me from
bringing to completion the iambic verses I had begun to compose—
the poetry I promised so long ago. In a manner not dissimilar, they
say, Anacreon of Teos burned with desire for Bathyllos of Samos—
Anacreon who lamented his passion very often on his hollow shell
in an uncomplicated meter. You yourself are hopelessly on fire; but if
the "flame" that burnt besieged Troy was no more gorgeous, then
rejoice in your fate! I am roasted by desire for Phryne, a freedwoman, who is not content with just one lover.

The poem's scaffolding consists in the *aporia* (*inertia*) of the speaker
who is interdicted (*vetat*) from composing *iambi*. The term *carmen*,
which occurs in apposition to *iambos*, here signifies "a kind of poetry and not merely a poem" ("un genre de poésie, et non pas
simplement un poème": Olivier 1917, 135). In other words, Horace
is once more engaged in an act of disavowing a literary kind. Since
the demotion of invective poetry takes place within the framework
of an "iambic" poem in an Archilochean meter,[69] the overall effect
of the epode is subversive: the poet surrenders to a more compelling Muse of a radically different persuasion.

    That the *iambi* are interdicted when already in progress (*inceptos*)
is, of course, a recurrent motif of such staged disavowals, as is the
invention of a divine agent for the interdiction itself (*deus, deus nam
me vetat*). The author's confessed failure to consummate an ongoing *carmen* is the pretext for his reorientation to a new generic imperative—erotic verse. By this familiar route, Horace divulges his
nascent attraction for the kind of erotic lyric that later comes to occupy a central place in the *Odes*.

The impulse to write amatory verse is, in principle, predicated on a prior love relationship, real or fictitious. In Ovid's charming parody of this predication (*Am.* 1.2), Cupid deliberately shoots the hapless poet with a dart—a logically necessary prelude to the composition of *Amores*. Horace's prostrate speaker is similarly shown at the outset in the grip of an oppressive *amor* that an unnamed god will channel into its natural literary outlet in "Anacreontic" love-lyric. His description of *inertia* is full of verbal overtones of Greek predecessors, such as Archilochus and Sappho,[70] whose overwhelming passions purportedly brought them close to death. The Augustan poet's *aporia*, however, is soon revealed as highly selective: it applies to one type of composition but not to another. Thus the self-presentation of the writer as abject lover becomes warrant for a radical shift from the predominantly invective mode of the *Epodes* to the more muted tones of the *Odes*. It is no accident that *Ep.* 14 is preceded in the collection by another poem (*Horrida tempestas*) whose structure and argument also anticipate the universe of the *Carmina*.

The way in which Horace manages to negotiate the shift by pleading the exigencies of erotic bondage is superficially reminiscent of the elegiac poets, as my comparison with Ovid's parodic version in the *Amores* suggests. With his usual sophistication, Horace foreshadows the answer to his indirect rhetorical question to Maecenas with his use of the adjective *mollis*—a typically elegiac catchword—to inaugurate the poem. *Mollis* immediately places in the foreground the stance of enervation, and thus prepares the way for the final image of the poet being weakened (*macerat*) in the fiery crucible of *amor*. Between the initial "soft" and the concluding "soften," we are treated to a grossly exaggerated version of the craven *amator* typical of elegiac discourse. The plaintive modality we associate chiefly, though not exclusively, with elegy also resonates in the verb *flevit*, ascribed to the passionate effusions of the love-struck Anacreon ("qui persaepe . . . *flevit* amorem," 11)—the term *flevit* signifying, in this context, *flebiter cecinit* ("sang mournfully").[71] The explicit invocation of the Anacreontic model adds a nuance to the new generic inflection, for it serves notice that Horace proposes to handle the erotic theme, not in the distraught strains of a Catullus[72] or a Propertius, but rather in the light-hearted and convivial manner of an Anacreon. Thus the point of convergence between Horace's new orientation and that of the ele-

gists is accidental rather than substantial, despite the surface resemblances in diction mentioned above (*mollis; flevit amorem*). The
recent convert to love-poetry will find his own distinctive voice in
the vast grove of Eros that has preceded him.

Horace in this epode provides a subtle rehearsal of the kind of
wordplay and symbolic nomenclature that is later characteristic of
the *Odes* as I have interpreted them. "Phryne", for example, who is
billed as the speaker's current flame, fits in all too harmoniously
with the recurrent fire-imagery of the poem (cf. *arsisse*, 9; *ureris,
ignis*, 13; *accendit*, 14); for the first syllable of her name recalls the
Greek word for "roast" or "parch" (cf. φρύγω and the words *arente
fauce* in line 4). The fact that Phryne is also the name of a well-
known Greek courtesan (cf. Propertius C. 2.6.6) adds, as it were,
more fuel to the fire, and nicely matches the idea of her "roasting"
the poet to softness (*macerat*) by her inflammatory arts. Maecenas's
unnamed "flame" (*ignis*), by contrast, is likened to the paragon of
Helen whose power to ignite is the occasion for a double entendre
in the expression *accendit obsessam Ilion* (fire of love; fire that burnt
the Trojan citadel). This trifling with metaphorical clichés as well as
the portrayal of a love-bond between the speaker and a *libertina* are
in keeping with the direction that Horace's poetics will take in
many of the convivial odes. The indulgence in the love-theme is
authenticated by the pointed reference to the model of Anacreon—
a poet who, as befits his iconographic status in Archaic vase-paint-
ing, came to typify a certain kind of liberated Dionysiac minstrel.[73]
The conversion to "Anacreontic" literary pursuits, in turn, is mediated by the speaker's initial disavowal of iambic contumely.

CRIMINOSIS . . . IAMBIS (C. 1.16)

> O matre pulchra filia pulchrior,
> quem criminosis cumque voles modum
>   pones iambis, sive flamma
>   sive mari libet Hadriano.
>
> non Dindymene, non adytis quatit   5
> mentem sacerdotum incola Pythius,
>   non Liber aeque, non acuta
>   sic geminant Corybantes aera,
>
> tristes ut irae, quas neque Noricus
> deterret ensis nec mare naufragum   10
>   nec saevus ignis nec tremendo
>   Iuppiter ipse ruens tumultu.

fertur Prometheus addere principi
limo coactus particulam undique
    desectam et insani leonis   15
        vim stomacho apposuisse nostro.
irae Thyesten exitio gravi
stravere et altis urbibus ultimae
    stetere causae cur perirent
        funditus imprimeretque muris   20
hostile aratrum exercitus insolens.
compesce mentem: me quoque pectoris
    temptavit in dulci iuventa
        fervor et in celeris iambos
misit furentem: nunc ego mitibus   25
mutare quaero tristia, dum mihi
    fias recantatis amica
        opprobriis animumque reddas.

O daughter more beautiful than a beautiful mother, please put an
end to those invective iambic poems in whatever way you will,
whether with fire or with the Adriatic sea! Neither the goddess
Cybele at Didymus, nor Apollo in residence at Pytho, who from his
inner sanctum shakes the mind of his priestesses, nor Bacchus, nor
even the Corybantes that clash together their high-pitched cymbals,
so incite the emotions as does gloomy anger, which is checked neither by Noric sword, nor a sea that causes shipwrecks, nor ferocious
fire, nor Jupiter himself as he rushes down with dreadful uproar.
Prometheus, they say, when he was forced to add a segment taken
from each creature to our primal clay, inserted the violence of a rav-
ing lion into our spleen. Anger brought down Thyestes in a heavy
doom, and anger has been the ultimate reason why lofty cities have
been totally destroyed and riotous armies have dug their ploughs
into their walls. Suppress your rage: I too in my sweet youthful
prime succumbed to hot-headed emotions and was driven by anger
to compose hasty invectives; now I seek to change gloomy verses for
mild ones, and retract my slurs—provided you become my sweetheart and give me back your affection.

Though this poem has been traditionally categorized as belonging to the "genre" of the so-called palinode,[74] its line of argument
brings it securely within the orbit of odes I have been analyzing as
representative of generic disavowal (the rhetorical handmaiden of
assimilation). The speaker strenuously dissociates himself from
the production of defamatory verse (*iambi*), and claims a present
desire to cultivate "mild" compositions ("nunc ego *mitibus* / mutare
quaero *tristia*," 25–26). The vexed question of whether the *iambi*

referred to in the first stanza (*criminosis* . . . *iambis*) should be ascribed to the speaker or the addressee need not be definitively resolved here, though the strict logic of the culminating *me quoque* in line 22 strongly supports those who, with the late L. A. MacKay, favor the latter reading.[75] With either alternative, it remains true that the poet is ultimately concerned to distance himself from iambic invective such as we find, by his own admission, in the *Epodes*, some of which he claims to have rashly composed *in dulci iuventa*.

The poem's central focus on *ira* and its doleful consequences is all of a piece with the generic abnegation, for iambic poetry, from Archilochus and Hipponax onwards, is characterized by practitioners and critics alike as presupposing an angry *persona*. To quote Horace himself from a passage reviewing the iambic tradition (*Ars Poetica* 79): "Archilochum proprio rabies armavit iambo" ("Anger provided Archilochus with its weapons of invective"). Brink and others have argued (conclusively, in my judgment) that *proprio* is to be construed here as conferring ownership of *rabies* on the genre itself rather than on its representative composer, Archilochus.[76] Rage, then, is endemic to *iambi*, and by expatiating on its dire sequelae, Horace is not indulging in purely gratuitous digression, but rather constructing a hyperbolic foil against which to contrast the seductive charm of love-lyric. Of course, a crucial aspect of that "charm," as it turns out, lies in its potential to win back the female addressee as a love-partner ("dum mihi / fias . . . amica", 26–28). The partially hidden agenda of the poem, however, is twofold, comprising an erotic and a literary dimension. The poet hopes to persuade the woman to relinquish her anger and recommit her affection to him (*animumque reddas*); at the same time, he seeks to accomplish this seduction through a mild variety of *carmen* that will "cancel out" (*recantare*)[77] the negative effects of vituperative song.

Horace's firm repudiation of his former iambic manner is therefore self-serving in more ways than one. In its retrospective aspect, it sharply defines the mature *persona* of love-lyric as he reaffirms his current generic predilections while dissociating himself from the "mad" compositions of his iambic phase. As a subtle token of his poetic transmutation, he apparently alludes, in the very first line of the ode, to an epode by Archilochus (recovered in part on the famous Cologne papyrus)[78] that blatantly flattered a Lycambid in order to seduce her. The Archilochean reference may be viewed as part of the strategy of assimilation since it is here employed in a lyric context that suggests the speaker's "sincerity," whereas in its original iambic context it was presumably intended to defame. In short, Horace's eloquent appeal to the beautiful unnamed woman to lay aside her anger (*compesce mentem*) merges with, and becomes indistinguishable from, the discourse of disavowal that caps the ode (*me quoque . . .*). With the pivotal *nunc ego* of the final strophe, erotic desire, on the one hand, and lyric intention, on the other, are made to flow together in a single stream that takes the reader to a horizon far removed from the extravagant outbursts of Archilochean *iambos*.

CODA

The overall aim of this chapter has been to demonstrate the pervasiveness of the subterfuge of exclusion/inclusion (disavowal/assimilation) rather than to account for every instance of its use in the *Odes* and *Epodes*. Since there is some degree of overlap between what I have been calling the "rhetoric of disavowal" and certain "modes of authentication" (the topic of the next chapter), I shall be returning intermittently to some of the ideas first broached here under the more general category of "modes of assimilation."

2

Modes of Authentication

In chapter 1, I delineated some of the principal schemes by which the poet of the *Odes* privileges lyric discourse at the expense of other genres. I shall now shift my analytical focus to a set of related procedures that have as their outcome the authentication of the poet's peculiar calling. My analysis will be elastic enough to include poems that seek not only to justify the lyric vocation in general, but also to determine its particular scope within the boundaries of the Horatian *carmen*. From this viewpoint, Horace's adroit use of motifs and figures from early Greek lyric and his exploitation of the reputations of various poetic antecedents will play a crucial part in my investigations.

AUTOBIOGRAPHICAL *MYTHOS*

A highly effective means of establishing one's authenticity as a *vates* is to relate quasi-autobiographical incidents that can be seen as exemplary for the brand of poetry in which one is currently engaged. In this sophisticated form of self-presentation, the speaker narrates or alludes to episodes in his life with the object of investing it with coherence and authority. I shall refer to this coherent biographical pattern as *mythos* in the neutral, value-free sense of the word—that is, without any prejudgment as to the truth or falsity of the related events. The *mythos* may or may not coincide with actual incidents in the life of Horace;[1] the crucial circumstance determining its construction is the need to conform to a prestigious conception of what constitutes the career of a genuine poet.

SEDES PIORUM: THE SELECT COMPANY
OF LYRISTS (C. 2.13)

Ille et nefasto te posuit die,
quicumque primum, et sacrilega manu

produxit, arbos, in nepotum
　　perniciem opprobriumque pagi;
illum et parentis crediderim sui　　　　　　　　　5
fregisse cervicem et penetralia
　　sparsisse nocturno cruore
　　　　hospitis; ille venena Colcha

et quidquid usquam concipitur nefas
tractavit, agro qui statuit meo　　　　　　　　　10
　　te triste lignum, te caducum
　　　　in domini caput immerentis.

quid quisque vitet numquam homini satis
cautum est in horas: navita Bosphorum
　　Poenus perhorrescit neque ultra　　　　　　15
　　　　caeca timet aliunde fata;

miles sagittas et celerem fugam
Parthi, catenas Parthus et Italum
　　robur; sed improvisa leti
　　　　vis rapuit rapietque gentes.　　　　　　　20

quam paene furvae regna Proserpinae
et iudicantem vidimus Aeacum
　　sedesque discriptas piorum et
　　　　Aeoliis fidibus querentem

Sappho puellis de popularibus,　　　　　　　　25
et te sonantem plenius aureo
　　Alcaee, plectro dura navis,
　　　　dura fugae mala, dura belli!

utrumque sacro digna silentio
mirantur umbrae dicere; sed magis　　　　　　　30
　　pugnas et exactos tyrannos
　　　　densum umeris bibit aure vulgus.

quid mirum, ubi illis carminibus stupens
demittit atras belua centiceps
　　auris et intorti capillis　　　　　　　　　　35
　　　　Eumenidum recreantur angues?

quin et Prometheus et Pelopis parens
dulci laborum decipitur sono,
　　nec curat Orion leones
　　　　aut timidos agitare lyncas.　　　　　　　40

Whoever that man was that first planted you, did the deed on an ill-omened day, and with sacrilegious hand cultivated you to bring destruction upon later generations and infamy to the countryside. I would believe he broke his own father's neck and spattered the inner chambers of his house at night with the blood of a guest; he has surely meddled with Colchian poisons and whatever brand of wrong-doing is anywhere conceived—that person who placed you on my farm, you wretched log, ready to fall upon your undeserving master's head. No man can ever take adequate precautions every hour of the day against what he wants to avoid. The sailor from Carthage is terrified of the Bosporus and has no further fear of a blind fate from a different source; the soldier fears the Parthians' arrows and their rapid retreat; the Parthian fears enslavement and Italian might; but the unforeseen force of death has carried off, and will forever carry off, humankind. How close I came to seeing dark Proserpine's kingdom, and Aeacus passing judgment, and the abodes reserved for the devout, and Sappho complaining on the Aeolian lyre of her compatriot girls, and you, Alcaeus, sounding forth in a fuller register with your golden pick about the hardships of seafaring, the evil hardships of flight, the hardships of warfare! The shades of the underworld marvel at the songs of both bards—songs worthy of holy silence; but the densely packed crowd, shoulder to shoulder, more readily drinks in with the ear tales of battles and the expulsion of tyrants. Small wonder, when the hundred-headed beast, struck dumb with awe at those very songs, lets his black ears droop, and the snakes entwined in the hair of the Eumenides are charmed and refreshed. Prometheus, moreover, and Pelops' father are distracted from their toils by the sweet sound; and Orion does not care to hunt lions or timid lynxes.

Part of the submerged agenda of this complex ode is to advance the far from modest claim that the poet of the *Odes* ought to be venerated on a par with those giants of Lesbian lyric, Sappho and Alcaeus.[2] The escape from premature death and the vision of the underworld merely furnish a witty narrative pretext for what is, at bottom, the Roman bard's strong prognosis of his future immortality. Despite an initial impression of inorganic transition and disconnectedness, the main thematic segments of the ode are mutually supportive of the central argument.

Before I move on to defend the underlying unity of the poem, it is important to take cognizance of the painstaking, quadripartite symmetry that the composer has built into the design of the ten strophic units. Two equal portions (A and B), each comprising five stanzas, readily break down, in terms of thought and syntactic markers, into matching subgroups of three and two stanzas, respectively:

A:	1	(three)	2	(two)
B:	1	(three)	2	(two)

The first subgroup of three stanzas (A1) features a speaker who fulminates against the obscure planter of the *arbos* (1–12); in the next (A2) the speaker switches to calm, gnomic reflections on the inexorability and unpredictability of death. The second half of the poem (the latter five stanzas) also subdivides neatly into two subgroups isomorphic with the first half: three stanzas (B1) are devoted to describing the performance of Alcaeus and Sappho in the *sedes piorum* (21–32); the final two (B2), introduced by the rhetorical *quid mirum?* vastly amplify the underworld audience to encompass fabulous monsters and legendary *impii* (33–40). Between the opening and closing sections, moreover, there is a demonstrable effort at "ring composition"—an important aspect of the design that I hope to bring to the fore in what follows.

On this remarkably symmetrical grid, the poet superimposes the theme of *pietas* and its opposite. The full connotations of the word *pius* and its cognates in this thematic context will be explored in due course. Suffice it to note, at this juncture, that, with the exception of the gnomic transition (A2), the *pius*/*impius* dichotomy is material to the basic topic of each segment:

	Impius	*Pius*
A1	Tree-planter Analogues (parricide, poisoner, guest-slayer)	Speaker (cf. *sacrilega manu*)
B1		Alcaeus, Sappho (cf. *sedes piorum*)
B2	Sinners in the underworld (Prometheus, Tantalus, Orion)	

To spell out the scheme in more explicit terms: in A1 the planter of the tree and the nameless *impii* to whom he is likened almost violate the sacrosanctity of the poet; in B1 the Lesbian poets in the underworld are included in the category of *pii* (cf. *sedes piorum*); in B2 we hear of legendary figures who have committed acts of notable impiety against the gods (Tantalus, Prometheus, Orion). The transgressors of *pietas*, both anonymous and named, frame an inner Elysium devoted to the select group of those rewarded for their *pietas*.

The coherence that appears so pronounced at the thematic level is not, however, immediately apparent at the levels of tone and mood. The incongruity, for instance, in the speaker's emotions as between parts A1 and B2 is at once glaring and (we may assume) deliberate. As Nisbet and Hubbard correctly observe at the conclusion of their commentary on the ode: "The poem ends in harmony and peace, a marvellous contrast to the boisterous humour of the opening stanzas." A focal challenge for the interpreter, then, is to account for the tonal discrepancy between parts of an ode that, in respect to design and thematic structure, is fundamentally consistent.

A. 1–20

Perhaps the most significant aspect of the speaker's invective directed against the tree-planter is the one least explored by the majority of critics—its *generic* affiliations with the manner and matter of Horace's *iambi*.[3] The indignant speaker who explodes into extravagant hyperbole against a defenseless opponent closely resembles the vehement denouncer of garlic in the hilarious salvo of *Ep.* 3 (1–8):

> Parentis olim si quis impia manu
>   senile guttur fregerit,
> edit cicutis alium nocentius.
>   o dura messorum ilia!
> quid hoc veneni saevit in praecordiis?
>   num viperinus his cruor
> incoctus herbis me fefellit? an malas
>   Canidia tractavit dapes?

If anyone should break the neck of his old father with sacrilegious hand, let him consume garlic, a substance more harmful than hemlock. Oh, those tough-gutted reapers! What kind of poison is this that rages in my entrails? Can viper's blood have been inadvertently cooked in with these herbs, or did Canidia meddle with the abominable feast?

In this travesty of more earnest invective, Horace urges that garlic replace the less potent hemlock as a punishment for parricides! He goes on to liken the plant to poison and makes the exorbitant analogy with the brews of the legendary Medea (9–12):

ut Argonautas praeter omnis candidum
  Medea mirata est ducem,
ignota tauris illigaturum iuga
  perunxit hoc Iasonem

When Medea was spellbound by the Argonauts' leader, Jason, the
fairest of them all, she surely smeared him with this stuff as he was
about to bind the unfamiliar yoke on the bulls.

The parricide comparison with its reference to filial impiety (*impia
manu*) reappears with minor variations in the opening stanzas of
C. 2.13.1–12. The reworking of motifs from the epode is far from
trivial: *sacrilega manu* directly recalls *impia manu;* the grisly assas-
sination is depicted in similar anatomical detail (cf. "parentis . . .
sui *fregisse cervicem*" and "senile *guttur fregerit*"); the mention of
poison (*venenum*) is common to both, as is its association with
the arch-sorceress Medea (alluded to anonymously in the ode in the
phrase *venena Colcha*, though explicitly named in the epode); the
verb *tractavit*, applied to the planter's hypothetical potions, has
earlier described the imaginary confections of Canidia. In sum, we
are confronted with what looks like a deliberate intertextual stratagem: the ode commences with an imitation, in Alcaics, of the earlier manner of "iambic" invective.

The rationale for this generic interchange is, in my view, to be
sought in the ode's prompt abandonment of this very invective in
favor of the lyric reflections that come to predominate in the sequel. By shifting conclusively from pseudo-angry expostulation to
mellow generalization, the speaker has craftily promoted the brief
of lyric, which thereby emerges as the superior response to life's
vicissitudes. The ramifications of the speaker's conversion to phi-
losophizing and his positive reaction to his mortality are critical: they involve a revision of the same speaker's earlier "iambic"
stance, which entailed an unreflecting, negative attitude to the
near-catastrophe. Thus the discrepancy in tone that readers commonly experience in the ode is strictly related to an ulterior program of upgrading lyric (the genre of the present) at the expense of
the early experiments in *iambi* (the genre of the past). At bottom,
the vindication of Lesbian *carmen*—the centerpiece of the ode—
rests on the implicit demotion of the invective posture and, in this
respect, may be compared with the more overt "disavowal" techniques I have explored in the preceding chapter. In effect, the ode's

prelude succeeds in assimilating, in order to set aside, the irrelevant fortissimi of the "iambic" persona. By this interpretation, the "I" of the poem is not univocal: instead, the distinct voice of the lyrist, which utters the *sententiae* of 13–20, is heard to transcend the animus of the iambographic voice in 1–12.

The gnomic section that follows the outburst (13–20) is, as customary in the *Odes*, pivotal in its double function of refining what precedes and making more explicit the succeeding lyric program. The passage is tidily enclosed by two matching *sententiae* that purvey, *grosso modo*, the same message—the ineluctability of death for humankind. Between the framing maxims is ensconced an elliptical priamel, which, though largely unrecognized as such, is important to the developing argument.[4] Sailor and soldier are mentioned as two representative types in a list of "other" vocations that Horace elsewhere extends (cf. C. 1.1). The abbreviated foil, with its land/sea "complementary," serves as a globalizing device: the other vocations are tokens for immature attitudes that will provide a contrast to the mature insights of the philosophical lyrist. It is axiomatic that the priamel comes to a "cap" in a climactic term (often pronominal). In this case, the poet has decapitated the form and in place of a culminating "me" opposed to the differentiated mass of humanity, he interposes the idealized, capsule portraits of Alcaeus and Sappho. The main consequence of Horace's elliptical treatment of both foil and cap is to bolster the cause of Lesbian *melos* by glorifying its most prestigious practitioners. In short, the truncated priamel creates an expectation that is partly fulfilled (or displaced) in the concrete description of the two acknowledged masters of the preferred genre.

As far as content is concerned, the aphorisms on death, compounded with their concrete exemplifications, emphasize the futility of avoidance (*vitet*), of precautionary measures (*cautum est*), and of fear (*perhorrescit; timet*). These philosophical admonishments are self- as well as other-regarding. If taken by the reader in relation to the preceding lines, they cast an ironic light on the speaker's opening remonstrations against the tree-planter; for it is apparent that a person who was mentally fortified by his metaphysical stance—the counterexample to the *navita* and the *miles*—would be less prone to be overexcited and abusive over the matter of his near-demise. The critique of the attitudes of representative "others" (sailor; soldier) suggests that the appropriate (poetic) response to a close brush with death is to reflect on the law of vicissitude, or even to turn the event into an occasion for celebration, as the lyric poet does in *C. 2.7* (*O saepe mecum*). The observations that constitute the gnomic passage, then, function as a corrective to the prior posture of abusive overreaction.

As "lyric" acceptance of mortality has prevailed in the poem itself over "iambic" spleen, the suitably chastened speaker is free to indulge in eschatological fantasies, albeit of a selective kind.[5] The underworld vision (*quam paene vidimus . . .*) is quite narrowly circumscribed to a privileged *locus*—the abodes of the *pii* (*sedesque discriptas piorum*). Elsewhere in the *Odes,* the salient linkage of poets and *pietas*[6] makes the epithet *pius* virtually a token of the *vates.* In the ambiance of 2.13, the *pii* who become the focus of the hypothetical visit are none other than the representative lyric bards, Alcaeus and Sappho. Since the characterization of these twin *lyrici vates* is carefully slanted so as to convey a peculiar sense of the thematic range of Lesbian lyric, a thorough scrutiny of the passage (lines 21–32) may prove instructive for understanding Horace's view of his relation to the tradition.

The speaker's description of the two poets in performance is both polarized and reductive: his "Sappho" intones plaintive love-songs and his "Alcaeus" relates the hardships of the soldier's life. The thematic reduction is deliberately severe. The educated reader is expected to be aware of the much wider range of subjects in the historical corpus of Sappho, no less than in that of her compatriot Alcaeus.[7] In the case of the latter, Horace might have opted for the sympotic poetry, for example, as representative of that poet's muse. Why then does he choose baldly to assign war to Alcaeus and love to Sappho, with a concomitant antithesis between a grander (*plenius*) and a plainer style (*querentem*)?[8] If Horace reduces in order to achieve a starker polarity, we must further inquire as to the raison d'être of such a bifurcation of the tradition. The answer lies, in part, in the innate rhetoric of polar description: we tend to interpret the two extremes as co-defining a whole. Thus Alcaeus and Sappho here stand, not so much for the historical *lyrici,* as for two complementary generic poles available to Horace within the Lesbian tradition—namely, a more public-oriented variety, concerned with the welfare of the *polis* (tyrants, wars, etc.), and a more inner-directed, personal one, involved with light, and often erotic subject matter. With the strategic polarization of the tradition corresponds the splitting of the imaginary audience into two contrasted groups. On one side, the Alcaean manner has a greater popular appeal (*sed magis . . . volgus*); on the other, the more intimate Sapphic songs demand, by implication, a more elite audience of *sophoi*.

The crucial conclusion to be extracted from Horace's picture of a disproportionate reception for the two immortal bards is that he is not primarily concerned to adjudicate in favor of either practitioner of *melos*.[9] Rather than stating an outright preference, he is seeking to define the kind of sophisticated (and necessarily elite) audience of *docti* that is required for the variety of light lyric he himself espouses in the *Odes*. This interpretation of the scene accords with the programmatic statement of *C.* 1.1, where Horace similarly defines his select audience (30–32):

> me gelidum nemus
> nympharumque leves cum Satyris chori
> secernunt populo

> [For my part], the cool grove and the light songs of nymphs as they dance with Satyrs set me apart from the crowd.

In a nutshell, the bifurcated tradition and its differentiated audience of few/many reflect both Horace's assessment of the scope of his own lyric (mainly light, but capable of sounding *plenius*) and his forecast of its future reception (lacking in mass appeal, but appreciated by the *docti*). Under the alibi of describing the *Nachleben* of his Lesbian models, he subtly discloses his own orientation and ideal audience. Thus the hypothetical episode in the afterlife is a charter for a lyric praxis already enshrined in the *Odes* themselves.

The concluding portion of the ode (B2) continues the design of enhancing *melos* by portraying its *global* effects, as distinct from its effects on specialized audiences in the fortunate groves of the *pii*. By proving that lyric has the power to move even such mythical figures as Cerberus and the Eumenides, the speaker succeeds in universalizing that power, for if such intractable monsters are charmed and refreshed (*recreantur*) by *carmina*, then everyone can be assumed to be amenable to such compelling strains.[10] The *dynamis* of lyric, then, is revealed as irresistible. In making this larger claim, Horace leans, textually, on the image of the *vates* that Virgil adumbrates in his account of the *katabasis* (descent into the under-world) of Orpheus in *Georgics* 4.481–84:

> quin ipsae stupuere domus atque intima Leti
> Tartara caeruleosque implexae crinibus anguis
> Eumenides, tenuitque inhians tria Cerberus ora,
> atque Ixionii vento rota constitit orbis.

> Even the abodes of Death, the innermost reaches of Tartarus, were
> dumbfounded, and the Eumenides whose hair is entwined with
> dark blue snakes, and gaping Cerberus held open his three mouths,
> and Ixion's wheel ceased to rotate in the wind.

The literary borrowings (the charming of the Eumenidean snakes;
the stupefaction of Cerberus) amount to more than a complimen-
tary nod to Horace's friend and fellow-poet. The Virgilian echoes of
motif and diction help to magnify the aura of Lesbian poetry by
affiliating its effects with those of the all-puissant Orpheus. This
Orphic image of the *vates*, when transposed to a cadre of lyric performance, confers authority on the latter and stamps it with a seal
of authenticity.

If the penultimate stanza reveals the miraculous and universal
dynamis inherent in lyric by expanding its audience almost indefi-
nitely, the closing lines (39–40) not only augment the list of unlikely auditors (*quin et . . .*), but also negotiate a return, implicitly,
to the theme of impiety, which predominated in the opening lines
of the poem:

> quin et Prometheus et Pelopis parens
> dulci laborum decipitur sono;
>   nec curat Orion leones
>   aut timidos agitare lyncas.

> Prometheus, moreover, and Pelops's father are distracted from their
> toils by the sweet sound; and Orion does not care to hunt lions or
> timid lynxes.

Prometheus, Tantalus, and Orion are far from otiose increments
to the catalogue of improbable, but appreciative, listeners. They ex-
emplify legendary sufferers who have committed famous acts of
impiety against the most exalted of Olympian deities. The very periphrasis used for Tantalus, *Pelopis parens*, reverberates with the
parentis of line 5. Moreover, the named *impii* of the underworld
myth recall the even more violent and hypothetical unnamed *impii*

to whom the tree-planter was humorously compared in 5–12. The rehearsal of the motif of notorious offenders (a variety of ring composition) accomplishes more than a neat sense of recapitulation and formal closure. It also provides a coup de grace to the angry "iambic" speaker, who has given way to the superior lyric voice. Certain of the most famous *impii,* it now appears, prove susceptible to the prevailing power of *carmina;* hence, in retrospect, even the notorious tree-planter, who has been assimilated to the status of the grand sinners, would ultimately have been vulnerable to such sweet compulsion. The poem's final vignette, therefore, completes the movement of replacing ineffectual recriminations with the affirmation of a *dulcis sonus* that magically enforces the enduring destiny of the lyric tradition to which Horace is heir.

The perfect icon of the transformation that has taken place in the poem is the snake-entwined hair of the Furies. These fearful goddesses, who incarnate the principle of vengeance for blood guilt and, inter alia, violent crimes against kin, are the appropriate agents of the kind of punishment that would be meted out to the nefarious tree-planter and his mythical analogues who commit parricide and other heinous crimes. When therefore they make an appearance towards the end of the ode as the euphemistically named "Eumenides" ("The Gracious Ones"), whose venomous and angry snakes have been rendered placid by sweet song, we may perceive, above and beyond the Virgilian tag, the total transcendence of "iambographic" *ira.*

My interpretation of the tree episode and its sequel in C. 2.13 assumes that its primary function is to certify the speaker's authenticity as a composer of "sweet" lyric against the backdrop of a discredited discourse of invective. In the other three odes that make reference to the tree episode, it is invariably the status of the speaker *qua* poet that guarantees his salvation. Thus (a) in C. 2.17, Horace attributes his escape from death to the god Faunus, whom he characterizes as *Mercurialium custos virorum* ("guardian of men devoted to Mercury"), where the epithet *Mercurialium* points to the function of Mercury as the protector of poets; (b) in C. 3.4 (to be discussed more fully below), Calliope and the Muses are alleged to be responsible for the poet's rescue, since he is *amicum fontibus et choris;* while (c) in C. 3.8, Bacchus (who is, of course, a special patron of the Horatian *carmen*) is the recipient of the poet's vow of a thanksgiving sacrifice and feast in celebration of the same event.

In view of the recurrent motif of rescue, why the odd variation, one might legitimately ask, in the particular divinity who is allotted the role of poet's savior? The impression Horace seems to convey is that Mercury (with Faunus), Calliope (with the Muses), and Bacchus are, for the purposes of an exemplary salvation function, interchangeable. In other words, the episode acquires its meaning only in respect to its emblematic character. The rescuing *numen* varies, but the significance of the rescue remains constant. In place of a pseudo-historicity that would fix the incident in canonic terms, we have a malleable episode that is analogous to a mythical event in the way its underlying meaning persists from one variant to the next. The tree episode, then, is partly constitutive of a biographical *mythos* designed to accredit the speaker as fully worthy of the Greek melic tradition whose mantle he has assumed.

SUB LAURU MEA: THE ESCAPE FROM *BELLUM* (C. 2.7)

O saepe mecum tempus in ultimum
deducte Bruto militiae duce,
    quis te redonavit Quiritem
      dis patriis Italoque caelo,

Pompei, meorum prime sodalium?   5
cum quo morantem saepe diem mero
    fregi coronatus nitentis
      malobathro Syrio capillos.

tecum Philippos et celerem fugam
sensi relicta non bene parmula,   10
    cum fracta virtus, et minaces
      turpe solum tetigere mento.

sed me per hostis Mercurius celer
denso paventem sustulit aere;
    te rursus in bellum resorbens   15
      unda fretis tulit aestuosis.

ergo obligatam redde Iovi dapem
longaque fessum militia latus
    depone sub lauru mea, nec
      parce cadis tibi destinatis.   20

oblivioso levia Massico
ciboria exple; funde capacibus
    unguenta de conchis. quis udo
      deproperare apio coronas

curatve myrto? quem Venus arbitrum   25
dicet bibendi? non ego sanius
bacchabor Edonis: recepto
dulce mihi furere est amico.

You who were often misled with me into extreme peril when Brutus led our troops—who has restored you as a civilian to your ancestral gods and the sky of Italy, O Pompey, foremost of my companions, with whom I often broke up the lingering day by means of unmixed wine, my hair crowned with a wreath and resplendent with Syrian nard? With you I experienced Philippi and swift flight, my shield having been left behind unceremoniously, when our prowess was broken, and menacing warriors touched the base earth with their chins. But me, as I lay overcome with fear, swift Mercury bore up in a thick cloud through the enemy lines; while you the wave of warfare sucked back into the fray and bore over seething waters. Now, therefore, render unto Jupiter the feast you owe him, and lay down your limbs, weary with long service in the wars, beneath my laurel, and do not be sparing with the wine jars that have been earmarked for you. Fill the burnished goblets to the full with Massic wine that induces amnesia; pour out the perfumed oils from large containers. Who will hasten to provide us with wreaths of moist celery or of myrtle? Whom will the "Venus" [the best throw of the dice] elect as master of the symposium? I, for one, shall carouse no less wildly than the [Thracian] Edoni. When a friend has been recovered, I take sweet pleasure in going mad.

Nowhere is Horace's desire to shape an episode in accordance with a prototype more evident than in his account of his escape from the battle of Philippi—an account embedded in a convivial ode of a kind well represented in the *Odes*. The strictly sympotic aspects of the poem do not concern us at this stage in the argument; instead, I shall concentrate on the ways in which the lyric vocation is sanctioned and vindicated. The Philippi episode constitutes a litmus test of my concept of a mythologized *bios*, for the very reason that it alludes to a documented historical experience—Horace's participation in the battle on the losing, Republican side. It is therefore all the more telling that an incident that afforded such an opportunity for historical concreteness should have been so schematized as to conform to a timeless conventional model—the lyric poet's emblematic gesture of abandoning his shield. For the composer of C. 2.7, the actual experience of Philippi (*Philippos . . . sensi*) is comprehensively mediated through a topos that received its first definitive (extant) formulation in Archilochus 5 W.

Since Horace's ode manifestly contains at least one verbal echo of the Archilochean diction (line 10: *relicta;* cf. κάλλιπον), it is appropriate to compare the prototype in order to clarify the deeper ramifications of Horace's allusion:

> ἀσπίδι μὲν Σαΐων τις ἀγάλλεται, ἣν παρὰ θάμνωι,
> ἔντος ἀμώμητον, κάλλιπον οὐκ ἐθέλων·
> αὐτὸν δ' ἐξεσάωσα. τί μοι μέλει ἀσπὶς ἐκείνη;
> ἐρρέτω· ἐξαῦτις κτήσομαι οὐ κακίω.

Some member of the Saioi tribe takes delight in my shield, which I left, involuntarily, behind a bush—an object in perfect condition! My person, however, I kept intact. What does that shield matter to me? So much for that! By and by I shall get another just as good.

As Hermann Fränkel perceived so clearly, the meaning of the gesture for Archilochus, and by extension, for ancient lyric, resides in its authoritative redefinition of values (Fränkel 136–37). In leaving behind his shield (or, to be precise, in announcing the event in elegiac verse), the Archaic poet breaks iconoclastically with a heroic value-system in which death in battle was regarded as more honorable than an inglorious life. Homer's Achilles had already posed a challenge to that ethos from within the domain of epic (see my analysis of Cheiron's advice to his ward in chapter 1). In his thoughtful discussion, Fränkel eloquently compares Achilles' mordant words rejecting a heroic death in battle (*Il.* 9.408ff.) with the Archilochean text and concludes:

> The Achilles of the Iliad is only toying with the idea that life could be dearer to him than honor; Archilochus seriously balances the value of life against an exaggerated notion of honor, draws a realistic conclusion, and acts accordingly; and at once, in a tone of aggressive challenge, he proclaims to all the world what he has done.

The Greek poet outlandishly flaunts a major difference in philosophical orientation between epic, on the one hand, and lyric, on the other (to employ the latter term in the extended sense to which Fränkel also subscribes). That difference, which is already foreshadowed in the *Iliad* with Achilles' jaundiced critique, becomes the proud badge of the lyric ethical position from Archilochus onwards. In promulgating the shift, Archilochus relies on the epic norms as a foil for articulating the rival (lyric) attitude.

Horace, whose imitation of Archilochean postures is by no means circumscribed to the genre of *iambos*, situates himself unambiguously within the lyric tradition of the *rhipsaspis* (the soldier/poet who jettisons his shield) that included among its eminent exemplars Alcaeus and Anacreon.[11] In so doing, however, he is not simply replicating a topos for the sake of displaying his erudition. For him, the reaffirmation of the primacy of life (and the corollary, the demotion of heroic death in battle) is fundamental to the whole lyric stance as he sustains it throughout the *Carmina*.

Certain details in Horace's variant of the topos confirm his grasp of the underlying meaning of the conventional gesture of the lyric *rhipsaspis*. The fact, for instance, that the shield is denoted by the diminutive *parmula* is a sign of the speaker's disparagement of an object that would normally have elicited pride from a Roman soldier no less than from an ancient Spartan or Homeric hero. The glaringly anachronistic vocable (the *parmula* was obsolete in the Roman army of Horace's day and, in any event, was technically inappropriate to infantry!) conspires, in the words of Nisbet and Hubbard, "to remove Horace's account from the world of real campaigning." Though the *parmula* is not the historical equivalent of an archaic Greek hoplite *aspis*, both accoutrements belong to the same "paradigmatic set" within the universe of signification created by the lyric tradition. The variations that occur in the convention (the shield, for example, is "left behind" by Archilochus and Horace, and "thrown away" by Alcaeus and also, apparently, Anacreon) are in themselves of negligible import. What the gesture signifies remains, in its broad outline, stable: a radical devaluation of the warrior ethos and posthumous glory, together with an enhancement of the value of life in the present.

Although Horace's gesture of abandoning the *parmula* is schematized pseudo-biography rather than reportage, we need not conclude that the speaker is either merely flippant, on the one hand, or utterly earnest, on the other. To say that the Philippi episode is "schematized pseudo-biography" (*mythos*) is not, of course, to assert or deny its actual occurrence. It is a matter of historical record that the battle occurred in Thrace—not far from the spot where Archilochus is presumed to have fled the enemy![12] This is just the kind of coincidence that a clever poet delights in exploiting. The self-deprecation expressed in the phrase *relicta non bene parmula* ("my shield having been left behind unceremoniously") is vintage Horace in its sophisticated yoking of the comic and the pathetic. Whereas the litotes *non bene* openly acknowledges the shamefulness of the gesture in terms of the normal conception of *virtus*, the Archilochean tag *relicta* and the well-placed diminutive *parmula* facetiously advertise the poet's allegiance to a competing order of values.

The same grotesque humor informs the account of the destruction of martial *virtus* at Philippi (11–12):

> cum fracta virtus, et minaces
> turpe solum tetigere mento.

when our prowess was broken, and menacing warriors touched the base earth with their chins.

Fracta—a violent metaphor of disruption—is made to reverberate with the perfect *fregi* in the previous strophe, where the context was a robust drinking bout ("cum quo morantem saepe diem mero / *fregi*": "with whom I often broke up the lingering day by means of unmixed wine"). The startling repetition of a word within consecutive stanzas is deliberate and laden with significance for the argument as a whole. Time, Horace's metaphor seems to suggest, can be intermittently "broken" or interrupted by a life-affirming symposium; military *virtus*, however, once broken, loses all meaning and, like the hapless Humpty Dumpty, cannot be reconstituted as such. The ignominious death of haughty warriors (*minaces*)[13] does not, in this view of martial enterprise, compensate for a life mortgaged to an illusory honor. In a word, the Philippi debacle is recast in the mold of an emblematic "lyric" event. The true hero is not the stolid seeker after *virtus* on the battlefield, but the chastened singer who, like Alcaeus or Anacreon, apprehends the paramount value of human life in the here and now. As Archilochus succinctly and irreverently puts it in another fragment that Horace evidently knew (133 W):

> οὔτις αἰδοῖος μετ᾽ ἀστῶν οὐδὲ περίφημος θανὼν
> γίνεται· χάριν δὲ μᾶλλον τοῦ ζοοῦ διώκομεν
> ⟨οἱ⟩ ζοοί, κάκιστα δ᾽ αἰεὶ τῶι θανόντι γίνεται.

Once dead, a man is no more respected by his fellow-citizens nor held in high repute; alive, we pursue the favor of the living; for the dead, there remains only dishonor.

The *charis* of the living, then, is precisely the end lyric enterprise strives to fulfill, and that C. 2.7 is ultimately designed to celebrate.

In the way he organizes the discourse on lyric values (symbolized in the *charis* of the symposium), Horace avails himself of a structuring device dear to the Augustans: he constructs an "opposition" between the military and the poetic vocations. As I observed in the parallel case of war/eros, the opposition helps to set the contours of lyric in bold relief. The convergent (and later, divergent) destinies of the speaker and addressee are symmetrically represented in a carefully balanced antithesis. Thus the three opening stanzas are devoted to the union of the *amici*, and a corresponding final three to the anticipated celebration of their reunion. The middle stanza, the fourth, focusses on the violent disunion of the friends on the battlefield. All seven stanzas are predicated on the rhetorical antinomy between *bellum* and *convivium*.

As a means of marking the eventual disjunction of the comrades-in-arms, the singer harps, at the outset, on the contrary— that is, the prior convergence of the experiences of the two bosom *sodales*. The preposition *cum*, strategically reiterated in emphatic positions, binds together this opening motif of close union:

I	II	III
me*cum*	*cum* quo	te*cum*
(1)	(6)	(9)

Stanzas I and III, which allude to the friends' joint (and unsuccessful) experiences on the battlefield stand as a somber frame within which the radiant picture of their joint (and successful) experiences in the symposium is inserted (stanza II: cf. *nitentes . . . capillos*). In the period of time when the friends were united, there was already an ominous bifurcation in the quality of their life-style as Horace subtly portrays it. For though both kinds of activity, the military and the convivial, were continual and alternating (a point Horace stresses by the repetition of *saepe* at lines 1 and 6), the military portion encompassed both mortal danger (cf. line 1: *tempus in ultimum*) and failure (hinted at in the ironic wordplay in line 2: *deducte . . . duce*). Before he proceeds to describe their subsequent separation, the poet previews the vocational alternatives open to them in terms prejudicial to the military. The slant in the account is most noticeable in the ironic use of verbal repetition to highlight fundamental differences. As the repeated *saepe* opposes the re-enacted symposium to frequent defeat in warfare, so also, as I have previously observed, the repeated metaphor of fracture (*fregi/fracta*) opposes the ultimate futility of soldierly prowess to the viability of the convivial mode of being.

The central and intermediary fourth stanza narrates the abrupt sundering of the speaker and addressee as a consequence of the decisive defeat at Philippi. Here Horace is at pains to articulate the disjunction (as earlier the conjunction) by counterbalancing the pronouns *me* and *te* and allocating two lines each to their disparate destinies (13–16):

> sed *me* per hostis Mercurius celer
> denso paventem *sustulit* aere;
>   *te* rursus in bellum resorbens
>   unda fretis *tulit* aestuosis.

But *me*, as I lay overcome with fear, swift Mercury *bore up* in a thick cloud through the enemy lines; *you* the wave of warfare sucked back into the fray and *bore* over seething waters.

The contrasting (and cognate) perfects *sustulit* and *tulit* drive home the disparity, as does the reappearance of the epithet *celer*, which had modified *fugam* in the previous stanza, but now is attached to the savior god, Mercury. "Swift Mercury" and "swift flight"—the iteration is one of several in this remarkable poem in which the use of the same word in differing contexts is a much exploited technical device.[14] In the case of *celer*, the effect is to show the poet and deity acting in concert at the very moment when the unity of the two comrades is being disrupted.

The separation of the comrades is a crucial turning-point in their lives. Pompeius is carried off by the figurative wave into further warfare, while his friend Horace is carried off by Mercury to a life devoted to the peaceful cultivation of the Muse. The radical dissociation of the military and convivial spheres of existence has, for Horace, not merely a diachronic (i.e., historical) significance, but a synchronic one as well, insofar as vocational alternatives are concerned. The sympotic way of life is inextricably intertwined with lyric performance. This essential facet of the contrast in life-styles becomes most pronounced in the fifth stanza, where the singer plays on the symbolic import of the laurel tree (17–20):

> ergo obligatam redde Iovi dapem
> longaque fessum militia latus
> depone *sub lauru mea,* nec
> parce cadis tibi destinatis.

Now, therefore, render unto Jupiter the feast you owe him, and lay down your limbs, weary with long service in the wars, *beneath my laurel,* and do not be sparing with the wine jars that have been earmarked for you.

Despite efforts on the part of some commentators to limit the reference to a purely literal level (i.e., the shade of an actual laurel on Horace's estate), there is scarcely any doubt that the phrase *sub lauru mea* is, in context, deliberately ambiguous.[15] The decisive Horatian passage for the heraldic coupling of the laurel with the poetic function is the envoi of *C.* 3.30, the lines that formally conclude the *tribiblos* (14–16):

> sume superbiam
> quaesitam meritis et mihi Delphica
> lauro cinge volens, Melpomene, comam.

Assume the proud esteem earned by your merits and with Delphic laurel, O Melpomene, be pleased to bind my hair.

If further substantiation of the link is deemed necessary, we may compare the situation that Horace portrays in *C.* 3.4.37–40, where Augustus is invited to refresh himself after the labors of protracted campaigning:

> vos Caesarem altum, militia simul
> fessas cohortis abdidit oppidis,
> finire quaerentem labores
> Pierio recreatis antro.

[You, O Muses,] as soon as exalted Caesar has hidden away his cohorts, weary with military service, in the towns, and he seeks to put an end to his toils, you refresh him in the Pierian cave.

Here the phrase *militia . . . fessas* clearly echoes the line *longaque fessum militia latus* in the poem under discussion. The echo suggests that *Pierio antro* may be the structural analogue of *sub lauru mea.* Both Pierian cave and shady laurel are manifest emblems for the lyric verse that is to provide solace and recreation for the war-weary soldier.

The role of the god Mercury in saving the speaker from mortal danger is in itself a vindication of the poet's calling. As mythical inventor of the lyre, the god has a clear *parti pris* in the destiny of bards, and he is specifically invoked in this aspect in more than one ode. Horace even goes so far as to designate poets as a class by the pseudo-eponymous term *Mercuriales viri* (*C.* 2.17.29; and see my discussion above on *C.* 2.13.23 ff.). His timely salvation through the intervention of Mercury is therefore a signal event in the bio-mythography of the poem, since it confers the stamp of authenticity on the métier of the lyrist.[16] The motif of the rescue, which reads in Horace's self-deprecatory account like a caricature of an epic type-scene (e.g., Aphrodite's rescue of Paris in the *Iliad*), contributes to the primary design of valorizing lyric in relation to heroic verse. At the moment of his salvation, the poet portrays himself as blatantly anti-heroic, even fearful (cf. *paventem*); hence Mercury's gesture demonstrates the irrelevance of heroic *virtus* and the overriding concern to safeguard the sacrosanct artist. In a nutshell, Mercurial men—in Horace's idiosyncratic sense of that epithet—are under special auspices, and are thereby in a unique position to extend the laurel to those who are lucky enough to escape death in battle.

The topic of escape from death is, of course, subliminally present throughout the ode and helps to animate the anticipated festival of thanksgiving. In the way he leads into the topic in the first two lines, Horace may be punning subtly on the words *deducte* and *Bruto* as a means of downgrading military generalship (*militiae duce*) and upgrading "lighter" activities. A primordial meaning of *brutus* is "heavy" (gravis).[17] *Deductus,* on the other hand, has well-documented literary associations in the critical lexicon of the Augustans with the "light" genre (*genus tenue*).[18] The effect of Brutus's "heavy-handed" generalship is, paradoxically, to reduce his follower, Pompeius, to a status pathetically deprived of grandeur (*deducte,* in transparent interplay with *duce*). The diminishment of the soldier who followed "Brutus" prepares the former to become, once again, a fitting *sodalis* to the light-hearted symposiast.

Archilochus in a famous fragment (1 W) had boasted of being able to combine successfully the disparate roles of soldier and poet:

εἰμὶ δ᾽ ἐγὼ θεράπων μὲν Ἐνυαλίοιο ἄνακτος
καὶ Μουσέων ἐρατὸν δῶρον ἐπιστάμενος,

I am, to be sure, a servant of Lord Enyalios [the war-god]; I am no
less a servant of the Muses, and am conversant with their ador-
able gift.

Horace, in a conspicuous and perhaps self-conscious departure
from that claim, posits the *incompatibility* of the two roles. *O saepe
mecum* is the Roman poet's refined effort to demonstrate the viability of his own *imbellis lyra.*[19]

ANIMOSUS INFANS: THE CHILDHOOD OF
A *LAUDATOR* (C. 3.4)

The prooemium of *C.* 3.4 constitutes an ornate illustration of the
poet's use of a quasi-autobiographical event to authenticate the
mode of discourse he has undertaken to compose. To apprehend
the function of the miraculous scene from infancy that Horace relates in lines 9–13, it will be expedient to analyze the entire first
half of the ode (1–40), in which the stage is elaborately set for a
Pindaric-style encomium of Augustus. For the sake of convenience,
I shall consider each of the ten introductory stanzas in turn in the
hope that diachronic analysis will reveal the coherent design of the
prooemium as a whole.

I

> Descende caelo et dic age tibia
> regina longum Calliope melos,
> seu voce nunc mavis acuta,
> seu fidibus citharave Phoebi.
> (1–4)

Descend from heaven, Queen Calliope, and sing, if you please, a
lengthy ode on the flute, whether you now opt for a high tone or for
the strings and lyre of Apollo.

The term *longum melos* immediately demarcates the generic scope
of *C.* 3.4. The epithet *longum* announces an intention to compose a
song that will test the outer limits of the poet's lyric range (the
poem is actually the longest of the *Carmina*). An unusually long
poem obviously requires special rhetorical justification within the
predominant aesthetic norms of the short, light lyric. To an audi-

ence of Augustan *docti, longum* would, of course, imply far more than mere length: certain stylistic and thematic exigencies would be expected to come into play. By demanding such an extensive poem of Calliope, the lyrist is preparing us for a daring experiment in panegyric in the grand manner.

To this end, the disjunctive clauses (*seu . . . seu*) have a precise, augmentative function that is often obscured in the copious litera-ture on the ode. By offering the Muse a choice between two alter-natives,[20] the singer indicates his supreme confidence in his own ability to adopt whatever level of tone is appropriate to the theme at hand. The bifurcation of the lyric repertoire into discrete modes (emblematized by the *tibia/cithara* contrast) is, for Horace, a con-sistent practice in contexts emphasizing the versatility of his *inge-nium*. Two prominent instances may convey this ulterior meaning of the antithesis between musical instruments.

(a) In the inaugural ode, *C.* 1.1, poetic achievement is alleged to depend upon the Muses' generosity to the singer, and that achievement is formally dichotomized (32–34):

> si neque *tibias*
> Euterpe cohibet nec Polyhymnia
> Lesboum refugit tendere *barbiton.*

so long as neither Euterpe restrains *the flutes* nor Polyhymnia shuns from tuning *the lyre* of Lesbos.

The dichotomy (*tibia/barbitos*) is, at bottom, a rhetorical means of expressing a totality. The speaker is asserting thereby the extent of his potential lyric range.

(b) In an early Pindarizing encomium of the *princeps, C.* 1.12, the Muse (here named Clio) is deferentially accorded a choice of in-struments at the inception of the song (1–3):

> Quem virum aut heroa *lyra* vel acri
> *tibia* sumis celebrare, Clio?
> quem deum?

What man or hero, what god do you undertake to praise, O Clio, either on the *lyre* or the high-toned *flute?*

By projecting the option of musical accompaniment onto the Muse, Horace marks his present decision to extend the scope of the *car-*

men to include the loftier strains (associated with the *tibia*) along with the quieter melodies that typify the *lyra*.

To revert to the diction of *Descende caelo:* the bold overture relies on a conventional code wherein a proffered choice of musical alternatives (wind versus strings) has come to signify a claim of omnicompetence on the part of the bard. In this regard, the carefully chosen attributive *acutus*, as applied to the voice of Calliope, points, like its contextual synonym *acer* (cf. *acri tibia* in *C.* 1.12, cited above), to a metaphorically "high" level of melic expression.

II

> auditis an me ludit amabilis
> insania? audire et videor pios
>   errare per lucos, amoenae
>   quos et aquae subeunt et aurae.
>   (5–8)

Do you hear, or is a pleasurable madness playing with me? I seem to hear and to be wandering through sacred groves, traversed by delightful waters and breezes.

As in many "kletic" (invocatory) hymns in which a god is summoned from a *sedes* (whether celestial or terrestrial), the strategy of the singer is to pronounce a self-fulfilling request. In Sappho's celebrated hymn to Aphrodite, for example, the goddess's timely appearance in the poem is a kind of preemptive guarantee of its magical efficacy.[21] The request of the poet in such kletic contexts is self-fulfilling in the sense that it accomplishes its purpose in the very act of utterance. It is this fiction of the immanent reification of the appeal (*descende; dic*) that Horace proceeds to dramatize in the second strophe when he suddenly addresses his audience with the double question, *auditis . . . insania?*[22] The listeners are, in effect, being asked to verify the epiphany of the Muse (hence the competence of the bard) by acknowledging the evidence of the unfolding *melos*. By a comparable ruse, Pindar secures assent to the efficacy of his own art by a peremptory opening command to the singers in *P.* 6.1: ʾΑκούσατʼ ("Listen!").

With the response *audire et videor* ("I seem to hear"), the composer of *C.* 3.4 advances the substantial claim to be speaking with the voice of Calliope, or, in other words, to be already engaged in a *melos longum* fit to be situated in a grander tradition. The implied idea of comparability with the best in such a tradition emerges most clearly in the topos of the poet "wandering through *sacred groves*" ("*pios* errare per lucos"). A plurality of groves (or stylized *loci amoeni*) suggests abundance of inspiration, and *pius*, as so often in the *Odes*, is not so much a moral, as a literary badge of competence. Although there is an ostensible touch of modesty in *videor* (as also perhaps in the hint of possible self-delusion in *ludit*), the preponderant effect of the strophe is to establish the poetic credentials of the singer. A fine parallel from Greek lyric to Horace's subterfuge of indicating Calliope's manifestation in the poem is to be found in a line of Alcman (30 *PMG*), where the Muse, who is characterized as "high-toned Siren," is said to have sounded in the song itself:

ἁ Μῶσα κέκλαγ᾽ ἁ λίγηα Σηρήν

The Muse has sounded, the high-toned Siren[23]

The first two stanzas, then, are intimately bound together in terms of a double objective—to alert the audience to the fact that the present *carmen* will be (a) extraordinarily long and (b) fully within the creative powers of the singer of the *Odes*.

III–V

> me fabulosae Vulture in Apulo
> nutricis extra limen Apuliae[24]
>   ludo fatigatumque somno
>   fronte nova puerum palumbes
>
> texere, mirum quod foret omnibus,
> quicumque celsae nidum Acherontiae
>   saltusque Bantinos et arvum
>   pingue tenent humilis Forenti,
>
> ut tuto ab atris corpore viperis
> dormirem et ursis, ut premerer sacra
>   lauroque collataque myrto
>   non sine dis animosus infans.
>   (9–20)

When I was a baby boy I strayed on Mount Voltur beyond the threshold of nurse Apulia where, worn out with play, I fell asleep and was covered over with new leaves by the legendary doves—des-

tined to become a wonder to all who inhabit lofty Acherontia's nest,
and Bantia's glades, and the fertile field of low-lying Forentum—a
wonder as to how I slept with my body safe from black snakes and
bears, how I was tucked in under a heap of sacred laurel and myrtle
leaves, an infant imbued with spirit through divine grace.

Strophes III through V comprise a single, lengthy period culminating in the afflatus of *animosus infans*. The very complexity of the
syntax (witness the exfoliating subordinate clauses, *quod . . . ut . . .
ut*) mirrors the grandiloquence predicated in the implied theophany. In form, no less than in substance, elaboration is the order of
the day. The whole edifice is proudly vaulted by the pronoun *me* at
one end and the substantive *infans* at the other—both referring to
the central persona in the episode, the poetic wunderkind. In con-
templating the structure, I shall focus on a few elements that have a
crucial bearing on the topic of my analysis.

Coming immediately after the initial *me*, the modifier *fabulosae*
brands the narrative to follow as legendary in status and warns the
audience against a mundane reading of the incident. As if this were
not sufficient, the *mirum* of the next stanza boldly stresses the marvellous dimension of the account. What Horace in fact presents
under the guise of autobiography is a paradigmatic *Erlebnis*. The
miraculous episode of doves covering the sleeping infant with
leaves conforms in its essentials to a conventional fable illustrating
the charmed childhood of the bard. To be protected from harm
through divine intercession (especially on the part of the Muses)
is a conventional sign of election to the distinguished company
of poets (such as Ibycus, Simonides, Pindar, and Stesichorus) to
whom tradition assigned similar prophylactic episodes. Horace's
variant of the "Muses' protégé" motif has its palpably light side,
despite the heavy baggage of an almost pompous syntax. We are
surely meant to smile as we are treated to a catalogue of surrounding districts whose inhabitants are destined to wonder at the pro-
digious infant (13–16). The imparting of local color to a timeless
narrative pattern is a Horatian signature that, as often, comes per-
ilously close to self-caricature.

In its root function, the narrative recalls the passage in the *Integer vitae* (C. 1.22) where the sacrosanct poet is magically protected
from a portentous wolf[25] (as compared to the boars and vipers of
this episode) after wandering beyond the bounds of his estate (cf.

extra terminum with *extra limen*). Whereas the speaker in the short ode to Lalage is saved thanks to his fidelity to love-melodies, he is preserved in the *longum melos* in order to compose an elevated praise-poem on the ruler. At either end of the scale of composition, the salvation motif is a narrative "signifier" that serves to mark the poet off as one who is predestined to fulfill a special role.

The semi-humorous handling of the biographical fable does not detract from its underlying significance. To prove his precocious commitment to the literary calling, the speaker identifies the "new foliage" (mentioned in 12: *fronde nova*) as none other than the laurel and the myrtle (19: *lauroque collataque myrto*), two plants that bear symbolic associations with Apollo and Venus respectively. The "sacred laurel" is, of course, especially to the purpose in view of the fact that Apollo's *cithara* has been specified as an instrumental option in the beginning gambit (*seu fidibus citharave Phoebi*). Thus it is the floral emblem of the mythological "leader of the Muses" that the doves select to spread over the sleeping child. By such semiotic precision, Horace contrives to reemphasize the level of performance at which he proposes to engage the hearer—a level that the epithet *animosus*, with its suggestion of high inspiration, also enhances.[26]

VI–VII

> vester, Camenae, vester in arduos
> tollor Sabinos, seu mihi frigidum
>   Praeneste seu Tibur supinum
>   seu liquidae placuere Baiae.
> vestris amicum fontibus et choris
> non me Philippis versa acies retro,
>   devota non exstinxit arbos,
>   nec Sicula Palinurus unda.
>   (21–28)

With you—yes, you—I rise to the Sabine heights, whether I am drawn to cool Praeneste, or sloping Tibur, or clear Baiae. As devoted friend of your fountains and dancing-choirs, I was not annihilated by the rout at Philippi, nor by the accursed tree, nor by the Sicilian waves around Cape Palinurus.

The triple repetition of *vester* in this section of the ode (a standard feature of hymnal style) buttresses the main point that the poet wishes to bring home—the *continuity* of his inspiration from childhood onward. The shift of tense from past to present in *tollor* (22), and the reversion to the perfect in *exstinxit* (27), together extend the temporal scope of the Muses' tutelage to embrace the poet's entire career. These two stanzas place the earlier (childhood) episode within the general perspective of a consistent *bios*. A possible inference from the apostrophe to the Camenae (the local, Italian version of the Muses) is that they are ultimately responsible for the original act of salvation (the doves' strewing of leaves), and are probably also to be extrapolated from the unnamed divinities in 20 (*non sine dis*) who succor the *animosus infans*. Be that as it may, the seventh stanza goes even further in vindicating a lifelong covenant between the bard and the Muses, insofar as it brings together three later biographical episodes of magical salvation (from the field of Philippi, from the falling tree, from shipwreck).[27] The systematic alignment of these episodes in the same passage is additional corroboration (if such is required) of Horace's appropriation of biographical topoi to ratify the integrity of his artistic inspiration. An important consequence of the aggregation of escapes is to place all the events in the same paradigmatic set.

The sequence of toponyms in the sixth strophe (Sabine Hills, Praeneste, Tibur, Baiae) is much more than a straightforward list of Horace's favorite haunts. The fact that the poet is accompanied, if not actually transported, by the Muses to these localities (*tollor*) is tantamount to regarding the latter as quasi-sanctified *sedes* of the divinities themselves. The key word *placuere* in 24, along with the freedom of choice expressed in the cola *seu . . . seu . . . seu*, conspires to enhance the aura of a divine conveyance from one cult-center to the next. In a nutshell, Horace is at pains to qualify the several *loci* as conducive to lyric creativity. As in the opening strophe, the disjunctives formalize the fiction that the Muses' transfer to various poetic locales is unrestricted and voluntary.

Over and above the mutual devotion of poet and goddesses of poetry, there is a literary nuance to be observed in the topographical arrangement itself. Horace has ordered the haunts in a graduated series from highest to lowest. Each level in the descending order is signposted with an appropriate adjective (*arduos; frigidum; supinum; liquidae*). If the graded declension were unique to this passage of the ode, it would be relatively easy to discount it as otiose.

The same ordering principle, however, can be shown to be operative in the fourth stanza, where the speaker proceeds from the heights of Acherontia (*celsae; nidum*) to the lower-lying Forentum (*humilis*). Why the two hierarchical enumerations of familiar places in such close succession? The answer, we may legitimately surmise, lies in Horace's desire to schematize the all-inclusive range of his muse. As the miracle of his childhood election has been manifest at all regional levels, so his allegiance to the practice of poetry remains intact at whatever *locus amoenus* he, as a mature composer, chooses to sojourn.

VIII–IX

> utcumque mecum vos eritis, libens
> insanientem navita Bosphorum
>   temptabo et urentis harenas
>   litoris Assyrii viator,
> visam Britannos hospitibus feros
> et laetum equino sanguine Concanum,
>   visam pharetratos Gelonos
>   et Scythicum inviolatus amnem.
>   (29–36)

Whenever you are with me I shall freely, as a sailor, explore the raging Bosporus and, as a land-voyager, the burning sands of the Assyrian shore; I shall visit intact the Britons that are unfriendly to strangers, the Concanians that delight in the blood of horses; I shall visit the quiver-bearing Geloni and the Scythian river.

In the twin geographical catalogues of strophes VIII and IX, the idea of an inseparable bond (*amicitia*) between poet and muses neatly converges with that of unrestricted thematic range. The almost banal topos, "I am willing to go anywhere with a true friend," acquires a fresh modulation when the faithful *amici* to whom the speaker is devoted are identical with his creative sponsors, Calliope and her sisters.[28] From this viewpoint, the hypothetical voyages limned in the asseveration of friendship turn into tropes for literary exploration (cf. *temptabo*). The careful distribution of places—the potential itinerary of the author—is itself fraught with significance, for the tribes mentioned are situated on the remote borders of the Roman world.[29] The use of extremes is, from a rhetorical point of view, very economical, in that it sustains at least three interrelated points: (1) no place is too inhospitable or savage when friendship is at stake (extremity of devotion), (2) no "place" is inaccessible to the lyrist (poetic omnicompetence), and (3) tribes on the borders of empire are themes germane to the occasion (implicit eulogy of the military accomplishments of Augustus's regime). The second point, in particular, is made by Horace in virtually the same form in a prominent ode predicting his posthumous fame (*C.* 2.20.13–20):

> iam Daedaleo notior Icaro
> visam gementis litora Bosphori
>   Syrtesque Gaetulas canorus
>   ales Hyperboreosque campos.
> me Colchus et qui dissimulat metum
> Marsae cohortis Dacus et ultimi
>   noscent Geloni, me peritus
>   discet Hiber Rhodanique potor.

Already better known than Icarus, son of Daedalus, I, a melodious swan, shall visit the shores of the groaning Bosporus, and the Gaetulian Syrtes, and the Hyperborean fields. The Colchian will get to know me, and the Dacian, who conceals his fear of Marsian cohorts; my poems will be taught to clever Spaniards and to men that drink the Rhône's waters.

The map is different in some respects but the purpose of the catalogue is the same: the "visits" (cf. anaphora of *visam* in 3.4) are proof of the global puissance of his art.[30] In the context of *Descende caelo*, globalization is achieved not only by indicating spatial extremes, but also by the familiar device of the "dichotomized whole" (*navita/viator*: 30; 32). In a word, the geographical code of "ubiquity," as elaborated here, serves the primary goal of enlarging the parameters of lyric discourse.

I have earlier characterized the entire first half of the poem as prooemial. The very length of the introduction is, in retrospect, part and parcel of the eulogistic design. Only a magnificent subject would necessitate so qualified a bard and so prolonged an overture. Taking his cue from his model Pindar, Horace culminates the proem in a resounding "name-cap" (to borrow the terminology of Bundy):

X

> Vos *Caesarem altum*, militia simul
> fessas cohortis abdidit oppidis,

finire quaerentem labores
Pierio recreatis antro.
(37–40)

[You, O Muses,] as soon as *exalted Caesar* has hidden away his cohorts, weary with military service, in the towns, and he seeks to put
an end to his toils, you refresh him in the Pierian cave.

By lauding Caesar as *altum*, the writer plays upon a dual connotation of the epithet: the *laudandus* is exalted above ordinary mortals
and, at the same time, he becomes the exalted subject of an encomium. Thus the *melos longum* finds its ultimate validation in the
"height" of its postponed theme.

When he attributes the lyric refreshment of the ruler to the
Muses (*Pierio recreatis antro*), Horace politely continues the fiction
that his own craft is a function of its divine source. To put it more
unambiguously than the text does, the Muses here operate as in-
termediaries for the poet. It is clearly the composer of *C.* 3.4 who
now proffers the ruler the refreshing *melos* that will be an antidote
to his *labores*. In this powerfully oblique method, the old epinikian
cliché of present song as compensation for previous *ponos* is transmuted into the picture of the Muses entertaining a war-weary Augustus in an idealized setting. The sheer immodesty of Horace's
vaunt explains why he has gone to such great lengths to authenticate his art and parade his credentials. The remainder of the ode
(which I have excluded from the present analysis) is given over
to an extensive narration of the Gigantomachy (the battle of the
Olympian gods against the Giants), in which the role of Augustus
in establishing peace is shown to be analogous to Jupiter's mythic
restoration of cosmic order. The absolute mastery that the poet displays throughout in his handling of elevated discourse fully justifies his initial pose as the vehicle of *regina Calliope*.

CREDITI POSTERI: THE CREDIBILITY OF THE
LAUDATOR (C. 2.19; 3.25)

In two closely allied odes in the dithyrambic vein (*Bacchum in remotis* and *Quo me Bacche rapis*), we see Horace enlisting the language of ritual possession in the service of high encomium (of god
and ruler respectively). The preludes of both poems subtly validate
abnormal excursions into the grand style by appeals to "authentic"
Dionysiac experience. These excursions belong to a category of ode

in which Horace, in diametric contrast to the "disavowals" I have analyzed, explicitly *avows* his aptitude for more elevated composition. The apologetic basis for such ostensible inconsistency is the claim of overpowering *ekstasis*. Let us examine the prooemium of C. 2.19 in the light of this apologetic.

The ode purports to describe an epiphanic experience that we, the audience of posterity, are expressly called upon to credit (1–4):

> Bacchum in remotis carmina rupibus
> vidi docentem—*credite posteri*—
> Nymphasque discentis et auris
> capripedum Satyrorum acutas.

I have seen Bacchus teaching poems on remote cliffs—*believe me, posterity*—and the nymphs, his pupils, and the pointed ears of the goat-footed Satyrs.

The parenthetical injunction, *credite posteri*, is decisive for the interpretation of the poem insofar as it playfully foregrounds the issue of the sincerity of the lyric speaker. Horace's claim to be giving an eyewitness report of a vision (*vidi*) has provoked contradictory responses from readers. Whereas the skeptics reject it outright as a mere pose, the believers are inclined to take the verb *vidi* in a more literal sense.[31] A more appropriate response to the aside, in my view, entails not merely a "willing suspension of disbelief" (in this case, disbelief in the insincerity of the claim!), but a readiness to reformulate the whole issue of credibility in terms of rhetorical strategy. What, we may ask, does the speaker stand to gain by presenting himself as a bacchant in the grip of religious frenzy? If we provisionally assent to the genuineness of the vision, does this implicit contract between reader and poet deepen our perception of the unfolding *carmen*?

When we examine the putative vision at close range, we are immediately struck by its preponderantly literary modality. Horace, it transpires, has witnessed what is, at bottom, a poetry lesson, with Bacchus in the role of instructor (*docentem*) and nymphs and satyrs playing the part of attentive pupils (*discentes*). As *praeceptor*—or, more precisely, *chorodidaskalos* (Fraenkel, 199)—the god imparts his knowledge of *carmina*, the generic term that Horace applies to his own lyric oeuvre. The self-reflexive aspect of *Bacchum . . . carmina docentem* is crucial: the privileged attendance at the master class vouchsafes the purity of the transmission and, by extension, the authenticity of the current *carmen*, which, by the very fact that it continues to engage an audience of *posteri*, vindicates the original appeal (*credite!*). Once again, Horace has, with typical badinage, presented a quasi-autobiographical scenario that is cunningly germane to the poetic agenda. The strictly conventional side of the accrediting "vision" is, of course, salient: it is not difficult to illustrate the motif of the poet learning his or her métier from a divine source. As Mark Griffith has prudently reminded us, however, even such a widely credited *Erlebnis* as Hesiod's famous vision on Mount Helicon cannot be presumed to reflect hard information of a biographical nature (e.g., that Hesiod was a shepherd) (Griffith 1983). Within the framework of lyric singer and ideal audience (*posteri*), the reported theophany serves to encode a pact in terms of which the ensuing hymn is to be adjudicated. By acceding to the speaker's pitch for credence, we legitimate not so much the genuineness of the vision itself as the quality of its product—a *carmen* that exhibits the hallmarks of the grand style.

The concentration on the credentials of the speaker reaches a fortissimo in the second stanza (5–8):

> Euhoe, recenti mens trepidat metu
> plenoque Bacchi pectore turbidum
> laetatur: Euhoe, parce Liber,
> parce gravi metuende thyrso!

Euhoe! my mind quivers with a novel fear and a wild ecstasy agitates my heart, fully possessed by Bacchus. Euhoe! be gentle, Liber, be gentle, O god to be feared for your heavy thyrsus!

If the vision of the opening lines has placed the speaker in the charmed elite of Bacchus's auditors and pupils (cf. *C.* 1.1.29–34), the description of ritual possession in the succeeding verses puts a further stamp of approval on the inspired discourse that erupts from the enraptured bard. The vocable *Euhoe* and the sudden transition to the present tense are dramatic evidence of the benefits of the initiation into Bacchic *poiēsis*. By alleging a genuine religious experience, the speaker wins the right to tune his utterance to the higher registers of lyric.

The rhetorical insistence on legitimacy is marked in the text by the anaphoric repetition of *fas* in lines 9 and 13:

fas pervicaces est mihi Thyiadas
vinique fontem lactis et uberes
cantare rivos atque truncis
lapsa cavis iterare mella:
fas et beatae coniugis additum
stellis honorem tectaque Penthei
disiecta non leni ruina
Thracis et exitium Lycurgi.

It is meet for me to sing and sing again of enthused bacchants, of a fountain flowing with wine and copious streams of milk, and honey dripping from hollow trunks. *It is meet* also to sing of the crowning glory of a blessed spouse—glory added to the stars—and of Pentheus's palace demolished in a violent overthrow, and the destruction of Thracian Lycurgus.

The phrase *fas est . . . cantare* makes it transparent, in retrospect, that the function of the description of ecstasy was to bestow permission on the bard to hymn the marvellous *dynameis* of the god. The very fact that the enunciated themes of the hymnal encomium contain distinct reminiscences of choral passages in Euripides' *Bacchae* bears out the latent purpose of the preamble.[32] If such tragic matter and manner can be accommodated within the purview of the slender *carmen*, then the Dionysiac exordium has accomplished its major objective of preparing the audience for the upward tonal expansion of the lyric repertoire.

Although my analysis has so far been focussed on the rhetoric of the prelude, a brief glance at the main body of the hymn proper will reveal the extent to which it is commensurate with the extravagant promises of the overture. As is conventional in hymnal technique, the speaker is at pains to universalize the power of the divinity. To this end, he employs the usual "dichotomized wholes" such as land/sea (17–18) and peace/war (25–28). He also systematically includes all the major compartments of the cosmos in enumerating the god's sphere of influence. Thus the terrestrial powers of Bacchus are extended to the celestial domain by the mention of his role in the Gigantomachia (21–25). The final upgrading of his *numen* to embrace the underworld is reserved for the delightful diminuendo of the last strophe (28–31):

te vidit insons Cerberus aureo
cornu decorum leniter atterens

> caudam et recedentis trilingui
> ore pedes tetigitque crura.

A harmless Cerberus has seen you, splendid with your golden horn,
a Cerberus who rubbed you gently with his tail, and touched your
feet and legs with his triple tongue as you went on your way.

The Cerberus vignette gracefully completes our sense of the totality of Dionysus's range of influence (earth, heaven, underworld).
At the same time, the range of the god's power is coterminous with
that of the lyric discourse itself. Like the subdued monsters of *Ille et
nefasto* (C. 2.13.33–36) who constitute a surprise element in the audience of lyric, the chastened and fawning Cerberus of the hymn's
finale symbolizes the irresistible puissance of Dionysiac *carmina*
transmitted to posterity by the well-schooled singer. As is typical
of Horatian closures, the key repetition, *vidi* (line 2) and *vidit* (line
29), ensures that the original vision of the speaker intersects with
the scene of the miniature *katabasis*.

In the twin ode to Bacchus (C. 3.25), we encounter the same
elaborate vindication of a grander mode of composition. The prelude, though curtailed, takes as its point of departure the fiction of
the speaker's present rapture (1–3):

> Quo me, Bacche, rapis tui
> plenum? quae nemora aut quos agor in specus
> velox mente nova?

Where, O Bacchus, are you taking me, fully possessed by you? Into
what groves, into what caverns, am I being driven, at such speed,
with a mind that is new?

The many thematic common denominators between the two odes
are too obvious to require enumeration. Not so obvious, perhaps,
is their underlying function in a self-conscious poetic program. In
the shorter ode in book 3, the rhetorical questions addressed to the
god take the place of the symptoms of *ekstasis* in predisposing us to
accept the repercussions of inspiration. That the primary issues are
indeed the tenor of utterance and its generic manifestation becomes unequivocal with the thematic cadence (3–6):

> quibus
> antris egregii Caesaris audiar

> aeternum meditans decus
> stellis inserere et consilio Iovis?

In what grottoes shall I be heard rehearsing a song to place the eternal glory of illustrious Caesar among the stars and the council of Jove?

As the verb *meditare* ("rehearse") suggests, the eulogistic prospectus is fundamentally self-fulfilling and, despite the future cast of the verb *audiar*, we are probably not meant to indulge the speculation that some other encomium is projected (though such a possibility cannot, of course, be definitely excluded).[33] In outlining a laudatory agendum for Augustus's exploits, the poet ipso facto composes a pregnant lyric encomium, and the line between announcement and performance is virtually obliterated. Furthermore the diction of *decus stellis inserere* recalls the programmatic statement of C. 1.1, where the *laudandus* is Maecenas and the *laudator* shares the honor of deification: "quodsi me lyricis vatibus inseres / sublimi feriam sidera vertice" (lines 35–36: "but if you place me in the canon of lyric poets, I shall strike the stars with my uplifted head"). The praise of Caesar is therefore not deferred but actually immanent in the present performance, which, like the lyric refreshment proffered to the ruler in C. 3.4.40 takes place in the symbolic *antrum* (cf. *quibus antris* and *Pierio . . . antro*).

The technically hymnal segment of the ode delimits, as is customary, the god's sphere of influence (14–16):

> O Naiadum potens
> Baccharumque valentium
> proceras manibus vertere fraxinos

O you who have dominion over Naiads and Bacchants that have the power to uproot tall ash trees with their hands

Nymphs and Maenads constitute the select community over which Bacchus exercises his awesome power—a community into which the speaker has already inscribed himself by the portrayal of *enthusiasmos* (*me . . . tui plenum*). As in the corresponding case of the *Bacchum in remotis*, it soon becomes apparent that what the poet chiefly procures by the simulation of possession is the guarantee of lofty effusion (17–18):

nil parvum aut humili modo,
nil mortale loquar.

nothing trivial or in a pedestrian manner, nothing of mortal cast
shall I utter.

Horace obtains our assent to this audacious departure from the
hymnal norm by a clever sleight of hand; for formal considerations
would lead us to expect a "request" in the culminating portion of
the hymn. Instead, we receive the bold disavowal of light verse in
favor of more grandiloquent utterance. In sum, the ode not only
defines its own course, but underscores its innovative aspect (7–8):

dicam insigne recens adhuc
indictum ore alio.

My theme shall be illustrious and fresh, and hitherto unsung by the
mouth of another.

The exploration of unfamiliar lyric space (cf. *mente nova*, 3) is brilliantly expressed in the simile of a wandering, entranced Maenad
gazing at the wintry landscape of Thrace (8–14):

non secus in iugis
exsomnis stupet Euhias
Hebrum prospiciens et nive candidam
Thracen ac pede barbaro
lustratam Rhodopen, ut mihi devio
ripas et vacuum nemus
mirari libet.

Just as on high ridges the sleepless bacchant stays entranced, looking out over the river Hebrus and Thrace shining white with snow,
and Rhodope paced by barbarian feet, so I in my wanderings am
pleased to look in awe upon the banks and the unoccupied grove.

Irene Troxler-Keller, in particular, has rightly stressed the symbolic
character of the landscape here described (Troxler-Keller 1964, 52).
A salient feature of this *Dichterlandschaft* is the "empty grove" (*vacuum nemus*)—the counterpart, for the wandering poet (cf. *devio*),
of the hitherto unexplored terrain traversed or contemplated by the
rapt bacchant. The unoccupied grove at which the entranced poet
gazes in wonder (cf. *mirari libet*, 14, and *stupet*, 9) is the locus of a
new strain of exalted song exemplified by the *carmen* itself.

Such a new departure, Horace goes on to imply, inevitably involves the artist in serious, though pleasurable, risk (18–20):

> dulce periculum est,
> o Lenaee, sequi deum
> cingentem viridi tempora pampino.

It is a sweet danger, O Bacchus-of-the-winepress, to follow the god, crowning the temples with green vine-leaves.

The "sweet danger" for the speaker exists on two levels, which it is inexpedient to keep distinct: ecstatic religious experience and elevated lyric discourse. If my view of the poem's rhetoric is valid, the former ultimately serves as scaffolding for the latter. The follower of Bacchus ornamented with an ivy wreath is, in essence, the singer whose inspired voice will continue to be heard in the *antra* of posterity.

EMBLEMS OF THE LYRIC

Quasi-biographical episodes such as those I have considered in the previous section are an effective means of corroborating the authenticity of poetic inspiration. Equally instrumental in achieving the same end is what we may term, faute de mieux, the "objectification" of the work of art through recourse to prestigious lyric emblems. In selecting such emblems for his own poetic compositions, Horace does not hesitate to rely on traditional metaphors, such as the wreath, the fountain, and the sacrificial victim. The overlapping functions of these three fundamental emblems, in particular, will be the focus of attention in the succeeding pages.

A Garland for Lamia: *Corona* and Song in *C.* 1.26

To begin with the figure of the wreath, let us glance at a short ode, *C.* 1.26, whose symbolic import is unequivocal:

> Musis amicus tristitiam et metus
> tradam protervis in mare Creticum
> portare ventis, quis sub Arcto
> rex gelidae metuatur orae,

quid Tiridatem terreat, unice   5
securus. O quae fontibus integris
  gaudes, apricos necte flores,
    necte meo Lamiae coronam,

Piplei dulcis! nil sine te mei
prosunt honores: hunc fidibus novis,   10
  hunc Lesbio sacrare plectro
    teque tuasque decet sorores.

As the Muses' friend, I shall relegate sorrow and fears to the impet-
uous winds to be borne into the Cretan sea, with a singular lack of
concern for what king ruling over cold shores in the far north is causing anxiety, or what prospect alarms Tiridates. O you who delight
in fresh fountains, Muse of Pipla, weave bright flowers, weave a
garland for my Lamia! My accolades are worth nothing without you:
it is fitting that you and your sisters should hallow him with new
lyric song, him with the Lesbian pick.

From the standpoint of grammatical periods, no less than of the
sequence of ideas, the ode exhibits a lucid triadic plan: A, lines 1–6
(*Musis . . . securus*); B, lines 6–9 (*O quae . . . dulcis*); C, lines 9–12
(*nil sine me . . . sorores*) (cf. Syndikus, 252–53). All three syntac-
tic/thematic segments are closely interconnected by emphatic references to the Muses (line 1, *Musis amicus;* line 9, *Piplei dulcis;*
line 12, *sorores*). The first and last of these neatly ring the poem,
while the second is embedded in a hymnal invocation that occupies
the middle period of the ode. This clarity and cohesion on the formal level enhances the underlying argument, which turns, as we
shall see, on the rhetoric of the "self-fulfilling prophecy."

The hymnal portion hinges upon a request (expressed in the
conventional form of the imperative) that the Muse weave a *corona*
for the addressee: "necte flores / necte meo Lamiae coronam." The
garland is, of course, a stock metaphor in Greco-Roman literature
for a poem or a set of poems, and I shall spell out some of its
ramifications more fully below in connection with the *Persicos odi*
(*C.* 1.38). The actual fulfillment of the speaker's request—the
making of the wreath—takes place within the poem itself, for the
corona becomes immediately identifiable with the *carmen* in progress.[34] A parallel for this kind of self-fulfilling discourse is provided
by the prelude to *C.* 3.4 in which the speaker (also called an *amicus*
of the Muses) first summons Calliope and immediately thereafter
imagines her as manifest in the ongoing performance. A good deal

of the peculiar charm of this brief ode resides in the subtlety with which the coronal is transmuted into the verbal *honores* that the poet uses to enshrine his *laudandus*.[35] The transmutation is facilitated by counterbalanced cola: the *fontibus integris* that generally cause delight to the Muses prefigure the *fidibus novis*, which, in the immediate performance, constitute the particular source of pleasure—the encomium of Lamia. The resultant mixture of metaphors (wreath, fountain, lyre) may strike the modern sensibility, imbued with a radically different concept of imagistic consistency, as confusing, if not infelicitous. To a Roman audience, however, it is likely that fountain, wreath, and lyre comprised interchangeable emblems of poetic composition. As such, they successively complement, rather than contradict, each other.[36] In terms of a persuasive rhetoric, then, the final section of the ode marks the realization of the request—a realization that substantiates the tacit avowal of authenticity. Since the Muses are virtually a proxy for the poet, the latter accomplishes his ends through them and vice versa; by their timely intercession, the "integrity" of the poetic utterance is guaranteed. Hence, this newly fashioned *corona, C.* 1.26, will shine with the lustre of genuinely inspired wreaths of yore (apricos . . . *flores*).

The avowal of genuineness comes after, and is predicated upon, a preliminary disavowal, the thematic implications of which have not been fully articulated in the critical literature. The poem opens with an explicit characterization of the speaker as *Musis amicus* ("the Muses' friend"). It is in this special role that he performs the gesture of consigning certain alien events and their accompanying emotions to the winds. The future tense that expresses the gesture (*tradam*) carries a "voluntative" aspect, indicating a characteristic attitude on the part of the bard.[37] What is the nature of these concerns that are ritualistically cast off? If the poet's words are taken at face value, they refer to political and military affairs affecting remote borders of the empire. Such a description of what is relegated to oblivion is, however, fundamentally inadequate at a deeper level, since it overlooks the point that the Parthian and similar imbroglios are also *potential themes* that the writer is repudiating.[38] In fine, it is precisely as lyric spokesman that the speaker disavows *reges et proelia* ("kings and battles")—to borrow an apposite phrase that Virgil uses in the *recusatio* of *Ecl.* 6—represented here by the fortunes of Tiridates and the unnamed northern king. The items disavowed, in a word, are not politics and wars as such, but, more pertinently, the kind of bellicose subject matter that is deemed irrelevant to present lyric imperatives. The prelude to *C.* 2.11 is analogous in its rhetorical attack (1–4):

> Quid bellicosus Cantaber et Scythes,
> Hirpini Quincti, cogitet Hadria
>   divisus obiecto, remittas
>   quaerere . . .

Stop seeking to know, O Quinctius Hirpinus, what the war-mongering Cantabrians and the Scythians are planning, tribes separated from us by the intervening Adriatic . . .[39]

In *Musis amicus*, the peremptory exclusion of incompatible subjects (which would, however, be compatible with a more pretentious non-lyric genre) involves, on the plane of ethical values, the relegation of fear (cf. *metuatur; terreat*). Because philosophical issues are bound up with literary predilections in Horace's poetic system, the elimination of fear (and the fear of death is implicitly included here) goes *pari passu* with the exclusion of thematized battles between distant monarchs. Thus the poem seeks to vindicate the election of personal lyric on the basis of an outright disavowal of alien (politico-military) matter.

By the above reading, the brilliantly condensed *recusatio* of segment A is the logical obverse of B and C (the latter taken together as a positive affirmation of the poet's orientation). In the new poetic dispensation, the ode delimits what is germane to a lyric program and defines a crucial element in such a program as the banishment of unnecessary cares (*tristitiam et metus;* cf. the Teucer ode [*C.* 1.7.15–32]).

What Horace has proudly fashioned, in explicit contrast to a tedious account of military exploits in a far-off arena,[40] is a succinct eulogy of a friend within the confines of three Alcaic strophes. As a cornerstone of this "new-fangled" eulogy, the speaker incorporates a topos that is, ironically, more common to higher species of encomium—the absolute dependence of the *laudator* on his Muse: "nil sine te mei prosunt honores." By alleging that the poetic accolades bestowed by him are totally dependent on the Muses' collaboration, Horace attempts to adorn his new theme, Lamia, with an august and ancient motif of praise. He accomplishes this feat of solemn consecration (cf. *sacrare*) in the modest medium of Lesbian *melos* (*Lesbio . . . plectro*). It is the artful inclusion of the "high" within the precincts of the "low" that constitutes part of the novelty of the modest encomium of Lamia.

SIMPLEX MYRTUS: THE METAPHORICAL STRUCTURE OF *C.* 1.38

The *corona* as embodiment of the *carmen* is also the organizing principle that informs the short ode *Persicos odi:*

> Persicos odi, puer, apparatus,
> displicent nexae philyra coronae;
> mitte sectari, rosa quo locorum
>   sera moretur.
> simplici myrto nihil allabores   5
> sedulus cura: neque te ministrum
> dedecet myrtus neque me sub arta
>   vite bibentem.[41]

I detest Persian paraphernalia, my boy; wreaths woven on linden bark displease me; stop trying to track down those rare places where a late rose lingers on. Take care that in your zeal you work no extra ornament into the plain myrtle: myrtle is most fitting both to you, as you serve, and to me, as I drink, beneath the dense vine.

Whereas the ode to Lamia glorifies an individual for whom the Muses' wreath is expressly commissioned, the concluding ode of book 1 stands as a general statement of aesthetic principles—a kind of miniature *Ars poetica.* Since the figurative meaning of the ode has been called into question by some leading Horatian critics,[42] let us briefly review the most cogent evidence in support of the symbolic interpretation.

Among the most pertinent pieces of evidence, in my judgment, are parallel *loci* in the odes themselves. As we have just seen, the poem in honor of Lamia reifies the ongoing encomium in the form of a *corona.* In another ode from the first book, *C.* 1.7, Horace describes a lengthy encomiastic piece on the city of Athens in terms of an overelaborate wreath (5–7):

> sunt quibus unum opus est intactae Palladis urbem
>   carmine perpetuo celebrare et
> undique decerptam fronti praeponere olivam.

There are some whose only project is to celebrate the city of virgin Pallas Athene in continuous song, and to place upon their foreheads an olive wreath indiscriminately culled.

Here the antitype of the Hellenistic short poem—the *carmen perpetuum*—is metaphorized as an olive garland indiscriminately assembled (*undique decerptam*). The coronal figure in C. 1.7. occurs within a literary priamel that repudiates high encomiastic verse on distant and famous places in favor of lyric praise of one's own home. The wider ramifications of this priamel will be discussed in chapter 4; for the moment, suffice it to remark that the rejected examples of epideictic are a foil for the speaker's choice of a different type of song.

As an instance of the emblem operating in a non-lyric work of the Horatian corpus, a passage from the epistle to Florus is particularly illuminating. The authorial *persona* is ridiculing the vanity of poets who hypocritically compliment each other for self-serving ends. After an exchange of verses, each poet flatters the other (*Epist.* 2.2.99–101):

> discedo Alcaeus puncto illius; ille meo quis?
> quis nisi Callimachus? si plus adposcere visus,
> fit Mimnermus et optivo cognomine crescit.

I come away as an Alcaeus by that man's vote; and how does he emerge by mine? As a Callimachus, who else? If he seems to be making a more ambitious claim, he becomes a Mimnermus, and is magnified by the name he chooses.

The poets' alternate recitation of their compositions is, significantly enough, likened to the mutual presentation of *coronae* (91–96):[43]

> carmina compono, hic elegos. "mirabile visu
> caelatumque novem Musis opus!" aspice primum,
> quanto cum fastu, quanto molimine circum-
> spectemus vacuam Romanis vatibus aedem!
> mox etiam, si forte vacas, sequere et procul audi,
> quid ferat et quare *sibi nectat uterque coronam.*

I compose lyric poetry, he elegiac. "Marvellous to contemplate, a work inscribed by the nine Muses!" Note, first of all, with what pride, with what a fuss we look around the temple of Apollo, accessible now to Roman bards! Shortly, if you have time to spare, follow through and hear from a distance what each poet contributes, and why *each weaves a garland for himself.*

The tone of the lines is patently derogatory—the need for fulsome flattery has earlier been described as a kind of *furor* (line 90). Nevertheless, the *corona* is introduced as a trope for poetic performance in a manner so casual as to confirm its cliché status.

That the wreath-poem is a commonplace of Augustan poetry is incontestable in the face of such passages as Propertius 3.1.19–20:

> *mollia,* Pegasides, date vestro *serta* poetae:
> non faciet capiti *dura corona* meo.

> Muses of Pegasus's spring, bestow *soft wreaths* on your poet: a *hard garland* will not suit my head.

It is noteworthy that Propertius refines the stock metaphor by discriminating between hard and soft wreaths (*dura corona* / *mollia serta*), corresponding to epic and elegiac kinds, respectively. Prior to the Augustan period, the *stephanos* appears not simply as a reward for poetic achievement, but as an emblem of *poiēsis*, from Sappho to the composers of Hellenistic epigram (among whom Meleager with his garland is a conspicuous example).[44] Finally, a passage from Lucretius (which clearly influenced the language of the Lamia ode) characterizes the poetic composition in progress as an *insignem . . . coronam.* In short, the textual evidence from a wide range of pertinent sources—the Horatian corpus, contemporary Roman poetry, Greek and Roman antecedents—is so compelling that the onus of proof should be placed upon those who would deny the allegorical cast of the *Persicos odi.*

If we accept the metaphor as established, then the ode is best interpreted as a deceptively simple, but in fact densely packed, poetic manifesto. To unpack Horace's polysemous verses in a methodical way, it will be expedient to scrutinize the literary connotations of key words and phrases.

Persicos

The term *Persian* has manifold connotations on the social and cultural levels (e.g., remote, exotic, luxurious, ornate). Its literary-generic association with protracted composition is best glossed from the prologue to Callimachus's *Aetia*—the canonic text for Augustan critical programs—where the Persian *schoinos* (a unit of land measurement) is dismissed as a criterion of artistic excellence (lines 17–18 [Pfeiffer]):

ἔλλετε Βασκανίη,ς ὀλοὸν γένο,ς,· αὖθι δὲ τέχνῃ
κρίνετε,],μὴ σχοίν,ῳ Περσίδι τὴ,ν, σοφίην·

Away with you, destructive breed of Slander. Now then judge poetry by the standard of craft, not by the Persian measure.

Horace's dismissed accoutrements (*apparatus*) are more inclusive
than his model's concrete *schoinos*, and the objects envisaged are
obviously different, but the common referent of both metaphors is
the verbal *opus* that is large-scale and overblown.

Apparatus

In its primary denotation, *apparatus* refers to preparations—in this
case, for a feast. The analogy between elaborate appointments for a
banquet and stylistic attributes is by no means far-fetched: it is, in
fact, precisely paralleled as well as elucidated by a passage in
Cicero's *Orator* in which he attempts to define the practitioner of
the plain style (cf. Race 1978):

> Nam [orator subtilis] sic ut *in epularum apparatu* a magnificentia
> recedens non se parcum solum sed etiam elegantem videri volet, et
> eliget quibus utatur.
> (*Or.* 83)

> For, as *in the preparations for a banquet*, [the plain orator] will es-
> chew a show of magnificence out of a desire to seem not only par-
> simonious, but also elegant, and will select his ornaments for use
> accordingly.

As can readily be seen from the Ciceronian use of the banquet comparison, magnificence of preparation *in epularum apparatu* parallels
the ornate style of discourse, while a judicious restraint produces
the elegance and parsimony of the *oratio subtilis*. Cicero's *locus* furnishes a neat explanatory instrument for the exegesis of the phrase
Persicos apparatus, for both modifier and noun may acquire connotations of "magnificence" (see L&S s.v. *apparo* II.B).

Odi

The proem to the so-called Roman odes brandishes the word *odi*
as a way of excluding, at the outset, an unsophisticated audience
(*profanum vulgus*) before announcing an innovative poetic program
(*C.* 3.1.1–4):

Odi profanum vulgus et arceo;
favete linguis: carmina non prius
audita Musarum sacerdos
virginibus puerisque canto.

I detest and debar the uninitiated throng. Keep reverend silence: I,
the Muses' priest, am singing songs previously unheard to unmar-
ried girls and boys.

As employed to convey the poet's displeasure in the context of
C. 1.38, *odi* like the synonymous *displicent* in the succeeding line,
resonates with several passages in Greek epigram in which the authors dogmatically lay out their aesthetic tastes.[45] Perhaps the most
apt Hellenistic precedent for Horace's initial *odi* is the opening
couplet of an epigram of Callimachus (*Anth. Pal.* 12.43.1–2 = Gow-
Page 1041–42) expressing unequivocal distaste for epic poetry of
the "cyclic" variety:

Ἐχθαίρω τὸ ποίημα τὸ κυκλικὸν οὐδὲ κελεύθῳ
χαίρω τίς πολλοὺς ὧδε καὶ ὧδε φέρει·

I detest the "cyclic" poem; nor do I take pleasure in a path that carries many here and there.

The epigram goes on to list tastes in other matters, including the
character of love-partners. The main function of this and many
similar catalogues in Hellenistic epigram is to present a holistic
view of the cultivated person—the tastes enumerated add up to a
coherent pattern and embrace a repertoire of urbanity. Horace eschews a banal catalogue. Instead, he focuses on the purely literary
reflexion of discriminating taste in the metonymic *corona*. In this
respect, the choice of *displicent* to carry forward the idea of *odi* is
especially opportune when we consider the commonplace occurrence of the simple verb *placeo* in literary-critical contexts such as
Ars poetica 365: "haec placuit semel, haec decies repetita placebit"
("this [work] pleased once and for all, this [other] will please with
tenfold repetition").

Nexae philyra coronae

Since the bark of the *philyra* was used as a substructure of intricate
coronae, the metaphoric designation, "wreaths bound of linden
bark" categorizes poems of an ambitious scope and grandiloquent

texture. If *corona* is signifier for *carmen* in this poem, then the plural suggests a general statement of principles with respect to poetic credo. As with all such sweeping generalizations, exceptions are, of course, taken for granted. In this regard, it is hardly fortuitous that the preceding poem in the collection (the *Nunc est bibendum*) is an excursion into the "magnificences" of the high style on an exotic eastern subject—the defeat of the Egyptian queen Cleopatra (cf. Fraenkel, 297). Horace's reaffirmation, in the *Persicos odi*, of his central commitment to norms of plainness and brevity gains all the more in incisiveness from its juxtaposition to the elaborately wrought *corona* of *C.* 1.37. The final poem of book 1 places such exceptional departures within the perspective of the predominantly *oratio tenuis* of the *carmina* as a whole.[46]

Mitte sectari

Horace's diction once again contains a distinct (though commonly unnoticed) echo of the Callimachean prologue to the *Aetia* in lines adjacent to those cited above (19–20):

> μηδ' ἀπ' ἐμεῦ διφᾶ‚τε μέγα ψοφέουσαν ἀοιδήν
> τίκτεσθαι· βροντᾶ‚ν οὐκ ἐμόν, ‚ἀλλὰ‚ Διός.'

Do not look to me to engender a song that makes a mighty boom: thunder belongs not to me, but rather to Zeus.

The Greek verb διφᾶτε ("look for"; "search after") closely corresponds in meaning to Horace's frequentative, *sectari*. The echo imparts a broader generic connotation that prepares us to make a further analogy between the object of the search (the "late rose") and the nature of the inappropriate *poiēma*. The pursuit of the rose in out-of-the-way places is the counterpart to striving after remote, recherché themes and styles. The ideal poetic wreath, therefore, reflects an aspect of convivial lyric that is dear to Horace: it is to be woven from subjects that are close to hand and immediately relevant, as opposed to distant, absent, and exotic. The similarities of the latter to the subjects repudiated in the overture to the Lamia ode are salient.

Rosa . . . sera

The delayed epithet *sera* receives emphasis from its initial position in the closing line of the Sapphic strophe. What precisely does "lateness" imply for the poem's texture of ideas? The rose that is *sera* is, by definition, out of season. In a fundamental sense, it is *akairos*, hence inappropriate for a poetics of the here and now, with its focus on "the right thing at the right time." The rose's inappropriateness is, however, relative rather than absolute. Conventionally, as is well known, roses are supremely fitting for erotic-sympotic settings, and in a well-known fragment of Sappho, rose garlands symbolize the immortalizing honors conferred by the Muses of Aeolic verse.[47] Horace's point in dismissing the *rosa sera* is that a flower that has to be sought after because it is no longer in season has passed into the category of the rare and extravagant. On the level of style, then, the *rosa sera* may signify a violation of decorum as defined by the exigences of the *genus tenue*. It represents a seeking after ornateness and preciosity in a context that requires an unpretentious elegance. The action of lingering on (*moretur*), which characterizes the personified rose, perfectly matches the critique of an indiscriminate taste by extending to the temporal plane what had been expressed as a lack of containment on the spatial plane (*quo locorum*).

In my microscopic dissection of one half of Horace's *corona*, I have so far concentrated on the ambiguous meaning of discrete phrases and cola. Before subjecting the second strophe to a similar scrutiny, it may be profitable to step back from the picture and view lines 1–4 as a coherent whole. From this vantage point, the first strophe functions as an implicit disavowal: "a negative thesis of that which is not wished" to be completed by "a positive antithesis of that which is desired."[48] Magnificent *coronae* have been rejected as tokens of generically inappropriate poems in the grand manner. This exclusion lays the groundwork for the formulation of a superior aesthetic. The "positive" second strophe is no less dense in its semantic nuances than the first.

Simplici

Plainness (*simplicitas*) is generally acknowledged to be an ideal attribute both of style and of *modus vivendi* in Horace and the major Augustan poets (cf. Cairns 1979, 21). Since it is perhaps more familiar as a *communis locus* in the latter frame of reference, a brief validation of the stylistic aspect may prove useful. In the *Ars poe-*

tica, the speaker lays down the prescription that a poem should be *simplex* and *unum* (line 23). In context, the adjective *simplex* would seem to denote, to quote from Brink's commentary *ad loc.*, "of one kind, a thing that is not *varium*." In respect to the argument of the *Persicos odi*, it appears that the meaning "of one kind" sits well with the injunction that the wreath be composed from a single plant, the myrtle. The wreath of plain myrtle is thereby contrasted with the *nexae philyra coronae* as the one to the many, or, in literary terms, as a unified composition to one that is multiform and incoherent (the objective analogue of the *corona* whose elements are *undique decerptae*).

Nihil allabores

Since these words have been variously construed by leading philologists, I offer my own paraphrase of the sentence in which they occur as a preliminary to further interpretation: "Take care that, in your zeal, you work no extra ornament into the plain myrtle."[49] By this reading, meticulousness and *labor* are indeed attributed to the prospective wreath maker. Horace, however, is not inveighing against these attributes as such (which, as we shall see below, he ardently admires), but rather against their misapplication. *Labor*, he implies, ought to be directed at the proper object—not the rare poetic bloom, but the apposite myrtle. Properly understood, the unadorned style (*subtilis oratio*) is not essentially devoid of artifice or even *labor*; rather, as Cicero makes crystal clear (*Or.* 78), it should create the *impression* of unaffected grace:

> Nam ut mulieres [pulchriores] esse dicuntur nonnullae inornatae quas id ipsum deceat, sic haec subtilis oratio etiam incompta delectat; fit enim quiddam in utroque, quo sit venustius *sed non ut appareat*.

> For, just as certain women are said to be [handsomer when] unadorned—this very lack of adornment becomes them—so this plain style gives delight even when unembellished: there is something in both cases that lends greater charm, *but without revealing itself.*

In Horace's version of *subtilitas*, such *labor* as does go into poetic composition ought not to be spent on eye-catching ornament where a studied negligence and stylistic restraint are regarded at a premium.

Neque te . . . dedecet myrtus

The speaker's unique choice of myrtle for his poetic *corona* has more semantic weight than is suggested by the mere antinomy of one to many (see my discussion above on *simplex*). The word *myrtus* is conspicuously repeated in the penultimate line of the ode with an expanded range of signification. Through its regular association with the goddess of love, Venus, the emblematic plant serves to foreground the erotic theme in Horatian lyric (cf. *C.* 1.4.5–10). Poet and addressee, both garlanded with myrtle, divide between them the heraldic image of a sympotic verse in which Eros is a central component. In addition, the litotes *neque . . . dedecet* graphically registers the idea of appropriateness (decorum), which, as I have previously observed, comprehends both a thematic and a stylistic dimension. As Meleager says, in a poem that Horace demonstrably knew, "sweet is the myrtle of Callimachus" (*Anth. Pal.* 4.1.21–22 = Gow-Page 3946–47). In place of the hard-to-obtain rose is to be substituted the humble myrtle, which, like the amatory subject, lies ever close to hand.

Neque me sub arta / vite bibentem

That the final word of the ode (and of the book it closes) is the present participle *bibentem* (drinking) is scarcely fortuitous. As Pasquali accurately observed, the ode functions as a kind of envoi (*commiato*) to the collection as a whole (Pasquali, 324). The poet deliberately leaves the reader with a symbolic distillation of the preponderant character of his convivial Muse. In locating the quintessentially convivial gesture *sub arta vite* ("beneath the dense vine"), Horace obliquely embraces the motif of the shade, or protective *umbra*, which is the generative matrix of the lyric *carmen*.[50] The *Persicos odi*, then, stands as a monument to the disingenuously "plain" style that dissimulates deep layers of meaning beneath a surface transparency.

SACRIFICE AND SONG: *O FONS BANDUSIAE*

Horace's hymnal invocation of a spring (*C.* 3.13) is rightly venerated as a chef d'oeuvre of Latin lyric. In my effort to elucidate its deeper meaning, I propose to focus on the metonymic relation-ship it appears to posit between sacrificial victim and poem. That complex relationship derives, in part, from the "perlocutionary effect"—to adopt J. L. Austin's well-known concept—of the speak-er's utterances.[51] A preliminary glance at this aspect of the poem will provide the framework for my exegesis.

The ode's culminating strophe is a lucid example of what some linguistic theorists since Austin have characterized as a "speech act" (13–16):

> fies nobilium tu quoque fontium,
> *me dicente* cavis impositam ilicem
>   saxis, unde loquaces
>   lymphae desiliunt tuae.

you also shall be classed among illustrious fountains *by virtue of my describing* the oak tree placed over hollowed rocks, from which your vocal waters spring downwards.

The verb of saying *dicente*, though occurring in an ablative absolute construction, clearly functions as a "performative" in the sense that it brings about the very phenomenon it describes. The coup-ling of a predictive statement, *fies . . . fontium*, with the explicit performative *dicente* has the self-fulfilling effect of ennobling the addressee. As is evident from a paraphrase that brings out the causal function of the participle—for example, "you will be made illustrious by virtue of my describing . . ."—the act of ennobling is at one with, and is inscribed in, the declaration itself. In the strict-est sense, therefore, the recitation of the ode has the perlocution-ary effect of elevating the *fons Bandusiae* to the stature of Hippo-crene and the other *nobiles fontes* of Greek mythology.

If the speaker's utterances are magically efficacious, so presum-ably are those of the mimetic fountain, which, it transpires, is also endowed with the human capacity to speak (cf. *loquaces . . . lymphae*). Through the shared act of vivifying speech, poet and fountain come to mirror each other, or, to phrase it in a way that privileges the authorial voice, the fountain is made to reflect the "phatic" element in the composition—the manner in which the ode calls attention to its own "channel of communication" (Jakob-son 1960, 355). It is against the background of a self-reflexive dis-course that the entire infrastructure of the ode is to be interpreted.

What is more, some of the apparent paradoxes begin to evaporate as such when this dimension of the poem is accepted in all its repercussions.

One repercussion of the ennobling speech act is that the fountain is thereby equated with prestigious Greek "haunts of the Muses." This is tantamount to saying that the scene of the utterance becomes certified as an authentic (albeit Roman) locus of lyric creativity. The elevation process, however, actually begins in the initial lines, which, by their hymnal form, signal that the addressee is ipso facto lifted out of the world of the profane (1–3):

> O fons Bandusiae splendidior vitro
> dulci digne mero non sine floribus,
>   cras donaberis haedo . . .

O fountain of Bandusia, more resplendent than glass, deserving of mellow wine no less than flowers, tomorrow you will be offered a kid . . .

The expression *splendidior vitro* is doubly eulogistic in conventional terms. The "lustre" of the *laudandus* is a stock honorific metaphor, while the use of the comparative degree *splendidior* abbreviates the laudatory topos: "X is bright, but Y (my chosen subject) far outshines X."[52] As a resplendent, divinized object of veneration, the *fons* is declared worthy of ritual offerings and receives the promise of a sacrificial gift (*cras donaberis haedo*).

The understandable temptation to attach Horace's ritual oblations to a particular historical event—the festival of the Fontinalia—has led most commentators, despite the poet's noteworthy vagueness about the occasion, to ignore the thematic implications of the items concerned.[53] Unmixed wine, flowers, and young animal constitute the *sine quibus non* of the banqueting apparatus: the wine is destined to be mixed with water according to the dictates of the *magister bibendi;* the flowers will compose the obligatory wreaths worn by the participants; the sacrificed lamb will ultimately furnish the meat course. In fine, Horace's *fons* is to be honored with the irreducible tokens of convivial poetry. This ensemble of tokens, and not the presumed reference to an obscure festival, is what principally determines the speaker's choice of offerings.

If, indeed, Horace is primarily referring to basic ingredients of the banquet, what, we may well inquire, has become of the erotic motif, which, in my analysis of the *Persicos odi*, I have claimed to be equally essential to the sympotic nexus? The relative clause describing the sacrificial kid playfully thematizes *amor*, or, to be more precise, the anticipation of *amor* (4–5):

> cui frons turgida cornibus
> primis et venerem et proelia destinat

whose forehead, swelling with first horns, marks him out for mating and battles.

The pubescent kid, whose burgeoning horns are a sign of erotic-aggressive activity, incarnates, no less effectively (though more obliquely) than the wine and the flowers, a thematic component of the symposium. The way in which Horace subsumes the erotic motif is, however, fraught with paradox; for it is not merely love-acts, *venerem*, but also battles, *proelia*, that the kid is "destined" to perform. The conjoining of battles and *amor* may, at first blush, appear to be contradictory to the lyric posture, since the latter typically and vociferously disavows bellicosity. As we have seen, however, in my discussion of the technique of "incorporation" (cf. C. 2.12.26), "battles"—the disavowed other—are often included in the lyric domain at the level of metaphor. In this case, the "incorporation" is engineered by what may be interpreted as a hendiadys. Like the *proelia virginum* of C. 1.6.17, the *proelia Veneris* of the libidinous goat (cf. *lascivi suboles gregis*, 8) embody aggressive *amor*, or, more aptly put, they testify to the inclusiveness of the amatory theme.[54]

The speaker's paradoxical formulations do not end, however, with the transference of erotic *proelia* to the personified animal. Having temporarily become, by a metonymic and ludic sleight of hand, a potential participant in the *convivium* (an erotic player), the kid is abruptly restored to its original role in the destined symposium—namely, that of sacrificial victim (6–8):

> frustra: nam gelidos inficiet tibi
> rubro sanguine rivos
> lascivi suboles gregis.

in vain: for the progeny of the lusty herd will infuse your cool streams with red blood.

The explanatory *nam* clause, which glosses the pathetic *frustra*, contains a striking image that many critics have found disturbing, if not incongruous. The mixture of colors (red blood infusing white fountain), combined with the undercurrent of violence, seems to such readers an obtrusive element in an otherwise brilliant canvas. As far as the violence is concerned, the repulsion felt by the modern reader is doubtless anachronistic: blood sacrifice was so much an integral part of ancient society that Horace's lines are unlikely to have had intrinsic shock value to a contemporary audience. Anachronistic reactions aside, the commingling of the kid's blood with the pure waters of the fountain is presented so graphically as to invite speculation as to the speaker's rhetorical intent. From the perspective of my analysis, there are two primary structural explanations for Horace's note of pathos in portraying the transubstantiation of the kid: (a) the role of death as a standard foil to convivial celebration and (b) the figurative *fusion* of *fons* and victim, to which the death is logically prior.

In chapter 3, "Modes of Consolation," I shall examine at length the invariable introduction of "dark background"—usually in the form of a direct reference to death—in the context of a *carpe diem* argument. For my immediate purposes, it is sufficient to observe that, if I am right in reading the poem as an encapsulation of fundamental convivial motifs, then the presence of death is an obligatory part of such a rhetorical edifice. Like the erotic motif, the mortality topos is here transposed from the human to the animal sphere, and in the *frustra* we are made to feel empathy for the transience of the young personified *haedus*.

In addition to the inclusion of the mortality topos, there is another compelling raison d'être for the speaker's conspicuous conflation of the life-blood of the victim and the waters of the fountain. The animal, I have been arguing, has come to incarnate certain crucial features of erotic-sympotic lyric. As such, it is eminently transformable into, and in a sense, identifiable with, that other symbol of *poiēsis*, the *fons* itself. The mixture of liquids, blood and water, is strictly parallel to the mixture of metaphors. As my dissection of the Lamia ode indicates, the Horatian *carmen* is amenable to the interchange of emblems having the same referent. In the particular instance of the *fons Bandusiae*, the synecdochic transfiguration of the sacrificial victim into poetic fountain is quintessentially apt.

The transfusion of consecrated blood into sacred source serves to mark the process as deeply symbolic and to determine, once and for all, the metonymic status of the whole *sacrificio al fonte* (Pasquali's caption).

The second to last strophe, with its anaphoric *tu* predications, comprises the segment of the hymn devoted to the specification of the powers of the *numen* (9–12):

> te flagrantis atrox hora Caniculae
> nescit tangere, tu frigus amabile
>   fessis vomere tauris
>   praebes et pecori vago

> you cannot be touched by the ferocious season of the blazing Dog Star; you proffer your seductive coolness to the bulls weary with the ploughshare and to the wandering flock.

The numinous fountain, we learn, has the capacity to ward off excessive heat and to offer cool shade to the flocks. The *umbra* that protects the members of the larger community of man and animals is a pastoral motif that Horace often assimilates into his version of latinized Aeolic. In the ode to Tyndaris in which he wishes to sanctify his Sabine home as a favorite *sedes* of Arcadian Pan (= Faunus), he relies on a similar characterization (C. 1.17.1–4):

> Velox amoenum saepe Lucretilem
> mutat Lycaeo Faunus et igneam
>   defendit aestatem capellis
>   usque meis pluviosque ventos.

> Swift Faunus frequently changes Lycaeus for pleasant Lucretilis, and continually protects my she-goats from fiery summer heat and rainy winds.

In both poems the magically prophylactic power of song is in the forefront: extremely hot weather (*igneam aestatem; hora Caniculae*) is exorcised and the animals (*capellis; tauris, pecori vago*) are safely ensconced in the pastoral shade (cf. 1.17.17–18: "hic in reducta valle Caniculae / vitabis aestus"—"Here in a secluded valley you will avoid the heat of the Dog Star"). In these circumstances, the power of the *fons* to refresh the weary is an index of poetry's regenerative power (cf. the "recreative" role of the Muses in C. 3.4.37–40).

I began my inspection of the *fons Bandusiae* by stressing the phatic element in the composition, and I interpreted the climactic utterance *me dicente* . . . as an explicit "performative" (in the jargon of speech-act theory). To round off my treatment of the poem, let us now redirect attention to the *prophetic* tonality of the ode's finale.

The future tense in "*fies* nobilium tu quoque fontium" ("You also shall be classed among illustrious fountains") masks, as I have already emphasized, a self-fulfilling prophecy. In terms of the ode's substratum, the word *prophecy* here has a double application—religious as well as rhetorical. The religious character transcends the obviously hymnal structure of the invocation and its central motif of ritual sacrifice: it embraces the fundamental notion, widespread in antiquity, of the *mantic* function of song—a function closely associated with sacred springs. As Kambylis has amply attested, powers of prophecy—especially those linked to cult centers of Apollo and the Muses—were thought to be derived from sacred sources (Kambylis, 27–30). The mention of the oak "placed over hollow rocks" makes the prophetic function even more prominent in view of the oracular cult-affinities of the plant. Thus in the closing sentences of his ode, Horace is speaking in the role of a *promantis*, an inspired devotee of the Muses who has the authority to pronounce in oracular tones on things to come. As one who has manifestly imbibed the magic waters of the fountain, he is capable of predicting the immortality of his own *fons* and declaring its future status as *fons nobilis*. Thus the epithet *loquaces* that modifes the *lymphae* is not only self-reflexive (in the sense defined above) but also predictive in terms of the afterlife of the *carmen*, for the "talking waters" (the mantic eloquence inherent in lyric utterance)[55] continue to dazzle posterity with their splendor, just as the poet prognosticated.

Despite the uncertainty in the critical literature about the location and even the correct name of the actual source, Horace's encomium of the *fons Bandusiae* remains a coherent meditation on the inherent power of lyric discourse. As with the *corona* in the *Persicos odi*, the poet objectifies the creative performance and the *carmen* itself as a means of clarifying his lyric program and validating his achievement. At this level of abstraction, fountain and sacrificial victim fuse into a complex image that reflects the virtues and thematic obsessions of the artist.

PLAIN SACRIFICE, PLAIN SPEAKER:
THE CONCLUSION OF *C.* 4.2.

Horace's intricate encomium to Augustus, *Pindarum quisquis studet aemulari* (*C.* 4.2) terminates in a pictorial vignette in which two sets of sacrificial gifts, ascribed to the addressee and the speaker respectively, are vividly contrasted (53–60):

> te decem tauri totidemque vaccae,
> me tener solvet vitulus, relicta
> matre qui largis iuvenescit herbis
>   in mea vota,
>
> fronte curvatos imitatus ignis
> tertium lunae referentis ortum,
> qua notam duxit, niveus videri,
>   cetera fulvus.

You will be released with a sacrifice of ten bulls and as many cows; I with one of a tender calf that has left its mother and is maturing on broad meadows in fulfillment of my vows, its brow copying the fiery curve of the moon at its third rising: white as snow where it bears a mark, otherwise ruddy.

Since the ode as a whole is, in certain important respects, an apologia for the poet's lyric praxis, the sacrificial vignette is no otiose appendage; rather, it subtly incarnates (and resumes) substantive points in the preceding stanzas. To appreciate the organic connection between the juxtaposed sacrifices and the rest of the ode, it will be useful to recall certain features of the larger design.

Broadly speaking, the ode may be bisected into (a) a long proem "disavowing" the grand style of Pindar and (b) a bifurcated eulogy of the *princeps*, comprising (1) a specimen in the grand manner (allocated to the addressee) and (2) a specimen in the plain style (allocated to the speaker). The following diagram may help to articulate the scheme:

(a) Disavowal of the grand style   (1–32)

(b) Double encomium of Augustus   (33–60)
    (1) Grand-style specimen by addressee   (33–44)
    (2) Plain-style specimen by speaker   (45–60)

There is a formal symmetry between the final cadences of the
two main divisions: both utilize the device of polar metaphors—
namely, swan/bee (25–32) and cattle-hecatomb/calf (52–60). As we
shall see below in a partial examination of the text, these metaphorical codas, which express bipolar attitudes to the craft of poetry, are, at a deeper level, homologous, insofar as swan:: bee ~
hecatomb/calf. The poem's armature exhibits the careful *labor* that
is the main burden of the bee comparison.

The swan/bee opposition epitomizes the disavowal of the grandiloquent style, as represented by the Pindaric *corpus*. I have earlier
insisted on the "paradoxical intent" of such disavowals. Thus to
the conundrum posed by Pasquali, "Why does Horace imitate Pindar [*pindareggia*] at the very place where he advises against imitating Pindar?" (Pasquali, 782), there is a relatively straightforward
answer: the disavowal itself by virtue of its form reveals the speaker's actual competence to undertake precisely what he claims to be
incapable of doing. By simulating Pindaric *audacia* while ostensibly
distancing himself from it, Horace, so to speak, eats his cake and
has it too. The duplicity is, however, both undisguised and tongue-
in-cheek, and its main purpose is to set Pindar up as a generic foil
for the poet of the *Odes*. Despite the explicitness of the disjunctive
catalogue of Pindaric genres, the description of Pindar is hyperbolic and deliberately distorted.[56] It is obvious, for example, that
Horace did not believe (or want the reader to believe) that the poetry of the Theban bard was emancipated from all metrical constraints! (lines 11–12: "numerisque fertur / lege solutis"—"[Pin-
dar] is transported in meters free from rules"); nevertheless, a
legendary Pindar who is characterized as boundless and awesome,
like a force of nature, makes a perfect antitype to a poet who is primarily committed to small-scale, neatly honed *carmina*. Above all,
the portrait of the Greek artist as inspired genius bears out the
playful opening warning about the dangers of imitation (1–4):

> Pindarum quisquis studet aemulari,
> Iule, ceratis ope Daedalea
> nititur pennis vitreo daturus
> nomina ponto.

Whoever seeks to compete with Pindar, Iulus, relies on wings joined
with wax through Daedalus's offices, and is destined to give his
name to a glassy sea.

My epithet *playful* is meant to draw attention to Horace's penchant for mingling caricature and seriousness—the former even occasionally manifested as self-caricature. Thus the facetious rapprochement of the poet to an Icarus-figure (with its acknowledgement of anxiety about potential failure) actually forms part of the speaker's self-presentation in the final poem of book 2, in which he envisages his future metamorphosis into a bird—presumably a swan (*C.* 2.20.9–16):

> iam iam residunt cruribus asperae
> pelles, et album mutor in alitem
>   superne, nascunturque leves
>   per digitos umerosque plumae.
> iam Daedaleo notior Icaro
> visam gementis litora Bosphori
>   Syrtisque Gaetulas canorus
>   ales Hyperboreasque campos.

Now, even now, rough skin is beginning to cover my legs, and I am being transmuted into a white swan in my upper body, while smooth feathers are growing all through my fingers and shoulders. Now more famous than Icarus, son of Daedalus, I shall visit, in the shape of a melodious swan, the shores of the groaning Bosporus, and the Gaetulian Syrtes, and the Hyperborean fields.

In the generalizing *quisquis* (*whoever*) that launches *C.* 4.2, Horace may also intend us to be aware of his own controlled explorations on the Pindaric heights—including those of the unfolding poem.

Since the speaker's deferential nod to Pindaric grandeur is prelude to the counterportrait that commences with the self-descriptive *ego* (line 27), a careful examination of the swan/bee opposition is a prerequisite to a full understanding of the poem (25–32):

> multa Dircaeum levat aura cycnum,
> tendit, Antoni, quotiens in altos
>   nubium tractus: ego apis Matinae
>   more modoque
> grata carpentis thyma per laborem
> plurimum circa nemus uvidique
>   Tiburis ripas operosa parvus
>   carmina fingo.

No mean breeze, Antonius, raises aloft the swan of Dirce, as often as he makes for the clouds' high reaches: I, in the manner and style of the bee of Matinus, gathering the pleasant thyme with much effort around many a grove and the banks of watery Tibur—I, small artisan, produce well-crafted songs.

The Pindaric bird has been foreshadowed in the poem's inaugural image of the imitator as a doomed Icarus in flight (1–4). On one side, we are reminded of a human being pretending to be a bird, equipped with artificial wings ("ceratis ope Daedalea / nititur pennis"), on the other, we are shown a "real" bird soaring on the breeze into the empyrean. In the contrast between Daedalian contraption and natural wings lurks the venerable critical dichotomy between technique (*ars*) and innate ability (*ingenium; natura*) (Syndikus, 303–4). This implicit disjunction between pseudo-bird and swan is preliminary to the explicit confrontation between swan and bee.

Though the association of bee and poet is a hoary commonplace in Greek poetry,[57] its semantic scope is broader and its range more diverse than might appear from a superficial inspection. In the pseudo-biographical tradition, for instance, bees are frequently credited with nurturing infant poets; a related literary cliché metaphorizes the mature poetic product as honey. When the poet himself is compared to a bee (as is the case with 4.2), several different qualities—and not necessarily compatible ones—may be signified. In gathering nectar to make his honey, the bee-poet may be envisioned as displaying diligence, versatility, discrimination, constancy, or (inversely) caprice. Whether the author's emphasis is on the maker or the product, the particular inflection of the trope has to be extracted anew from each context.

In this regard, it is ironic that Horace's model, Pindar, employs the metaphor in a notable passage in a sense divergent from that of his imitator (*P.* 10.53–54 [Snell]):

> ἐγκωμίων γὰρ ἄωτος ὕμνων
> ἐπ᾽ ἄλλοτ᾽ ἄλλον ὥτε μέλισσα θύνει λόγον.

For the finest bloom of my praise-poems flits, like a bee, from one theme to another.

In this epilogic context the *laudator* deploys the bee image to express his feigned tendency to digress from his theme—a subterfuge that allows him to refocus attention on the overriding task of praise. It is evident from a passage in the short epistle to Florus (1.3.20–22) that Horace is quite content to apply the same metaphor to a poet who has lofty ambitions:

> ipse quid *audes?*
> quae circumvolitas agilis thyma? *non tibi parvum*
> *ingenium,* non incultum est et turpiter hirtum.

> What do you yourself *dare* to write? Around what thyme do you flit so busily? *Your poetic talent is by no means small;* it is not uncultivated or disgracefully uneven.

Like Pindar in the portrait of 4.2, Florus is characterized as a poet of *audacia* and the possessor of an *ingenium non parvum* (i.e., an exponent of the grand style). It is not inconceivable that the words *circumvolitas agilis* are an actual expansion of the Pindaric locution θύνει (flits) of *P.* 10. In any event, both the Pindaric *locus* and the apostrophe to Florus demonstrate that the bee metaphor was at home in the ambiance of the *genus grande;* hence Horace's appropriation of it in order to express the properties of a modest lyric endeavor is, on the surface at least, a deliberate deviation. In distinguishing his manner from Pindar's, the composer of the *Odes* has transposed the generic aura of the *paragone.*

Having adapted the bee metaphor to the requirements of his antithesis, Horace puts it to work to convey a cluster of related ideas about his poetic practice. The bee's choice of thyme, for instance, condenses an aesthetic project. In terms of style, it discloses a respect for decorum, since we have it on record that blossoming thyme was regarded in the ancient world as "most appropriate" for the making of honey.[58] In terms of subject matter (a closely related topic), it betrays a predilection for the quotidian (witness the herb's ready availability in ordinary meadows). That the abundant thyme is to be gathered in the environs of Tibur is an additional index of the lyrist's commitment to the immediate and proximate. In addition, the exclusive devotion to a single type of flower (as opposed to a plurality) suggests discriminating taste as well as good judgment. The last-mentioned qualities may ultimately have a literary ancestry in a passage in Simonides (much admired by Plutarch) where, if Fränkel's speculative reconstruction is on track, there may have been a reference to a bee-poet who deliberately bypasses glamorous, brightly colored blooms in favor of the common but virtuous thyme.[59] Thus, as with the selection of plain myrtle for the wreath in the *Persicos odi*, the adherence to the lowly thyme betokens the poet's "Attic" values and thematic fidelity.

When we shift our gaze from the ingredients of the *poetica mella* ("poetic honey")[60] to the maker of honey (the poet), other properties of the ideal lyrist come into focus. A crucial aspect of the bee's *modus operandi*, in Horace's account, is its industry—an aspect stressed by repetition: *laborem plurimum; carmina operosa.*[61] Painstaking composition is a seminal precept in the Callimachean view of art as a product of craft (*technē*), and in combining the idea with that of smallness (*parvus*), Horace is drawing on a well-formulated pattern of values (cf. Wehrli 1946; E. Reitzenstein 1931). The diligent bee of the *Carmina*, therefore, will eschew spontaneous effusions and prefer carefully crafted, small-scale compositions. The word *fingo*, which David West felicitously calls "the *mot propre* for the work of bees," is evocative of finesse as well as creativity (D. West 1967, 31).

Between the bee analogy and the sacrificial vignette, there intervenes, as I have schematized it, a dyadic encomium of the *princeps*. The first part (b1) continues the strategy of disavowal by other means: it ascribes a hypothetical (future) praise-poem to a more appropriate *laudator* (cf. the similar use of a surrogate in C. 1.6 [Varius] and C. 2.12 [Maecenas]). In this development the addressee, Antonius, is credited with a eulogy that is artfully summarized (33–44):

> concines *maiore poeta plectro*
> Caesarem, quandoque trahet feroces
> per sacrum clivum merita decorus
>   fronde Sygambros,
>
> quo nihil maius meliusque terris
> fata donavere bonique divi
> nec dabunt, quamvis redeant in aurum
>   tempora priscum.
>
> concines laetosque dies et Vrbis
> publicum ludum super impetrato
> fortis Augusti reditu forumque
>   litibus orbum.

You, *a poet of grander pick,* shall sing of Caesar, when, bedecked with well-deserved laurel, he will drag the fierce Sygambri up through the sacred slope—Caesar, than whom no greater or better gift has been, or will be, bestowed upon the earth by destiny or the kind gods, even though the age return to a primal gold. You shall sing of joyful days, and the public games in the City that will follow upon brave Augustus's long-awaited return, and the forum bereft of litigation.

In prefacing this specimen encomium, the speaker characterizes Antonius *qua* poet in a phrase reminiscent of the depiction of Alcaeus in *C.* 2.13.26 (cf. "maiore poeta plectro" with "te sonantem plenius aureo / Alcaeae, plectro"). Does the consistent attribution imply that the manner of Alcaeus is on a level with that of a Pindarizing poet? The answer is positive, provided we make allowances for the way in which "Alcaeus" is presented in varying rhetorical contexts. In the framework of the underworld vision of *C.* 2.13 (*Ille et nefasto*), to revert to a case I have earlier analyzed, Horace had schematized the stylistic range of Aeolic *melos* by polarizing Sappho and Alcaeus into representatives of a lighter (private) strain, on the one hand, and a heavier (public) one, on the other. A similar alignment of Alcaeus with a more elevated mode occurs in *C.* 4.9.5–12, where Pindar, Simonides, Alcaeus, and Stesichorus (in that order) are grouped together in contradistinction to a playful Anacreon and an amorous Sappho:

> non, si priores Maeonius tenet
> sedes Homerus, Pindaricae latent
>   Ceaeque et *Alcaei minaces*
>   Stesichorique graves *Camenae;*
> nec, si quid olim lusit Anacreon,
> delevit aetas; spirat adhuc amor
>   vivuntque commissi calores
>   Aeoliae fidibus puellae.

If Maeonian Homer holds pride of place, yet there is no eclipse of Pindar's muses, nor of Simonides', nor *of Alcaeus's, with their menacing tone,* nor Stesichorus's, with their heavy cadence. Nor has time erased whatever playful verses Anacreon once composed; love still breathes in song, and the passions the Aeolian woman committed to her lyre remain alive.

In such categorizations the lyrist is deliberately oversimplifying the respective oeuvres for purposes of slanting the discourse, and we are not meant to see these capsule portrayals as absolute opinions about the poets catalogued. The relativity of the Alcaeus sketch, in particular, becomes patent when we compare another such sketch in a different passage of the *Odes* where the same poet's fondness for erotic-sympotic lyric is couched in an almost Hellenistic garb (*C.* 1.32.9–12):

> Liberum et Musas Veneremque et illi
> semper haerentem puerum canebat
> et Lycum nigris oculis nigroque
> crine decorum.

He sang of Bacchus, the Muses, Venus, and the boy who always clings to her, and Lycus, handsome with his dark eyes and dark hair.

In the context of the grander specimen poem assigned to the bard Antonius in *Pindarum quisquis,* we are given a taste (disguised as a foretaste, *concines*) of what a "greater plectrum" might pick out if it undertook a public-spirited eulogy of a ruler. Horace's ulterior point is that his *Carmina* can indeed, despite the disclaimers, accommodate a higher strain of encomium, though in a less expansive and carefully limited format. The partial demonstration of the more ample program (the projected song of Antonius) works with all the cunning of a *praeteritio,* insofar as it succeeds in including an abbreviated encomium in the disavowed style.

The epitomized panegyric by Horace's proxy contains an exorbitant "vaunt" on the emperor's achievements that is not merely comparable to, but consciously exceeds, some of Pindar's famous compliments to Hieron and other eminent *laudandi* (37–40):[62]

> quo nihil maius meliusque terris
> fata donavere bonique divi
> nec dabunt, quamvis redeant in aurum
> tempora priscum.

[Caesar], than whom no greater or better gift has been, or will be, bestowed upon the earth by destiny or the kind gods, even though the age return to a primal gold.

Whereas Pindar normally restricts his cohorts of comparison to the living, Horace's embedded *laudator* rather confidently embraces the future as well (*nec dabunt*). The device of the surrogate, then, enables the Roman bard to incorporate (and even outdo) high-style hyperbole without seeming to breach generic decorum.

The extravagant vaunt in the grand-style portion is later counterbalanced by a restrained vaunt in the plain style (b2). In the second mini-encomium, which is presented as attached to the first in an ancillary way, a simple apostrophe making use of a pedestrian metaphor replaces a majestic, rotund relative clause (45–52):

> tum meae, si quid loquar audiendum,
> vocis accedet bona pars, et, "o Sol
> pulcher! o laudande!" canam, recepto
>   Caesare felix.
> terque, dum procedis, io Triumphe,
> non semel dicemus, io Triumphe,
> civitas omnis, dabimusque divis
>   tura benignis.[63]

Then, if I have anything to utter deserving of attention, my voice will join in its better register to yours, and I shall sing, "O Sun most fair, most worthy of praise!" in my happiness at Caesar's return. Not once, but three times over, while you advance in procession, we shall sing, O Triumph; the whole city shall sing your name, O Triumph; and we shall offer incense to favorable gods.

In terms of content, the straightforward identification of the ruler with the sun was already a commonplace of Hellenistic panegyric, and it was also prefigured in archaic lyric encomia.[64] By adopting the plain speech (and also rhythm)[65] of the common man, the *laudator* displays his "sincerity" in words stripped of fulsome flattery. The employment of the humble acclamation *io Triumphe* is even more telling from this point of view, for nothing could be more unpretentious than the heartfelt ritual tribute repeated in Roman triumphal processions. Cicero's plain orator makes an analogous appropriation of the speech of the ordinary person (*Or. 76*):

> Ac primum informandus est ille nobis quem solum quidem vocant
>   Atticum. Summissus est et humilis, consuetudinem imitans,
>   ab indisertis re plus quam opinione differens. Itaque eum qui
>   audiunt, quamvis ipsi infantes sint, tamen illo modo confidunt
>   se posse dicere.

> First we must characterize the type whom they define as exclusively "Attic." He is restrained and plain, taking ordinary usage as his model, yet more divergent, in actual fact, from the untrained speaker than is generally imagined. As a result the audience, although itself untrained in eloquence, are convinced they can speak in similar fashion.

Horace's terse praise of Augustus artfully composed in the popular strain is, in effect, no insignificant supplement to Antonius's eulogy, for, between them, the two specimens (the grand and the humble) chart the stylistic poles of a comprehensive epideictic project.

From bifurcated praise to bifurcated vows—the closing vignette of the ode (quoted at the start of this section) encapsulates important points in the antecedent account as I have analyzed it. Predictably, the grandiloquent *laudator* will offer a sacrifice consisting of twenty victims (*decem tauri totidemque vaccae*), while the plain speaker will devote a single calf (*vitulus*).[66] Once again the one is favorably contrasted to the many, as quality to mere quantity (note the stress laid on sheer numbers in *decem* and *totidem*). Moreover, the fact that the calf is tagged with the epithet *tener* is not without relevance. The tag clearly recapitulates the theme of Callimachean values (cf. Russell 1981, 56–57). The succeeding lines describing the victim in further detail carry forward the argument by their medium no less than their symbolic content. The picture of the tender calf is attentive to minutiae in a way that reflects a major preoccupation of Hellenistic aesthetics. As Wesley Trimpi (1973) has carefully documented in regard to rhetorical theory from Aristotle to Horace, the short poem, intended to be viewed at close range, invites a meticulous critic. Horace's precious victim stands for a kind of poem embodying aesthetic principles that encourage the reader to admire at close range the subtle craftsmanship (*labor*) with which he has constructed his work. In framing an analogy between sacrificial victim and poem, the poet of the *Odes* follows the precedent of his friend Virgil, who was even more explicit in his invocation of the metaphor in *Ecl.* 3.85–87:[67]

DAMOETAS: Pierides, *vitulam* lectori pascite vestro.
MENALCAS: Pollio et ipse facit nova carmina: pascite *taurum*,
iam cornu petat et pedibus qui spargit harenam.

DAMOETAS: Pierian muses, feed *a calf* for your reader.
MENALCAS: Even Pollio himself is composing new songs: feed *a bull,* that already attacks with his horns and scatters sand with his hooves.

There is more to the intricate honeycomb of the ode's final strophe than is summed up in the mode of description per se. The youthful calf's splendid appearance is polysemous. On the level of sustained imagery, the calf's "lunar" horns furnish a contrapuntal extension of the eulogy, for the synecdochic "moon" donated by the *laudator* is a reflection of its inspiration in the "sun" of the *laudandus.* From the vantage point of sacrificial cult, the color symbolism is demonstrably pertinent, since white bulls were normally required by triumphal ritual in honor of Jupiter.[68] Antonius's full-grown *tauri* may therefore be presumed to have been completely white; by contrast, Horace's newly weaned *vitulus* has its ritually significant pigmentation confined to a single (though conspicuous!) mark on the forehead ("qua notam duxit, *niveus* videri, / cetera fulvus"—*"white as snow* where it bears a mark, otherwise ruddy"). The circumscribed white spot between the horns is a metonymic marker that encodes the poem's restraint and judiciousness, while respecting the ritual exactitude prescribed for the occasion. At the same time, the description of the calf's double coloration apparently recalls Moschus's (Hellenistic) portrayal of the Jupiter-bull that abducted Europa.[69] The veiled allusion to a famous (and, paradoxically, "grand") bull incarnating the sky-god contributes to the unique value of the ostensibly modest victim, while raising it to a higher order. Thus the small creation (sacrifice or poem) turns out to be, after all, just as important in its own way as the great. With its subdued but sophisticated closure, the ode perfectly corroborates its own contention that an abbreviated encomium in the hands of a master can accomplish the purposes of a more expansive *epinikion.*

CODA

Horace was by no means unique among lyrists, ancient and modern, in devising sophisticated strategies for securing the reader's assent to the authenticity of his poetic voice.[70] The foregoing analyses of representative odes have aimed at illustrating the density of such strategies by focussing on two that are less apparent: the use of quasi-autobiographical *mythos* and the "objectification" of the *carmen* through resort to prestigious metaphors. More transparent examples of this mode include straightforward declarations on the part of the bard concerning his place in the tradition. The climax of the priamel in the dedicatory poem *C.* 1.1. is unabashedly explicit in this respect (29–36):

> me doctarum hederae praemia frontium
> dis miscent superis, me gelidum nemus
> nympharumque leves cum Satyris chori
> secernunt populo, si neque tibias
> Euterpe cohibet nec Polyhymnia
> Lesboum refugit tendere barbiton.
> *quodsi me lyricis vatibus inseres,*
> sublimi feriam sidera vertice.

Ivy wreaths, recompense for learned brows, allow me to mingle with the gods above; the cool grove and the light songs of nymphs as they dance with Satyrs set me apart from the crowd, so long as neither Euterpe restrains the flutes nor Polyhymnia shuns from tuning the lyre of Lesbos. *But if you place me in the canon of lyric poets,* I shall strike the stars with my uplifted head.

While decorously complimenting his patron, Horace in this key, programmatic passage seeks to guarantee for himself a privileged place in the canon of major lyrists (*lyricis vatibus*); simultaneously, he puts forward his strong claim to be the authentic Roman standard-bearer of Aeolic, and specifically Lesbian, *melos.*

3

Modes of Consolation:
Convivium and *carpe diem*

Convivial motifs are so pervasive in the *Odes* that they have come
to epitomize, for many readers, the veritable signature of the Horatian *carmen*. It is all the more important, therefore, that the deeper
structure of the Convivial ode be adequately analyzed, and its
philosophical underpinnings clearly delineated. *Carpe diem* poetry,
of which the banquet motif is the paramount emblem, is especially
vulnerable to trivialization, because the repeated exhortation to carouse lends itself to easy travesty by those who refuse to give due
credit to its symbolic dimensions. In this segment of my investigation, I shall consider the sympotic gesture in its rhetorical context.
The injunction (expressed or implied) to enjoy the here and now
will be related to the broader epistemological framework in which
it is grounded. In the course of the analysis, I hope to contribute to
the elucidation of several passages in the *Odes* that have been ob-
fuscated by misconceptions arising, in the main, from too literal a
reading of Horace's text.

THE *CARPE DIEM* ODE:
RHETORICAL SCHEMA

I shall seek to describe the economy of the *carpe diem* ode (hereafter
abbreviated *CD*) through a succinct example of the type, *Ep.* 13.
Once I have derived a basic schema from this representative instance, I shall proceed to look at its essential components from a
"synchronic" perspective—that is, I shall compare variants in parts
of the schema as they occur in similar odes distributed throughout
the collection. This approach will furnish us with a reliable foundation for interpreting a small number of odes (including some
viewed as problematic) that depend on the reader's prior awareness of the *CD* structure.

RAPIAMUS OCCASIONEM DE DIE:
EP. 13 REVISITED

I have previously discussed the latter portion of this epode (the embedded speech of Cheiron to Achilles) in terms of "generic remodeling" (see text and discussion in chapter 1 above). I now return to the poem in order to identify and unpack the exemplary *CD* motifs that pave the way for Cheiron's admonitions. The epode begins with a description of a severe winter storm (1–3):

> Horrida tempestas caelum contraxit et imbres
>   nivesque deducunt Iovem; nunc mare, nunc silvae
> Threicio Aquilone sonant.

A horrible storm has contracted the sky, and rain and snow bring down Jupiter; now the sea, now the woods resound with the North Wind from Thrace.

Immediately following this vivid description comes the injunction to the companions to "snatch the opportunity from the day" (3–5):

> rapiamus, amici,
>   occasionem de die,[1] dumque virent genua
> et decet, obducta solvatur fronte senectus.

let us snatch, my friends, the opportunity from the day, and while our knees are still in bloom and it is appropriate, let old age be loosened from the contracted brow.

In the interest of expository consistency, I shall refer to the descriptive component of *CD* odes as "scene" and the injunction as "prescription." The "prescription," we may note, is part of the "response" to the scene and is grounded in a general "insight" concerning the ephemeral nature of human existence. We may formulate this recurrent rhetorical schema (and terminology) as follows:

1. Scene   Description of nature
2. Response   (a) Insight
                 (b) Prescription

As initially presented, the form the prescription takes in the epode is vigorous and, at the same time, aphoristic. Though formally directed to the immediate community of assembled *amici*, the injunction is general in scope, as the temporal clause makes clear with its telescoping of the relevant "day" to include a man's entire youth (*dum . . . senectus*). Such an expansion of horizons is all the more salient since it comes on the heels of a "contraction" (cf. the imagery in the verbs *contraxit* and *deducunt*) caused by the aggressive onset of the wintry storm. The prescriptive apothegm, then, grows out of, but rapidly goes beyond, the particular occasion, which thereby functions as a kind of "scaffolding" (another key term in my unfolding repertoire of labels) on which the ethical norms of the poem are constructed. The scaffolding, in a word, is put there as temporary support for the edifice of values, and the unstated purpose of the scene is to generate an appropriate ethical response (cf. *et decet*). The insight, whether it is merely implicit, as here, or more explicitly formulated, acts as a logical bridge between the scene and the response. Thus the imagery of the *dum* clause adumbrates the central idea of the transience of mortal life, inasmuch as it subtly annexes the green season of spring (*virent genua*) as metaphorical counter to the white rigidity of a winter that is to be loosened (*solvatur*) in its incarnation on the brows of the old.

The first few lines of the epode, therefore, exhibit the fundamental structure typical of the *CD* tradition. The sympotic gesture that crowns that structure is counterpoised to the ineluctable circumstance of human mortality. It is this bare skeleton that Petronius, a demonstrably percipient reader of Horace, parodies when he makes Trimalchio compose, in the vertiginal context of the *Cena*, an extemporaneous ditty in the *CD* tradition (*Sat.* 34.10):

> eheu nos miseros, quam totus homuncio nil est!
> sic erimus cuncti, postquam nos auferet Orcus.
> ergo vivamus, dum licet esse bene.

Alas, we wretched humans: how poor little man is a complete nothing! So shall we all become after Hell takes us away. Let us therefore live, while we may do so well.

In the witty Petronian travesty, no less than in the Horatian exemplars, the *convivium* may be apprehended as a mode of consolation, not so much for a particular "death" (as is the case in the related literary subgenre of the *consolatio*), but for the specter of death in general. From this perspective, the presence of death, as recurrent motif, in the very bosom of the Horatian *convivium* is not indicative, as is sometimes supposed, of a gloomy disposition (as may be the case with Trimalchio) but, on the contrary, of an intense recommitment to the joys of the present.[2] In *Ep.* 13, Horace conjures up the specter of *mors* obliquely through his mention of old age (*senectus*).

In his convivial poetry, Horace regularly employs a binary development of theme that is comparable to what E. H. Gombrich has called, in the context of artistic representation, "schema" and "refinement."[3] The argument of the CD ode receives a brief preliminary sketch that includes scene, insight, and response; then, in a movement that I shall label the "reprise," the singer returns to the argument to refine and supplement it, often enlarging on the motifs that he used to introduce the schema. I shall illustrate this binary organization in some of my subsequent analyses of selected CD odes. In the poem under inspection, the speaker supplies us with a second prescription, this time around in more concrete terms than the first (6–7):

> tu vina Torquato move consule pressa meo:
> cetera mitte loqui.

You [my friend] bring in the wine pressed in the consulship of my Torquatus. Leave off speaking of other matters.

The order to bring out a vintage wine for immediate consumption is a particularization of the earlier global exhortation to harvest the fleeting moment. The cryptic proscription (exclusion) of all irrelevant discourse from the sympotic occasion (*cetera mitte loqui*) is a refinement that makes sense when we grasp its relation to the scene of the epode; for it is justified by the insight that the winter storm is itself subject to an ineluctable law—that of alternation (7–8):

> deus haec fortasse *benigna*
> reducet in sedem *vice.*

a god perchance will restore this all to a stable calm *with a benevolent change.*

The alternation principle (the word *vice* in its limited inflections recurs as a "motif signal"[4] in two other paradigmatic convivial odes) here functions as a corrective to the false view that the scene is somehow permanent rather than contingent. Though death, the oblique signified, is indeed ineluctable for mortals, winter, the signifier, is subject to change, even though the change is temporary and part of a natural cycle of alternation. If the severe winter storm will abate *benigna vice* through the independent agency of the gods, then human conduct should reflect that insight by opposing the convivial springtime of youth to the winter of discontented old age. The observation (and acceptance) of alternation as a principle in nature is a fundamental element in the consolatory strategy, since it undervalues the significance of winter (and by extension, death) in the larger scheme of things. By seeing the current winter through the larger lens of seasonal change, the speaker imparts a transcendental ethical value to the convivial response. The symbolic parameters of that response are later spelled out in greater detail with the reappearance of the word *nunc*, which is deliberately antithetical to the earlier (and repeated) *nunc* that marked the roaring of the storm (9–11):

> *nunc* et Achaemenio
> perfundi nardo iuvat et fide Cyllenea
> levare diris pectora sollicitudinibus.

Now it is pleasing to be anointed with Persian nard and to lighten the heart of dreadful anxieties by means of the Cyllenean lyre-string.

A paramount feature of the convivial response—seen as a complex of exemplary actions—is the timely performance of lyric poetry (*fide Cyllenea*), which will have the desirable effect of consoling both singer and audience by relieving their cares (*levare . . . sollicitudinibus*). The *convivium*, then, is the supreme mode of consolation, since it furnishes the ideal occasion for poetic discourse—the kind that is most pertinent to the task of alleviating the harsh realities of man's condition.

The basic scheme I have extrapolated from *Ep.* 13 is, as we have seen, triadic: scene—insight—response. The three interrelated components of the structure do not, of course, occur in an invariable sequence, nor does Horace develop them in any fixed proportional relation. The poet may elect to amplify or attenuate (and occasionally even delete) a part of the scheme. In principle, however, this triad of elements serves to co-define the subgenre of the CD ode and provide a framework for its characteristic motifs. Let us now extend our exploration of the economy of the type so as to bring out more fully the philosophical nuances in Horace's argument. Rather than giving a complete "diachronic" account of each of the poems, I intend to focus on important facets of the recurrent pattern, using individual passages as illustrations of the range of motivic variation we encounter in the *Odes*.

BENIGNA VICE: THE MOTIF OF ALTERNATION IN NATURE

In my discussion of *Ep.* 13, I observed that the poet's reminder of a potential change in nature helps to reorient and console the audience of symposiasts who are confronted by an overwhelming storm. An analogous deployment of the alternation motif occurs in the so-called Soracte ode (*C.* 1.9)—a tightly organized poem that has suffered unjustly at the hands of those critics who insist on ignoring its universal import at the expense of what they see as a peculiar (and heterogeneous) scenario. The first three strophes (lines 1–12) will provide us with an adequate context for understanding the ode's motif structure.

> Vides ut alta stet nive candidum
> Soracte nec iam sustineant onus
>   silvae laborantes, geluque
>   flumina constiterint acuto.
> dissolve frigus ligna super foco
> large reponens atque benignius
>   deprome quadrimum Sabina
>   O Thaliarche, merum diota.
> permitte divis cetera, qui simul
> stravere ventos aequore fervido
>   deproeliantis, nec cupressi
>   nec veteres agitantur orni.

You see how white Soracte stands in the deep snow; nor do the laboring woods bear the burden, and the rivers have frozen to a standstill with the sharp frost. Loosen up the cold, piling logs abundantly upon the hearth-fire and, in a more generous temper, bring out the four-year-old vintage, O Thaliarchus, from the Sabine storage jar. Leave the rest to the gods: for as soon as they have straightened out the winds that do battle over the seething sea, then neither cypresses nor ancient ash trees continue to be driven about.

The opening strophe constructs a wintry scene (partially imitated, as is well known, from an Alcaeus paradigm)[5] in which excessive snow and frost overwhelm the landscape, producing stasis and rigidity (cf. *stet*, stands; *constiterint*, have frozen to a standstill). The scene is both particular (we face Mount Soracte) and generic (traditional *CD* foil); in fine, the individual frozen landscape, like the storm-battered vista of *Ep.* 13, is the background for the pre-scriptive response to follow. The content of the prescription bears some resemblance, in detail, to that of the epode, especially in its peremptory command to serve a fine vintage wine (cf. *deprome . . . merum*). The Roman poet departs from the Alcaean model to create an imagistic congruity between scene and prescription; for in the ode the rigidity of winter is to be loosened up (*dissolve*) in the burning logs of the fireplace, just as the knotted brow of the frowning *senex* in *Ep.* 13 is to be loosened (*solvatur*) by youthful merry-making. The fact that the formal addressee, Thaliarchus, bears a name that signifies "Leader of the Symposium" is striking in its un-abashed self-referentiality, and serves to highlight the point that the proposed "solution" to the scene of winter is to be taken not as unique, but, on the contrary, as profoundly typical.

The speaker's ethical agenda is more evident when, in the third stanza, he insists on the unqualified exclusion of irrelevant con-cerns (*permitte divis cetera:* leave the rest to the gods). Like the pe-remptory proscription of irrelevant conversation in the epode, the blunt instruction circumscribes the *convivium* as a place where a privileged ethos is to be nurtured and celebrated. The exclusion ap-plies, inter alia, to idle speculation about the future. The clause that follows immediately on the instruction proffers a clarification of the circumscription (9–12):

> qui simul
> stravere ventos aequore fervido
> deproeliantis, nec cupressi
> nec veteres agitantur orni.

for as soon as they have straightened out the winds that do battle over the seething sea, then neither cypresses nor ancient ash trees continue to be driven about.

The gods, so the poet declares, are everywhere responsible for the process of alternation in nature, which in this instance takes the particular manifestation of storm/calm. In addition, the metaphor in *deproeliantis* (that do battle) also assimilates, in passing, the alternation war/peace. Thus, far from being trivial, the alternation motif, once its generic and (generalizing) aspect is fully understood, is central to the *CD* argument.[6] Since change in external nature (whether malign or benign) is totally beyond man's control, it ought not, so argues the poet, to be made the focus of anxious obsession. The implied insight, then, is much more than a mere demarcation of the spheres of human and divine *dynamis;* the unstated corollary is that man should not hope to appropriate a process of alternation that, fundamentally, would operate as a guarantor of immortality. The alternation motif is here contrapuntal, in retrospect, to the depiction of stasis in the opening scene. As the enlightened symposiast of the second stanza effects a change from cold to warmth (an action mimetic of, and anticipatory to, seasonal change), so the gods' representative move in the next stanza consoles the audience by stressing the eventuality of "benign" alternation. The recognition of regular and predictable change is the principle that grounds the cryptic injunctions.

Since the subject of seasonal change in respect to the outdoor scene of the final stanza has provoked hostile criticism from some philological quarters, let us round off our analysis with a brief digression on the issue of the ode's unity. Fraenkel's strictures may be taken as representative of those who see incongruity in the poem's closing picture:

> Line 18 *nunc et campus et areae* and what follows suggest a season wholly different from the severe winter at the beginning. This incongruity cannot be removed by any device of apologetic interpretation. To put it somewhat crudely: the "Hellenistic" ending of the ode and its "Alcaean" beginning have not really coalesced.
>
> (Fraenkel, 177)

Fraenkel's objections rest on the unstated assumption that unity of place is, or should be, the organizing principle of a Horatian ode. As we have seen, however, opening scenes, especially ones of winter, usually constitute scaffolding for the unfolding *CD* argument. The unity of the *CD* ode exists preponderantly on the level of ideas as they are conveyed in a nexus of interrelated motifs, and not on the level of the expository situation that may inaugurate that nexus. The idea embodied in the vignette ("enjoy yourself while you are still young") is intimately related to the gnomic sequence that precedes it (13–24):

> Quid sit futurum cras fuge quaerere et
> quem Fors dierum cumque dabit lucro
>   appone, nec dulcis amores
>   sperne puer neque tu choreas,
> donec virenti canities abest
> morosa. *nunc* et campus et areae
>   lenesque sub noctem susurri
>   composita repetantur hora,
> *nunc* et latentis proditor intimo
> gratus puellae risus ab angulo
>   pignusque dereptus lacertis
>   aut digito male pertinaci.

Avoid trying to know what will be tomorrow, and set down as credit whatsoever day Chance will bring you; while you are young, spurn neither sweet lovemaking nor dancing, as long as morose old age stays away from your green prime. *Now* make for the park and the squares and gentle whispers by nightfall at the trysting hour; *now* the pleasurable laugh from the intimate corner that gives away the hiding girl, and the love-token snatched from the shoulders or from a finger that fails to resist.

The urgent *nunc* that gives weight to the injunction has an inclusive, rather than restrictive significance ("while you are young" rather than "now, at the time of speaking")[7]—a point anticipated in the previous temporal clause that amplified the gnome ("donec *virenti* canities abest / morosa"). As in the analogous *dum* clause in *Ep.* 13, the expanded time frame annexes the countervision of a spring verdure (*virenti*), which, as transposed to the human body, provides an antidote to the inertia of winter, old age, and death. Thus the closing vignette of the ode—a young man and woman engaged in amorous play—provides a model, by way of the *reprise*, of an appropriate response to the message communicated by the scene.

In the Soracte ode, as we have shown, the central motif of polar alternation takes the explicit form of a gnomic statement concerning the gods' control of the calm/storm transmutation (9–12). The figure of a storm (*tempestas*) is a favorite signifier, for Horace, of the idea of potential reversibility. Whereas the *tempestas* of *Ep.* 13 is represented as actually taking place at the moment of speaking, in other variants it is anticipated as a future "malign" change, requiring a prophylactic response. Thus in *C.* 3.17, a densely constructed *CD* poem, the *tempestas* is prognosticated as imminent (9–16):

> *cras* foliis nemus
> multis et alga litus inutili
>   demissa *tempestas* ab Euro
>   sternet, aquae nisi fallit augur
>
> annosa cornix. dum potes, aridum
> compone lignum: *cras* Genium mero
>   curabis et porco bimestri
>   cum famulis operum solutis.

> *Tomorrow a storm* unleashed by the East Wind will strew the grove with many leaves, and the shore with useless seaweed, if the long-lived raven, prophetess of rain, does not deceive us. While you may, pile up dry wood; tomorrow you will take care of your Guardian Spirit with unmixed wine and a two-month-old pig, in the company of your slaves, released from their chores.

By mentioning, in the course of the prognosis, the longevity of the raven (*annosa cornix*) the speaker hints at the contrasting brevity of human life. The single word *annosa* condenses a topos often elaborated in *CD* contexts. As Steele Commager saw, the later reference to the pitifully abbreviated span of the animal that is to be sacrificed at the *convivium* (*porco bimestri*, 15) is also part of the same contrastive strategy (Commager, 261). By transposing the topic of longevity/brevity to the pair of animals (raven/pig), the poet deftly inserts a linear conception of time that is antithetical to an eternal and cyclical natural order. The actual content of the raven's prognosis—the shift from calm to storm—constitutes the motif ground, so to speak, for the convivial prescription that crowns the ode (*cras . . . solutis*). The *convivium*, like the storm that helps to define its existential context, is imagined as taking place in the very near future (cf. *cras*, 9 and 14). The lyrist has not, we may safely assume, relinquished his cherished view that the present, rather than the future, should be the dominant focus of human concern. On the contrary, the concrete response that he urges—the piling on of firewood—is indeed to be implemented at once, for both storm and antidotal banquet are imminent. His consistent contention is that since external change, whether benign or malign, actual or potential, is a law of nature, the sympotic ethos will always be a rational strategy for coping with the inevitable swings between polar states.

SPES LONGA: THE DENIAL OF DEATH

In building up the CD enthymeme on the premise (stated or implied) of human limit, Horace consistently inveighs against the consequences of the contrary viewpoint—the immature denial of death. The illusory hope for immortality—succinctly expressed in the repeated phrase *spes longa*—is indicted as the inappropriate response to the scene, and is often juxtaposed with the superior CD response, whose appropriateness is typically marked with the word *decet* or *iuvat*. The antinomy receives its clearest articulation in those odes that show its close correlation with two disparate conceptualizations of time: the cyclical versus the linear. C. 4.7.1–8 contains a relatively full elaboration of the correlation:

> Diffugere nives, redeunt iam gramina campis
>   arboribusque comae;
> *mutat terra vices*, et decrescentia ripas
>   flumina praetereunt;
> Gratia cum Nymphis geminisque sororibus audet
>   ducere nuda choros.
> *immortalia ne speres*, monet annus et almum
>   quae rapit hora diem.

The snows have dispersed; already grass is returning to the meadows and leaves to the trees; *the earth goes through its changes,* and the rivers decrease their flow between the banks; a Grace with her two sisters and the Nymphs dares to lead the dances in the nude. The yearly cycle and the hour that snatches the nurturing day warns us *not to hope for immortality.*

The preliminary scaffolding here consists in a scene of *transition* from winter to spring, with an emphasis on the regularity of the alternation (*mutat terra vices*, 4). In the vanguard of those beings who engage in the appropriate response are the Graces and Nymphs, who emerge early in the season to perform choral dances in the nude—a role they also play, alongside the goddess Venus, in C. 1.4.5–7:

> iam Cytherea choros ducit Venus imminente Luna,
> iunctaeque Nymphis Gratiae *decentes*
> alterno terram quatiunt pede . . .

Already Cytherean Venus leads the dances beneath the overhanging Moon, and the *becoming* Graces joined with the Nymphs shake the earth with alternating feet . . .

The exemplary dance of the divine figures in C. 4.7 reflects the insight that is made explicit by the personified *annus* (7–8):

> *immortalia ne speres,* monet annus et almum
> quae rapit hora diem.[8]

The yearly cycle and the hour that snatches the nurturing day warns us *not to hope for immortality.*

The lesson inscribed in the seasonal alternation (*annus*) receives a negative formulation: man is admonished not to hope for immortality. In the elaborate reprise that immediately follows, the cyclical progression of the four seasons (the inaugural motif of the ode) is taken up again and refined; as such it functions mainly as foil to the non-cyclical (linear) movement of mortal existence (9–16):

> frigora mitescunt Zephyris, ver proterit aestas
> *interitura* simul
> pomifer Autumnus fruges effuderit, et mox
> bruma recurrit iners.
> damna tamen celeres reparant caelestia lunae:
> *nos ubi decidimus*
> quo pius[9] Aeneas, quo Tullus dives et Ancus,
> pulvis et umbra sumus.

The cold grows mild with the coming of the Zephyrs; spring is trampled down by summer—summer *destined to die* as soon as fruit-bearing fall sheds its leaves, and shortly lifeless winter returns. Celestial losses, however, are repaired by swiftly changing moons; *when we have fallen down* to where good Aeneas, where affluent Tullus and Ancus fell—we become dust and shade.

The acute cognizance of the difference between death in the natural order (a reversible event) and death in the human sphere (an irreversible event) informs the counsel inherent in the *annus*—a point carried forward with great poignancy in the ironic trope of a summer "about to die" (*interitura*). The incommensurability of the two models of time appears even more flagrant when the speaker continues the figurative contamination by making fallen leaves a metaphor for human demise ("nos ubi *decidimus*"). The mutual contaminations on the level of imagery (of nature by human and, conversely, of human by nature) serve to flag the radical incompatibility of the two ontological domains. The recognition of difference between human self and natural "other" is also the expressed insight of Catullus's brief poem in the *CD* genre, *C.* 5.4–6:

> soles occidere et redire possunt:
> nobis cum semel occidit brevis lux
> nox est perpetua una dormienda.

Suns can set and rise again: when once our brief light has set, we must sleep for one night without end.

The generic insight, then, resides in the philosophical acceptance of the irreversible model, and the immature desire to assimilate nature's endless reversibility is what Horace means by the recurrent motif I have labeled *spes longa*.

The seemingly innocuous epithet *longus* often carries, in the *Odes*, a special nuance of pathos that connects it with the leitmotif of mortality (cf. Smith 1931, *ad C.* 3.11.38). To illustrate this important usage, we may observe the shade of meaning imparted to it in the words of Hypermnestra, the "noble" Danaid who chose to rescue her betrothed (3.11.33–39):

> una de multis face nuptiali
> digna periurum fuit in parentem
> splendide mendax et in omne virgo
>   nobilis aevum,
>
> "surge," quae dixit iuveni marito,
> "surge, ne *longus* tibi *somnus*, unde
> non times, detur . . ."

One only out of many proved worthy of the wedding torch: to her forsworn parent she was sublimely mendacious, a maiden illustrious for all time. "Arise," she said to her young husband, "arise, lest you be accorded a *long sleep* from an unsuspecting quarter . . ."

The narrative context makes it clear that *longus somnus* is an ironic euphemism here for "death." The same connotation of "eternal" adheres to the adjective in *C.* 4.9.25–28, where *nox longa* is periphrasis for *mors:*

> vixere fortes ante Agamemnona
> multi; sed omnes illacrimabiles
> urgentur ignotique *longa*
> *nocte*, carent quia vate sacro.

There were many brave men who lived before Agamemnon; but all of them, unwept and unknown are compassed by *long night* for lack of a sacred bard.

When Horace, in a typical understatement, ascribes the same modifier to the ineluctable sufferings of Sisyphus in the underworld, he is, of course, referring to an irreversible condition (2.14.17–20):

> visendus ater flumine languido
> Cocytos errans et Danai genus
> infame damnatusque *longi*
> Sisyphus Aeolides *laboris*.

We must visit the somber Cocytus, meandering with its sluggish stream, and the notorious offspring of Danaus, and Sisyphus, son of Aeolus, condemned to *long labor*.

The placement of *longi*, no less than the motif context—the irreversibility of death—leaves no doubt as to the span of time imagined by the speaker: Sisyphus's *labor* is conceived as absolute and infinite, despite the literal denotation of "long."

Mature acceptance (versus immature denial) of death is the controlling idea structuring the response in *C.* 1.11—the short poem that contains the famous dictum *carpe diem:*

> Tu ne quaesieris, scire nefas, quem mihi quem tibi
> finem di dederint, Leuconoe, nec Babylonios
> temptaris numeros. ut melius, quidquid erit pati,
> seu pluris hiemes seu tribuit Iuppiter ultimam
> quae nunc oppositis debilitat pumicibus mare   5
> Tyrrhenum: sapias, vina liques, et spatio brevi
> *spem longam* reseces. dum loquimur, fugerit invida
> aetas: carpe diem, quam minimum credula postero.

Do not ask (it is wrong to know) what end the gods have assigned to you or what to me, Leuconoe, and do not dabble in Babylonian calculations. How much better it is to endure whatever will be, whether Jupiter has allotted us more winters or whether this is our last that now wears down the Tyrrhenian sea against the opposing rocks. Be wise: decant the wine, and prune *long hope* to a brief span.

Even as we speak, envious time will have fled. Pluck the day, trusting as little as possible to tomorrow.

In this most crystalline of *CD* variants, all the major components of the structure are present in a highly compressed form. The circumscription of convivial discourse (questions about the future are strictly outlawed)[10] occurs first, and the scene—normally the opening gambit—here appears in the mid-course of the argument (lines 4–6). In the disjunctive formulation "seu *pluris* hiemes seu . . . *ultimam*," the lyrist suggests both the cyclical and the rectilinear models. That "winters" are the synecdochic measure of the entire *annus* is, of course, an oblique and parsimonious allusion to the motif of death. Horatian wisdom (*sapientia*), which I have been designating insight, is condensed in the prescription to take full part in the *convivium* (*sapias: vina liques*) and, as a corollary, to prune (*reseces*) the excessive growth of *spes longa*.

If the main function of the seasonal motif is to convey the idea of an unattainable cyclicality by differentiating man from the "other" (external nature), then the poet may, in principle, choose to exploit any point in the ongoing cycle. This varying of focus is precisely what Horace is at pains to do in the *CD* odes, sometimes depicting the dead of winter, sometimes the nascent spring, sometimes the liminal moment of transition between the two. Alcaeus, who provided Horace with his prime model for convivial poetry, had also varied his seasonal foil in similar fashion, and was not above including even midsummer in his repertoire.[11] For this reason, it is fundamentally misleading to characterize those Horatian odes that select a moment in the cycle (spring) as "spring poems," as though spring, per se, were the main subject of such *carmina*. Spring, like winter, subserves the *CD* argument by provoking an appropriate response from the sapient, as we see clearly in the "parade" ode, *C. 1.4*, that I have partially cited above (line 1):

> *Solvitur* acris hiems *grata vice* veris et Favoni

> Vicious winter *is being loosened by the pleasing change* of spring and the West Wind.

Spring, we note, is here the ascendant season, but the basal motif of alternation accomplishes the same cognitive role, as the recurrent tropes *solvitur* and *vice* make patent. Paradigmatic responses are soon led by Venus, Graces, and Nymphs (with the busy Vulcan serving as negative model) and the sympotic "solution" is promoted, in a marvellously congruent way, through the image of the floral wreaths that are to be composed from the loosened (*solutae*) earth:

> iam Cytherea choros ducit Venus imminente Luna,   5
> *iunctaeque Nymphis Gratiae decentes*
> alterno terram quatiunt pede, dum gravis Cyclopum
> Vulcanus ardens urit[12] officinas.
> nunc *decet* aut viridi nitidum caput impedire myrto
> aut flore *terrae* quem ferunt *solutae.*   10

Already Cytherean Venus leads the dances beneath the overhanging moon, and the *becoming* Graces joined with the Nymphs shake the earth with alternating feet, while glowing Vulcan fires up the workshops of the Cyclopes. Now *it is appropriate* to bind one's gleaming head either with green myrtle-wreaths or with flowers put forth *by the loosened earth.*

FORMS OF INDIRECT PRESCRIPTION

Because the lyric speaker frequently delivers his injunction in the imperative mood, it is relatively easy to overlook more subtle forms of purveying the *CD* "message." In bringing to the fore some of Horace's more oblique varieties of admonition, it will be useful to invoke the concept to which speech-act theory has given the name "illocutionary force."[13] The syntax of a sentence is not the only clue to its semantics, and in the context of *CD* poetry it is often the case that declarative sentences, especially when projected into the future, have the illocutionary force of exhortations. A clear instance of such indirection occurs in the last stanza of the well-known ode addressed to one Postumus (*C.* 2.14.25–28):

> *absumet heres* Caecuba *dignior*
> servata centum clavibus et mero
> tinget pavimentum superbo,
> pontificum potiore cenis.

Your more deserving heir will drink up the Caecuban vintage that you guarded with a hundred keys, and he will stain the pavement with a proud *cru*, superior to those served at the banquets of pontiffs.

On the surface, the speaker makes a sardonic prediction about what will happen to the addressee's unconsumed wine cellar; but with the use of the comparative *dignior* applied to the carousing heir, he also makes a value judgment that may be readily recast in the form: "Consume your vintage wine now before it is too late." A similar manipulation of the future tense concludes the ode addressed to Sestius (*C.* 1.4.14–20):

> o beate Sesti,
> vitae summa brevis *spem* nos vetat incohare *longam*.
>   iam te premet nox fabulaeque[14] Manes
> et domus exilis Plutonia; quo simul mearis,
>   *nec regna vini sortiere talis*,
> *nec tenerum Lycidan mirabere*, quo calet iuventus
>   nunc omnis et mox virgines tepebunt.

O fortunate Sestius, life's brief span forbids us to embark upon *unlimited hope*. Already night will compass you, and the legendary shades, and Pluto's insubstantial home; as soon as you arrive there, *you will neither win with the dice-throw the dominion over the wine, nor cast admiring looks at tender Lycidas*, for whom now all the young men are burning with desire, and shortly the young women will become warm.

The negative formulation (lines 18–19) sets up a catalogue of desirable things that Sestius will be ineligible for in the afterlife. Not surprisingly, these turn out to be a metonymic description of the convivial life (symposiarch; love-mate), and the reader is left in no doubt about the appropriate course of action to pursue in the present. To be precise, the illocutionary force of the prediction—as determined by the communicative context—is to exhort us to enjoy those things that will be precluded by death.[15]

In the Dellius ode (*C.* 2.3), where the elements of the *convivium* are partially listed in the *reprise* in an imperative format, several of the surrounding utterances of the speaker imply the same prescription through non-imperative formulations. For example, the disjunctive clauses in the second strophe serve to draw a sharp line between undesirable and desirable responses to the perception of death's inexorability (4–8):

> *moriture* Delli,
> *seu* maestus omni tempore vixeris,
> *seu* te in remoto gramine per dies
>   festos reclinatum bearis
>   interiore nota Falerni.

O Dellius *destined to die, whether* you spend your entire life feeling sad, *or whether* ensconced in a secluded meadow you make yourself happy on festal days with a rare vintage of Falernian.

The illocutionary import of the clause, despite the future perfect cast of the verbs, is not difficult to infer ("drink, rather than be sad"), and it is identical to that conveyed in the rhetorical questions to follow (9–12):

> quo pinus ingens albaque populus
> umbram hospitalem consociare amant
> ramis? quid obliquo laborat
> lympha fugax trepidare rivo?

Why do the huge pine and the white poplar love to join in creating a welcome shade with their branches? Why does the fleeing water labor under stress in the slanting stream?

The implicit response to the questions is that the seductive *locus amoenus* (shady trees; flowing water) exists as background to (and pretext for) the banquet *en plein air*. The indirect prescriptions, expressed in different grammatical forms, are mutually reinforcing and feed into the direct injunction in the following strophe (13–16):

> huc vina et unguenta et nimium brevis
> flores amoenae ferre iube rosae,
> dum res et aetas et sororum
> fila trium patiuntur atra.

To this spot, order wine to be brought, and perfumes, and the too-brief flowers of the lovely rose, as long as circumstances and age and the dark threads of the three sisters permit.

As a final illustration of the technique, we may return to C. 4.7, which, though it contains no formal, direct exhortation to the banquet, nevertheless approximates the topic through a powerful allusiveness (19–20):

> cuncta manus avidas fugient heredis, amico
> quae dederis animo.

All the offerings you will have made to your friendly guardian spirit will elude the greedy hands of your heir.

The *animus*, like the *Genius* that is to receive libations in the ode to Aelius Lamia, is the self that is to be nurtured from the convivial source. The mention of a prodigal heir, which is a common ancillary motif in *CD* poems, anticipates the death of the addressee (here anonymous), and hence is yet another economical way of reintroducing the topic of mortality. The single reference to the libation offered to the *animus*—a standard preliminary to the symposium—is all that Horace here needs to suggest the appropriate consolation for man's irreversible destiny.

AEQUO PEDE: THE MOTIF OF IMPARTIAL DEATH

The motif of death's impartiality is an integral part of the insight and is frequently articulated as a gnomic utterance (or sequence of utterances), as, for example, the forcefully alliterative *sententia* of C. 1.4.13–14:

> Pallida mors aequo pulsat pede pauperum tabernas
> regumque turris.

> Pale death beats with an even foot on the huts of the poor and the towers of the rich.

The manifest content of such a "gnomic foil" requires no extended treatment in this discussion; however, since the rhetorical apparatus that commonly frames the sentiment is occasionally misapprehended, it may be worthwhile to glance at a few representative instances.

Latin poetry, no less than Greek, is fond of a rhetorical mode of generalization that has been described under various names, including "merism" and "universalizing doublet." In modern linguistics, the term "complementary" has been proposed for the same device by John Lyons, and it is this less cumbersome expression that I shall adopt here (Lyons 1968, 460). Complementaries are dichotomized pairs used to convey the concept of a whole. Thus to express the idea "everyone," for instance, the speaker may utilize the dichotomy "rich and poor" or "young and old"; and the idea "everywhere" may be bifurcated into "land and sea," as in C. 3.4.29–32 where the omnipresence of the Muses to the poet is compartmentalized:

> *utcumque* mecum vos eritis, libens
> insanientem *navita* Bosphorum
> temptabo et urentis harenas
> litoris Assyrii *viator*

Whenever you are with me I shall freely, *as a sailor,* explore the raging Bosporus, and, *as a land-voyager,* the burning sands of the Assyrian shore.

An interesting occasional feature of such complementaries is that one member of the pair may be "marked," the other "unmarked" (Palmer 1981, 95–96). Thus the term *rich* in the pair rich/poor is the unmarked member because it is normally preferred in cases where we define the entire category of age (we normally say, "How old are you?" when asking someone's age, not "How young are you?"). When in classical verse the speaker specifies both members of such a pair, the universalizing function is not difficult to grasp. In many instances, in fact, the complementary is simply appended, by way of explanatory supplement, to a global utterance. For example, in C. 2.14.9–12 the obligatory journey across the Stygian wave—the trope for death—is made by dichotomized shades:

> unda, scilicet *omnibus,*
> quicumque terrae munere vescimur,
> enaviganda, *sive reges*
> *sive inopes erimus coloni.*

The water that *all* without exception must sail through—all of us who feed on the earth's bounty, *whether we be monarchs or indigent farmers.*

The whole is first defined (*omnibus . . . vescimur*), then broken down into the complementary: [rich] monarchs / indigent farmers. Similarly in the Dellius ode (C. 2.3), the complementary merely amplifies the generalizing *omnes,* though here the order is the inverse of the case just considered (21–28):

> *dives*ne prisco natus ab Inacho
> nil interest an *pauper* et infima
> de gente sub divo moreris,
> victima nil miserantis Orci.
> *omnes* eodem cogimur, *omnium*
> versatur urna serius ocius
> sors exitura et nos in aeternum
> exsilium impositura cumbae.

It doesn't matter whether you linger under the sky *as a rich man* tracing his descent to ancient Inachus, or *as a poor man* of the most humble origin—you are still a victim of unrelenting Orcus. We are *all* gathered to the same place; the lots of *all* are shaken about in the urn and are doomed to fall out sooner or later, and place us in the bark for an eternal exile.

The repeated *omnes* comes after the subdivision into rich/poor and, in effect, reemphasizes the globalizing function of the complementary.

In addition to these straightforward instances, the poet often elects to abbreviate the rhetorical apparatus of generalization. He does so primarily in two ways: (a) by deleting the explanatory *omnes* (and letting the complementary carry the onus of the generalization) or (b) by eliding one member (usually, but not invariably, the marked term) of the dichotomized pair. Failure to recognize the latter ellipsis (b) can sometimes contribute to problems of interpretation. C. 4.7.14–16 illustrates the technique:

> nos ubi decidimus
> quo pius Aeneas, quo Tullus dives et Ancus,
> pulvis et umbra sumus.

when we have fallen down to where good Aeneas, where affluent Tullus and Ancus fell—we become dust and shade.

The category "we" (*nos*) is, of course, inclusive of all mortals, and the clause that follows presents two truncated complementaries, *pius*/[*impius*] and *dives*/[*pauper*]. In the commonplace "all must die"—a standard topos of the *consolatio* as well as of CD poetry— the idea "even the good die" is often vividly rendered through a concrete exemplar, such as the hero Aeneas. The attribution of the modifier *dives* to Tullus is similarly motivated: the "rich" half of the dichotomy rich/poor suffices to adumbrate the concept of the whole of humankind. Some commentators understandably seek to document the wealth of the historical early monarch Tullus Hostilius (e.g., Kiessling-Heinze), but Horace is using the proper names Tullus and Ancus as tokens of wealthy persons (= *reges; divites*), and the plural *nos* is meant to be inclusive of the appropriate antonyms (such as *inopes; pauperes*).

The opening of C. 3.17, which is commonly regarded as enigmatic,[16] is an even more instructive example of an abbreviated complementary (1–9):

> Aeli vetusto *nobilis* ab Lamo,—
> quando et priores hinc Lamias ferunt
>   denominatos et nepotum
>   per memores genus omne fastus,
> auctore ab illo ducis originem,
> qui Formiarum moenia dicitur
>   princeps et innantem Maricae
>   litoribus tenuisse Lirim
>   *late tyrannus*

Aelius, *noble descendent* of ancient Lamus (since the elder generation of Lamiae as well as the entire lineage of grandsons are said to have taken their name from him throughout the annals of history)—you trace your origin to that founder who, they say, was the first to occupy the walls of Formiae and the Liris where it floats amid the shores of Marica: *a lord of wide dominion.*

Horace here lavishly (and facetiously) lauds the noble ancestry of the addressee in a parenthesis that comes to a ringing climax on the founder of the clan, who is described as "late *tyrannus.*" Immediately after the extravagant laudation, he switches to the alternation motif I have cited and discussed above, in which a coming *tempestas* is vividly depicted. What, then, is the logical connection, in terms of an underlying *CD* argument, between the mock-eulogistic opening and the *tempestas* motif? The answer is apparent once we posit the unexpressed gnome that may be extrapolated from the mention of Aelius's royal ancestor. The founder of the clan, though a powerful *tyrannus,* had to die, and though the speaker does not explicitly say so, the topos "even the *nobilis* or the *tyrannus* must face death" is the argumentative link between the two sections of the ode. Since "king" is usually the unmarked term in the common complementary king/commoner, the speaker can artfully position the single word, *tyrannus,* so as to elicit the reflection, "death is indiscriminate." In a highly compressed and oblique poem such as C. 3.17, the speaker safely dispenses with the gnomic transition because he can count on the audience's awareness of the motif nexus of the *CD* poem. The "noble" Aelius, therefore, embodies the idea of the irrelevance of birth to the fact of mortality—an idea that is archly foregrounded in the amusing hyperboles of the opening address. The effect of the genealogical parenthesis, then, is not so much to parody the pretentious pedigree of Lamia (cf. Kiessling-

Heinze *ad loc.*), but, more aptly, to emphasize the *nobilitas* theme as a foil to the impartiality of death.

MENS AEQUA: THE CONVIVIUM AND THE MEAN

In the Horatian worldview, the convivial response, in the broad sense in which I have been employing the term, is an icon of *sapientia*. Wisdom of this kind, however, is not to be regarded simplistically as a mere extrusion from the drinking-goblet; rather it flows from a deep-seated apprehension of, and adherence to, the "mean." The doctrine of the mean (*mediocritas*), which Horace adopted, with modifications, primarily from Aristotle, is fundamental to the system of values articulated, with a high degree of consistency, in the four books of the *Carmina*. To appreciate its centrality to the convivial poems, it is necessary to conduct a brief summary of Horace's treatment of the concept.

Horace does not, in the main, depart from the principles that Aristotle formulated in the *Nicomachean Ethics*, according to which the mean is to be viewed, not as an arithmetical fixed point between two extremes, but instead as a *relative* term that must be adjusted to the peculiar nature and circumstances of the human agent. This idea of a flexible criterion is not, of course, to be confused with more modern notions of total relativity or indeterminacy. We can perhaps best approximate the core of the Aristotelian conception through the following well-known definition from *Ethics* 1107a:[17]

> Virtue, then, is a deliberate mental disposition, situated in a mean relative to us, and determined by rational principle, and as the prudent man would determine it.

In an ode that is wholly discursive and not beholden to a convivial scaffolding (C. 2.10), Horace expounds a similar doctrine in a sequence of gnomic utterances combined with prescriptions:

> Rectius vives, Licini, neque altum
> semper urgendo neque, dum procellas
> cautus horrescis, nimium premendo
> litus iniquum.

> *auream* quisquis *mediocritatem*   5
> diligit, tutus caret obsoleti
> sordibus tecti, caret invidenda
>   sobrius aula.
>
> saepius ventis agitatur ingens
> pinus et celsae graviore casu   10
> decidunt turres feriuntque summos
>   fulgura montis.
>
> sperat infestis, metuit secundis
> *alteram sortem* bene praeparatum
> pectus. informis hiemes reducit   15
>   Iuppiter, idem
>
> summovet. non, si male nunc, et olim
> sic erit: quondam cithara tacentem
> suscitat Musam neque semper arcum
>   tendit Apollo.   20
>
> rebus angustis animosus atque
> fortis appare; sapienter idem
> contrahe vento nimium secundo
>   turgida vela.

You will live more properly, Licinius, neither by pressing out to mid-ocean at all times, nor by clinging too much to the hostile shore, while being overcautious and terrified of storms. Whoever loves *the golden mean* will safely eschew the squalor of a rundown house, and will prudently eschew a hallway that provokes envy. The huge pine tree is more often tossed about by winds, and tall towers fall down with a heavier fall; and lightning bolts strike the tops of mountains. The heart that is properly prepared for *vicissitude* is hopeful in bad times and fearful in good. Jupiter brings back hideous winters, but he also removes them. If things are bad now, they will not always be so: sometimes Apollo arouses the Muse from her silence with his lyre; nor does he always stretch his bow. In tight circumstances appear buoyant and brave; but you should wisely draw in your sails when they swell with a too-favorable wind.

In the pivotal fourth stanza (lines 13–16), we learn that the wise practitioner of the mean (*bene praeparatum pectus*) needs to adjust his conduct, and more particularly, his emotional life, to the certain expectation of *vicissitude* (*alteram sortem*). Just as the principle of alternation in external nature constitutes, as we have seen, the major insight on which the convivial response rests, so the principle of vicissitude in human affairs is the ground perception on which behavioral and emotional *mediocritas* are based. The analogy between the two arenas of change is implicit in the mention of Jupiter's role in removing and "bringing back" winters—an image that Horace also employs in the *CD* ode *Tu ne quaesieris* (cf. C. 1.11.4–5 with lines 15–17). Although *Rectius vives* is clearly not a convivial ode, the philosophy that it enunciates is one consonant with the insights expressed in the banquet poetry. Essential to this philosophy is the notion that the human agent can ensure a stable happiness only by preparing himself in advance for the inevitable alteration of things into the opposite state. Aware of the underlying mutability of human life, he constantly adjusts his emotions so as to experience both hope and fear, joy and sorrow, in the relevant proportions. Horace's lyric version of the emotional calculus owes a great deal to Archilochus's notable advice to his own *thumos* (128 W, lines 4–7):[18]

> καὶ μήτε νικέων ἀμφάδην ἀγάλλεο,
> μηδὲ νικηθεὶς ἐν οἴκωι καταπεσὼν ὀδύρεο,
> ἀλλὰ χαρτοῖσίν τε χαῖρε καὶ κακοῖσιν ἀσχάλα
> μὴ λίην, γίνωσκε δ᾽ οἷος ῥυσμὸς ἀνθρώπους ἔχει.

And neither exult openly in victory nor groan abjectly at home in defeat, but rejoice in your good fortune and grieve in your bad— without excess. Get to know the rhythm that controls human life.

In urging his *thumos* (cf. Horace's *pectus*) to avoid overweening joy in success, no less than excessive lament in adversity, Archilochus establishes a prestigious lyric antecedent for the Horatian speaker of *C.* 2.3 (the ode addressed to Dellius) who prefaces a call to the convivium with a similar ethical admonition (1–4):

> *Aequam* memento rebus in arduis
> servare *mentem,* non secus in bonis
>   ab insolenti temperatam
>   laetitia . . .

Remember in hard times to preserve *an even mind;* in easy times, likewise, a mind curbed from arrogant exultation . . .

Human vicissitude—the *rhusmos* of Archilochus—is the basic insight that determines the appropriate ethical response for both the archaic Greek lyrist and his Roman imitator.[19]

As applied specifically to the *CD* poem, the Horatian *aurea mediocritas* ("golden mean") is a controlling concept that enables the symposiast to attune his participatory fervor to the requirements of the occasion. There are times, for example, when the poet deems it appropriate to throw caution to the winds and indulge in drinking bouts that might, on another occasion, be considered excessive or even uncivilized. Thus the safe return of his bosom companion Pompeius from the wars warrants an unrestrained response (C. 2.7.21–28):

> oblivioso levia Massico
> ciboria exple; funde capacibus
>   unguenta de conchis. quis udo
>   deproperare apio coronas
>
> curatve myrto? quem Venus arbitrum
> dicet bibendi? *non ego sanius*
>   *bacchabor Edonis:* recepto
>   dulce mihi *furere* est amico.

Fill the burnished goblets to the full with Massic wine that induces amnesia; pour out the perfumed oils from large containers. Who will hasten to provide us with wreaths of moist celery or of myrtle? Whom will the "Venus" [the best throw of the dice] elect as master of the symposium? I, for one, shall carouse no less wildly than the [Thracian] Edoni. When a friend has been recovered, I take sweet pleasure in going mad.

Extreme indulgence is here characterized as a benign form of madness (*furere*), but the lyrist makes it clear that the unusual circumstances (*recepto . . . amico*) fully justify such intemperance.[20] The playful comparison of the poet's madness to that of Thracian bacchants is significant: Dionysiac frenzy, though archetypal for lack of emotional restraint, is nonetheless a product of ritual possession and so may be thought to accomplish purposes other than mere self-indulgence. Elsewhere in the *Odes*, however, Horace is not above using the wild conduct of ordinary, unpossessed Thracians at banquets as a negative stereotype of inappropriate excess.[21] The occasionally permissive attitude on the lyrist's part to inordinate imbibing is not, at bottom, inconsistent with the doctrine of *mediocritas* in either its Aristotelian or Horatian versions—hence the apparent paradox that a timely insanity passes as a perfectly acceptable form that *sapientia* may take in particular situations. Sympotic decorum may necessitate restraint no less than license, depending on the occasion. Thus whereas at C. 4.12.28 Horace can cheerfully pen the adage, on behalf of intemperance, "dulce est desipere in loco" ("It is a pleasure to be unwise on occasion"), he can also argue quite eloquently for the suppression of untimely overindulgence, as in the short ode eulogizing the vine (*C.* 1.18.7–11):

> ac ne quis *modici* transiliat munera Liberi,
> Centaurea monet cum Lapithis rixa super mero
> debellata, monet Sithoniis non levis Euhius,
> cum fas atque nefas exiguo fine libidinum
> discernunt avidi.

> And lest anyone transgress the precious bounds of *Bacchus who observes limit*, he should be warned by the brawl between Centaurs and Lapiths, which was fought out over unmixed wine; warned also by the not-so-gentle treatment that Bacchus metes out on the Sithonians, when in their rapacity they discriminate right from wrong by the thin line of their desires.

Liber modicus ("Bacchus who observes limit"), then, is a relative concept that can encompass divergent modes, if not actual poles, of conduct. The wise symposiast is the one who is able to judge what degree of indulgence is appropriate (*kairos*). In exercising his judgment relative to *modus* ("limit"), he will know both when to repress the orgiastic *tympanum* (*C.* 1.18.13–14) and when, inversely, to call for a forte on the same instrument.

A nice illustration of the "fine tuning" of convivial potations to the relative situation of the revelers—a "tuning" that may even vary between subgroups of revelers at the same symposium—occurs in the delightful *C.* 3.19. After an initial disavowal of heroic subject matter (comparable to the exclusion of inapposite discourse in *CD* contexts), the poet proposes an unequal carousal whose participants are to imbibe differing proportions of mixed to unmixed wine (9–18):

> da lunae propere novae,
> da noctis mediae, da, puer, auguris
>   Murenae: tribus aut novem
> miscentur cyathis pocula commodis.
>   qui Musas amat imparis,
> ternos ter cyathos *attonitus* petet
>   *vates*; tris prohibet supra
> rixarum metuens tangere Gratia
>   nudis iuncta sororibus.
> *insanire iuvat.*

Let's have a toast at once to the new moon, and one to midnight, and one, my boy, to Murena's appointment as augur: the goblets shall be mixed with suitable proportions of three or nine measuring cups. *The thunderstruck bard* who loves uneven numbers of Muses shall demand a portion of three times three measuring-cups. The Grace joined with her nude sisters, fearing brawls, interdicts one from touching more than three. *I take pleasure in mad celebration.*

The bard, who, like Archilochus in a well-known fragment, is "thunderstruck with wine,"[22] humorously arrogates to himself a proportionately stiffer combination while claiming that other more prudent guests should limit their intake lest they lapse into unseemly brawls! The outlandish implication is that poets, being specially privileged by the Muses, are entitled to a benign and wine-induced *insania* (with obvious wordplay involving the idea of poetic inspiration or *mania*).[23] The differential apportionment of the wine is both comical and instructive. The enlightened bard sets himself up as adjudicator of the sympotic mean as well as *arbiter bibendi*. In so doing, however, he lightly parodies his own insight concerning the relativity of the mean to individual status and shifting circumstances.

GRATAE VICES: THE ETHICAL PARAMETERS OF THE CENA (C. 3.29)

My partly "horizontal" treatment of the constituent motifs of the CD ode has provided a foundation for a revaluation of some of the more complex Horatian constructions in this subgenre. With these fundamental elements as a point of reference, let us inspect the motif texture of two odes (C. 3.29 and 4.12) that elaborate important facets of the design in divergent, but equally coherent, ways. A related task will be to elucidate a few apparent obscurities in respect to the organization of ideas in the two poems.

I begin with the lengthy *capolavoro*, C. 3.29 (*Tyrrhena regum progenies*). The importance of this ode within the edifice of the *tribiblos* as a whole is clearly marked by its privileged position in the series. As Pöschl and others have noted, C. 3.29 is the last ode preceding the *sphragis* (*Exegi monumentum*) that closes the collection. As a carefully placed capstone, it is egregiously programmatic, containing significant retrospective allusions to poems earlier in the order, most notably the prefatory *C.* 1.1, which is also addressed to Maecenas.[24]

The first two stanzas of the ode have elicited contrary opinions from leading Horatian exegetes in regard to tone and pertinence (1–8):

> Tyrrhena regum progenies, tibi
> non ante verso lene merum cado
>   cum flore, Maecenas, rosarum et
>   pressa tuis balanus capillis
>
> iamdudum apud me est. eripe te morae,
> nec semper udum Tibur et Aefulae
>   declive contempleris arvum et
>   Telegoni iuga parricidae.

Descendant of Etruscan kings, Maecenas: for you there has long since been sitting at my house a mellow vintage in a jar not yet sampled, along with the bloom of roses and exotic perfumes extracted for your hair. Stop your loitering! Do not always view moist Tibur, and Aefula's sloping field, and the ridges of Telegonus the parricide.

The question of the intended tone of the inaugural periphrasis, *Tyrrhena regum progenies,* has divided the critics, some regarding its pomposity as humorous, others as serious. In an important sense, the critical schism is beside the mark, since for the composer of the *Odes* seriousness and humor are by no means mutually exclusive. A sophisticated lyric voice, such as Horace's, is quite capable of exploiting the ambiguities of burlesque hyperbole in the service of a serious ethical position. Rephrasing the issue, then, in a spirit that accepts the serio-comic tonalities of the circumlocution, we may pose the more pertinent question, What is the *rhetorical* function of the genealogical motif in a poem that invites the addressee to a symposium? A paratactic presentation of motifs assumes a readership that is schooled in the conventions of the genre. In positing an ulterior connection, therefore, between the genealogical and the symposiastic motifs, we need to have recourse to the *CD* pattern as we know it from other odes. From this angle of vision, the speaker's emphasis on the nobility of Maecenas (apart from the transparent effect of ring composition with respect to the dedicatory poem) is both explicable and germane: the topic of an individual's birth is often an ancillary motif of the *CD* foil. As we have seen in the case of the ode to Aelius Lamia (*C.* 3.17), which contains an even more elaborate excursus on an addressee's pedigree, the tacit line of thought is that birth, like wealth, is irrelevant, in the long run, to the quality of one's life *qua* human being.

In my earlier discussion of the nobility of birth as a *CD* motif, I stressed the implicit *sententia*, "even the high-born must die"; so it is legitimate to inquire where, in the context of *C.* 3.29, the recurrent topic of ineluctable mortality makes its appearance. Horace brings the subject into the poem only by intimation, for the obvious consideration that it would be grossly improper (if not tactless) to harp loudly to one's close friend and patron upon the latter's demise, however much such reflection may be formally exigent. As an illustration of the insinuated, as opposed to the frontally treated topos of death, we may cite line 8, where the speaker is inviting Maecenas to come to his country estate. In describing a beautiful, desirable *locus amoenus*, Tusculum (a place on a par with Tibur and Aefula) by the periphrasis, *Telegoni iuga parricidae*, Horace seems at first blush to introduce a jarring, incongruous note to his blandishments. The mention of parricide—the inadvertent murder of Ulysses by his son Telegonus—forms a curious climax to the list of peaceful places antithetical to the metropolis. The dark cadence, then, is ostensibly dissonant. At the level of the convivial argument, however, a dark subtext dealing with death is profoundly organic to the foil. Within the structural universe of the *CD* ode, the ultimate demise of Ulysses is not an otiose mythological intrusion; rather it deftly displaces the topic of mortality onto a distant, exemplary epic hero. In this indirect mode of presentation, there is a double gain to the speaker, for he manages to include an obligatory motif (*mors*), while, at the same time, circumventing the indecorum of confronting his intimate friend with the specter of an imminent death. A similar display of delicacy qualifies the way in which the same topic is approached later on in the poem where the single word *mortalis*, along with the imagery of darkness associated with an unknown future, subtends, so to speak, the faint shadow of death (29–32):

> prudens futuri temporis exitum
> caliginosa nocte premit deus,
>   ridetque si *mortalis* ultra
>   fas trepidat.

Wisely does god envelop in dark night the issue of the future, and
he laughs if *a mortal being* is fearful beyond what is proper.

Much of the elusive charm of *Tyrhenna regum* resides, to my mind,
in the subtle modulations that the convivial theme undergoes in
this intricate envoi.

A further instance of such permutation is the manner in which
the scene is deployed in strophes V and VI (lines 17–24):

> iam clarus occultum Andromedae Pater[25]
> ostendit ignem, iam Procyon furit
>   et stella vesani Leonis,
>   sole dies referente siccos:
>
> iam pastor umbras cum grege languido
> rivumque fessus quaerit et horridi
>   dumeta Silvani, caretque
>   ripa vagis taciturna ventis.

Already does the bright Father of Andromeda display his hidden
fire; already does Procyon blaze furiously, and the star of raging Leo,
as the sun brings back dry days: already the tired herdsman with his
drooping flock seeks the shade and the river, and the thickets of
shaggy Silvanus; and the silent bank is bereft of wandering breezes.

The fifth strophe sketches a scene of midsummer, when the heat of
the Dog Star is oppressively manifest. This particular time of year
is, of course, also congenial to the symposium, since, as we have
previously demonstrated, any point in the cycle of seasonal recurrence may subserve the *CD* argument. Horace here effaces the explicit liaison between scene (midsummer) and festive response, but
his readers will have been attuned to such a bond by earlier *CD*
odes in the *tribiblos*—as well as by intertextual resonances with
passages in both Hesiod and Alcaeus.[26]
   If the heat of summer induces a thirst that will duly be quenched
by the contents of Horace's *cadus*, it also creates a strong desire for
a pastoral shade—the contrapuntal scene of the sixth stanza. The
cool *umbra* to which the tired (*fessus*) *pastor* will retire with his flock
is powerfully evocative of the universe of Virgil's *Bucolics*. By the
same token, the *umbra* of Virgilian pastoral, like that of the *Odes*, is
an emblematic locus of poetic creation no less than recreation.
Whether we recall Virgil's shepherds discussing which variety of
shade (elm or *antrum*) is more apposite to a contemplated singing-

exchange (as in the opening dialogue of *Ecl.* 5), or Horace's vignette of a tired chief of state in *C.* 3.4 who gratefully repairs to the shade of the lyric *antrum* to hear the Muses' refreshing strains, the melodious Alcaics of *C.* 3.29 surely evoked, for *doctus* Maecenas, the prospect of exemplary lyric performance as an integral component of the coming celebration.

In several *CD* poems, the speaker dismisses topics of conversation that are deemed extraneous to the festive ethos. Typically, such dismissed matter revolves around military disturbances at the remote corners of the Roman world. Horace softens the normally peremptory tone of such exclusions in this ode by juxtaposing the invitation to an attractive *locus* with a statement about the addressee's alien anxieties and fears (25–28):

> tu civitatem quis deceat status
> curas et Urbi sollicitus times
>   quid Seres et regnata Cyro
>   Bactra parent Tanaisque discors.

> You are concerned with what condition is suitable to the state, and you are anxious and fearful for the City, as to what the Seres may be hatching, and Bactra, where Cyrus reigned, and the seditious Tanais.

Horace does not here belabor the obvious conclusion—that the statesman would do well to put aside such anxieties. He does, however, make such an overt exhortation in the shorter, sister ode to *C.* 3.29 (also addressed to Maecenas), *Martiis caelebs* (*C.* 3.8.17):

> mitte civilis super urbe curas

> put aside your concerns over state and city

In the *Tyrrhena regum,* which, apart from echoing the *Martiis caelebs* at several points, also shares the identical convivial scaffolding (the anniversary of the poet's escape from the falling tree), the starkly prescriptive aspect of the message is toned down, though the string of maxims that the ode deploys tends to produce the illocutionary effect of admonition.

Many of the ode's central stanzas are devoted to variations on the theme of polar alternation in nature as I have analyzed it above. This imparts to the poem an aura of redundancy; yet the art of refining and varying the expression of basic insights is one of the great secrets of the Horatian lyric oeuvre. An overview of the poem's transformations of the alternation topos will shed some light on the latent design of the whole.

After a terse reminder to Maecenas to pay attention to the present rather than the future and to maintain an emotional mean ("quod adest memento / componere aequus": "remember to attend, with an even mind, to what is present," 32–33), the lyrist presents an extended trope of alternation in the form of the river Tiber at peace, and conversely, in dangerous flood (33–41):

> *cetera* fluminis
> ritu feruntur, *nunc* medio alveo
>   cum pace delabentis Etruscum
>   in mare, *nunc* lapides adesos
>
> stirpesque raptas et pecus et domos
> volventis una non sine montium
>   clamore vicinaeque silvae,
>   cum fera diluvies quietos
>
> irritat amnis.

The rest is carried along like a river, which *at one time* flows down peacefully in midstream to the Etruscan sea, *at another* rolls together eroded stones, torn off tree trunks, herds and homes—not without a clamor in the mountains and the adjacent woods, when the savage flood stirs up tranquil streams.

The river's oscillation between calm and flood (the key word *cetera* fixes it as a script for the future) is strictly homologous, within the *CD* armature, to the other natural models I have dissected earlier, such as storm/calm and rain/sunshine. In describing the appropriate response of the self-controlled *sapiens* whose felicity flows from his ethical orientation, Horace makes his embedded spokesman employ another variant of the alternation image (41–48):

> ille potens sui
> laetusque deget, cui licet in diem
>   dixisse "vixi: *cras vel atra*
>   *nube polum Pater occupato*
>
> *vel sole puro;* non tamen irritum,
> quodcumque retro est, efficiet neque
>   diffinget infectumque reddet,
>   quod fugiens semel hora vexit."

That person will live in happiness and self-control who from day to day can say: "I have lived: *tomorrow let the Father invest the sky with*

dark clouds or with bright sun. He will not make void whatever is behind us, nor will he take apart and undo what the fleeting hour once
has brought our way."

The embedded citation corresponds, in terms of its insight, with
the bard's repeated observations in the *Carmina*. That insight,
though deceptively simple, is double-sided. The alternation, dark
skies / clear skies, sets up the natural "other" that functions as foil
to the self's internally stable pursuit of a present fulfilment; at the
same time, the irreversibility of the past for the human subject—in
short, the ontological difference between man and nature, between
linear and cyclical "chronotypes"—is forcefully reemphasized. The
crisp reference to the "fleeting hour," in which the word *semel* is
typical and decisive ("quod fugiens *semel* hora vexit"), constitutes
another veiled acknowledgment of mortality.

I turn now to the climactic verses in which the goddess Fortuna
makes a dramatic entry in a gnomic context (49–52):

> Fortuna saevo laeta negotio et
> ludum insolentem ludere pertinax
>   transmutat incertos honores,
>   nunc mihi, nunc alii benigna.

Fortune, who delights in her cruel task and is persistent in playing
her mocking game, interchanges her unstable honors: generous now
to me, now to a different person.

The crucial point to be stressed in regard to this much-discussed
portrayal is its organic relationship to what precedes. The figure of
personified fortune is simply the hypostatization of the principle of
vicissitude that is fundamental to the *CD* foil as I have delineated
it. My analysis has stressed the successive, figurative models of
polar alternation in the *Tyrrhena regum* (season, river, weather).
These mutually reinforcing pictures culminate in the vivid representation of a joyously sadistic *Fortuna*, who mocks humankind for
her own amusement. So far in my discussion of the motif of predictable transmutation, I have consistently applied the term *alternation* to polar shifts in the natural order, while reserving the term
vicissitude to the analogous phenomenon in the human sphere. The
separate labels, though necessary to a tidy analysis, are at bottom
somewhat artificial, since the same underlying process is operative
in both orders of existence. Whereas in many poems I have exam-

ined, the poet articulates the *divergence* between human and natural spheres, in this more complex ode, he is concerned rather to reveal their intersection in respect to the dynamic of oscillation. In the human arena, no less than in the skies' meteorological register, a "benign" turn of events is perceived as unstable ("Fortuna . . . nunc mihi, nunc alii benigna"). In tune with the growing sense of definitive summation in this ode, the poet goes on to place his own deliberate conduct in the forefront of the lyric meditation (53–56):

> laudo manentem; si celeris quatit
> pennas, resigno quae dedit et mea
> virtute me involvo probamque
> pauperiem sine dote quaero.

I praise her inasmuch as she stays with me. If she rustles her swift wings, I forsake what she has bestowed and, enveloping myself in my integrity, I court a decent modesty of means that comes without a dowry.

The blunt response of the speaker, as enlightened *praeceptor*, to a malign event (*si celeris quatit pennas*) is to renounce Fortune's ephemeral gifts and, by turning inward to his own *aretē* (*virtus*), to choose a life of modest means (*pauperiem sine dote*). Such an "involutional" move is not merely defensive (on the plane of behavior) but also assertive (at the level of metaphor); for it is notorious that Horace's self-characterizations in terms of virtue (cf. epithets such as *integer* and *pius*) are closely allied to his commitment to the vocation of poetry (see chapter 2 above). The image invoked in the verb *resigno* reflects this double aspect of the speaker's gesture, since it derives from, and refers to, the sphere of writing (cf. *signum* = seal; and the connotation *resigno* = *rescribo*).[27] Thus the culminating figures of the ode contribute to a reaffirmation of the poet's vocation—a fitting lyric "monument" (if I may anticipate the *sphragis* of the final ode) with which to signal the close of the *tribiblos*.

The semantic scope of the bard's *virtus* becomes even more perspicuous in the last two strophes, where he deliberately distinguishes his values from those of others (57–64):

> *non est meum*, si mugiat Africis
> malus procellis, ad miseras preces
> decurrere et votis pacisci
> ne Cypriae Tyriaeque merces

> addant avaro divitias mari.
> tunc me biremis praesidio scaphae
> tutum per Aegaeos tumultus
> aura feret geminusque Pollux.

It is not my way to descend to abject prayers whenever the mast makes moan under the storms of the South Wind, or to procure by vows that my wares from Cyprus or Tyre do not add riches to the greedy sea: safe and protected in my two-oared craft, I shall be borne thence through the tumultuous Aegean by the breezes and by twin Pollux.

Surprisingly, the received opinion on these lines radically misconstrues the scaffolding by envisaging the speaker as on board a merchant vessel. Nothing could be less characteristic of *Horatius lyricus* than to assume the *persona* of an acquisitive *mercator* in charge of a ship laden with Tyrian and Cypriot wares! The *mercator* figure who dreads the inevitable storm, but is too fundamentally greedy to renounce his commercial activities at sea, is profoundly antipodal to the poet, who is content with *pauperies*. Like the type of the restless *mercator* of *C.* 1.1, whom he is meant unequivocally to recall, the sailor-merchant of *C.* 3.29 is, by implication, also *indocilis pauperiem pati*. What we have before us in the close of the *Tyrrhena regum* is none other than a radically abbreviated "priamel" containing a single, but readily recognizable foil term: the wretched *mercator* juxtaposed to the "virtuous" (i.e., enlightened and distinctly unacquisitive) poet-sage. The conflation of speaker and *mercator* in the critical literature (and therewith the destruction of a basic dichotomy that Horace consistently maintains throughout the *Odes*) is the result, it would appear, of a misinterpretation of the final vignette: the poet at sea in his small bark (*scapha*). Because of the common denominator in the imagery—both the bard and his foil are represented as voyagers at sea—the vast majority of commentators have assumed an identity between the two "sailors." This accounts for the prevalent view that the *scapha* is a small, detachable lifeboat that Horace, the *mercator*, resorts to in the course of the violent storm. The time has come for interpreters to jettison this absurd reconstruction of a unitary "situation" and to pay attention instead to the antithetical typology—materialist *mercator*, on the one hand, and anti-materialist poet-voyager on the other. The poet-at-sea is a commonplace image in lyric, and Horace reintroduces it in this epilogic context as a way of differentiating poet from "other."[28] The very fragility of the poet's vessel—the light *scapha* in contrast to the presumably large commercial *navis*—is a topos that serves to emphasize the unique *security* of the bard who, as usual, is magically protected (cf. *praesidio; tutum*). A significant dimension of that protection is, however, neither mysterious nor magical: it is provided by Maecenas, generous patron of the poet, who has been previously characterized as *praesidium* in the dedicatory poem (*C.* 1.1.1). Thus the two-oared skiff in which the poet sails secure regardless of nature's alternations (stormy seas) is a metaphor for Horace's life as *vates* and the supreme emblem of the interdependence of poet and patron. *C.* 3.29 is a poem that commences with an invitation to a celebration and proceeds to explore the wider philosophical dimensions of conviviality. In retrospect, the lyric *convivium* becomes a microcosm for a certain plane of human existence in which poetry and ethical values intersect.

DULCE EST DESIPERE IN LOCO:
HORACE TO VIRGIL (*C.* 4.12)

The broader significance of the *convivium* within the cosmos of the *Odes* is gracefully summed up in the motival modulations of *C.* 4.12 (*Iam veris comites*). This richly allusive poem, which is addressed to the poet Virgil,[29] constitutes the final example in the entire collection of the *CD* subgenre and is therefore important as a distillation of certain central lyric norms. As an elegant formulation of the convivial enthymeme, the ode repays a less than casual scrutiny, despite its surface aura of facetiousness and sophisticated banter. A partially diachronic account of each of its strophes is in order.

I

> Iam veris comites, quae mare temperant
> impellunt animae lintea Thraciae;
> iam nec prata rigent nec fluvii strepunt
>   hiberna nive turgidi.
>
> (1–4)

Already spring's companions, the Thracian breezes that moderate the sea, are propelling the sails; already neither do the meadows freeze over, nor do the rivers roar, swollen with wintry snow.

The poem's point of embarcation is a very familiar motif—the signs of a newly emergent spring. Because of its well-documented resemblances to a group of Hellenistic epigrams that ritualistically portray the coming of spring in trite formulae,[30] many critics have unreflectingly adopted the facile category *Frühlingsgedicht* for the first three stanzas of the ode, if not the poem as a whole. As I have advocated earlier, however, the inaugural picture of a spring season is a standard scene whose programmatic function is to construct a foil for the ensuing invitation to a banquet (the appropriate response). The ulterior signification of the spring motif, in terms of the semiotics of the convivial ode, is to be sought in the root notion of alternation, rather than in the particular season. This reading receives validation in the verb *temperant*, conspicuously placed at the end of line 1, which implies that there has indeed been a raging storm over the ocean (and therein hints at the alternation storm/calm). The subsequent recollection of a frozen wintry scene (lines 3–4) makes the dramatic changeover from malign to benign season even more salient. The contrastive temporal signposts, highlighted by anaphora (*iam*/*iam nec*) further demarcate the gap between the two consecutive seasons and buttress the assertion that the "theme" of the opening is not the advent of spring as such, but rather the observation of recurrent *vices*. The motif of transmutation unfolds within the *cadre* of the sea/land complementary—the first two lines depicting a recently pacified *seascape* (*mare*), the next two a previously icebound *landscape* (*prata; fluvii*). Unmistakable verbal reminiscences of earlier *CD* scenes, such as those inaugurating C. 1.4 and 1.9 (discussed above), help to clarify the generic and structural affiliations of *Iam veris comites*.

II–III

The second and third strophes of the ode are contrapuntally organized and are best cited side by side:

> nidum ponit Ityn flebiter gemens
> infelix avis et Cecropiae domus
> aeternum opprobrium, quod male barbaras
>   regum est ulta libidines.
> dicunt in tenero gramine pinguium
> custodes ovium carmina fistula

delectantque deum cui pecus et nigri
colles Arcadiae placent.

(5–12)

The unlucky swallow, mournfully bemoaning Itys, is building her nest—eternal shame on the house of Cecrops, because she exacted evil vengeance on the barbarous lust of kings. On the tender grass the guardians of the well-fed sheep play their songs on the pipe and bring pleasure to the god who delights in the herds and the dark hills of Arcadia.

These two strophes describe alternative responses to the seasonal *vices*. As such they furnish a carefully tempered basis for comparison with the stanza to follow in which, as we shall shortly see, the speaker's own preferred response is revealed. What is instructive about the first two responses, as far as the normative *CD* pattern is concerned, is that they both indirectly refer to the domain of poetry. Whereas, for instance, in an early ode, *Solvitur acris hiems* (*C.* 1.4), the poet describes antithetical responses to spring's advent at the level of divine conduct (Vulcan bustles off to work in the forges of the Cyclopes, while his mate Venus more appropriately leads nude dances with the Nymphs and Graces), in the vernal context of *C.* 4.12 the bifurcated responses are distinctly vocal, or, to be more precise, melodic. The bifurcation articulates two major strains of *song*, both uttered in direct response to the tokens of changing nature—the mournful strain of the nightingale versus the bucolic strain of the shepherds.[31] The juxtaposed responses, then, are complementary and, at the same time, divergent. While both involve a literary subtext (Philomela's song and shepherds' ditties) the essential tones of their respective *carmina* (line 10) are disparate: the nightingale's melodies are lugubrious laments for a dead person, the shepherds' are "bucolic" compositions such as bring delight to the woodland god Pan (*delectant,* 11). The contraposition of different melodic strains is fraught with meaning for the evolving argument of the ode. To apprehend this meaning in all its intertextual density, we need first to pay some attention to the Virgilian echoes that reverberate throughout both species of *carmina*.

To begin with the nightingale: the song of the *infelix avis*, behind whom lies the story of the metamorphosed Philomela,[32] recalls the abbreviated version of the same tale that caps the embedded Silenus song of Virgil's *Eclogues* 6.78–81:

> aut ut mutatos Terei narraverit artus,
> quas illi Philomela dapes, quae dona pararit,
> quo cursu deserta petiverit et quibus ante
> infelix sua tecta super volitaverit alis?

or how he told the story of Tereus's altered limbs; what banquets, what gifts Philomela prepared for him; by what route she made for desert places, and on what wings she, unlucky [bird], earlier flitted about her own rooftops?

Horace's original audience, which presumably included Virgil himself, would have been more than superficially familiar with the *Eclogues*. Among the *Eclogues*, moreover, the sixth is avowedly programmatic in ways that notoriously pose a typological enigma. The central embedded song attributed to the figure of Silenus, like the generic disavowal that prefaces it, is thoroughly "neoteric" in character, and this poetic affiliation is legitimated, so to speak, by the subsequent appearance of the prime elegiac founder-poet himself, Cornelius Gallus. This is not the place to unravel the complexities of *Ecl.* 6, or to offer a definitive account of the reasons why Virgil there thematizes a contemporary poet as part of a catalogue of mythological subjects. The point of intersection between *C.* 4.12 and *Ecl.* 6 may be found in the observation that Virgil's experiment in transgressing the conventional boundaries of the bucolic genre goes far in the direction of celebrating (if not actually appropriating) the neoteric/elegiac style and subject matter. In brief, Horace's recollection of the Philomela tale, as mediated, in turn, by Silenus's recollected narrative, accomplishes the double objective of honoring the addressee, the poet Virgil, and highlighting the anomalous elegiac/neoteric strain that inserted specimen puts into prominence.

The quasi-elegiac cast of the Philomela lament is not, however, completely determined by Virgilian allusion. The *content* of the song, as adumbrated by Horace, includes several locutions that point in the same direction. The adverb *flebiliter,* qualifying the participle *gemens,* is virtually a catchword of the genre and recalls such stereotyped designations as *flebiles modi* ascribed to it in the Valgius ode (see chapter 1 above). By itself, of course, the single word *flebiliter* and its cognates do not invariably connote elegiac modes of verse; however, in the context of a sad song ritualistically performed with each recurrence of a season, it is difficult to dissociate the purely mythological aspect of Philomela's lament from the corresponding literary mode that had become synonymous with a querulous tone. All the more so, of course, when we take cognizance of the fact that Philomela's complaint implies a denial of death—or at least, a refusal to relinquish mourning. Exorbitant grief over a deceased loved one (and in this case, a grief that extends even to eternity) is the very attitude that Horace deplores in the elegiac poems (*Amores*) of his friend Valgius. Like the ode to Valgius, the invitation to Virgil includes an allusion to a passage in the Orpheus episode in *G.* 4: the distraught singer who remains unconsoled is compared to a *maerens philomela*. The perennial nature of the bird's lament in *C.* 4.12 (cf. *aeternum opprobrium*) is an indictment of the figure of the perpetual mourner—a figure that is once again to be contrasted with the lyric minstrel who is able to transcend mourning. The view that Philomela's song is meant to be *representative* of a certain type (literary and philosophical) receives added support at the grammatical level in the *quod* clause (lines 7–8), where the generalizing dimension of the mythical episode is captured in the use of the plural *regum*.

If the Philomela song is basically paradigmatic in the ways I have suggested, the strophe that follows is no less representative of a certain identifiable poetic orientation. The words *dicunt . . . carmina* could hardly be more explicit in this regard, and even a casual reader of Virgil's *Eclogues* can instantly recognize the transparent generic ambiance: poet-shepherds performing melodies on the *fistula* that bring delight to the Arcadian god, Pan![33] More particularly, the phraseology of *pinguium custodes ovium* ("guardians of the well-fed sheep") in the context of the bucolic poetry may also have served to refocus lines 4–5 of the programmatic proem of *Ecl.* 6 (itself derivative of the *Aetia* prologue of Callimachus), in which shepherd-poets are admonished to keep their sheep fat while cultivating a slender genre:

> pastorem, Tityre, *pinguis*
> pascere oportet *ovis*, deductum *dicere carmen*.

A shepherd, Tityrus, ought to keep his *sheep well fed, but to perform a song* that is slender.

The italicized words all recur, *mutatis mutandis*, in the first two lines of Horace's third strophe, and when we compound these specific allusions with the well-known neoteric associations of the epithet *tener* (line 9) and *deductum* (*Ecl.* 6.5), we are left in no doubt as to the stylistic and thematic affiliations of the *melos* here paraded by the poet of the *Odes*.

In these two densely allusive stanzas, then, Horace has artfully placed side by side two alternative melodic responses, which we may conveniently characterize, *grosso modo,* as elegiac and bucolic respectively. Both strains are intertextually related to Virgilian poetry, though, as I have observed, the elegiac mode is filtered through the experimental prism that is *Ecl.* 6—a hexameter poem that foregrounds the potential point of convergence between Gallus's amatory elegy and the remodeled Virgilian bucolic. Taken together, the two strophes pay oblique but memorable tribute to Virgil's incomparable art, while serving as the perfect foil for the different *carmina* that the melodious singer of the *Odes* has chosen to compose.

The strictly *poetic* component of the speaker's alternative response is, however, partly occluded in this ode, for Horace limits his advertisement of the drinking party explicitly to items such as the choice of wine and unguent (13–20):

> adduxere sitim tempora, Vergili;
> sed pressum Calibus ducere Liberum
> si gestis, iuvenem nobilium cliens,
>   nardo vina merebere.
>
> nardi parvus onyx eliciet cadum,
> qui nunc Sulpiciis accubat horreis,
> spes donare novas largus amaraque
>   curarum eluere efficax.

The time of year has brought on a thirst, dear Virgil; but if you, a protégé of noble youth, are eagerly anticipating draughts of Bacchus pressed at Cales, you shall best earn such fine vintages with nard. A wee onyx box of nard will draw forth a wine jar, which at the moment rests in the storerooms of Sulpicius—a jar wide enough to sponsor new hopes and efficient in washing away bitter anxieties.

The elision of alternative song is only apparent, however, since Horace's counteroffering to the musical strains of others is, besides the actual symposium, the ode itself, which constitutes a highly polished example of sympotic "invitational" verse. As William Race has persuasively shown in connection with *C.* 1.20 (*Vile po-*

tabis),[34] the unpretentious *cadus* that Horace offers to Virgil may very well be an emblem of symposiastic poetry that has within it the capacity to dissipate bitter anxieties (*amaraque curarum eluere efficax*). The capaciousness of this particular wine jar (it is *largus* in respect to its ability to give hope and banish cares) evinces an unstinting attitude on the part of the host. The contents of the *cadus* will generate not an indeterminate feeling of optimism, but *spes novas*—that is, these hopes are to be proximate, fresh, and readily apprehensible, unlike the *spes longas* that are vitiated by an unrealizable fantasy of immortality. The thirst (*sitim*) that the poet experiences can be readily quenched in the immediate present.

If the projected *convivium* stimulates the appropriate kind of *spes*, it also exemplifies the Horatian (and, more broadly, Augustan) topos of the disavowal of wealth (21–24):

> ad quae si properas gaudia, cum tua
> velox merce veni: non ego te meis
> immunem meditor tingere poculis,
>   plena dives ut in domo.

If such delights prompt you, come quickly with your barter. If you show up empty-handed, I do not propose to mimic a wealthy man in an opulent house by steeping you in my goblets.

The disavowal renders explicit what the speaker has hitherto implied in the charming bagatelle in which Virgil is forewarned that if he wishes to consume an expensive vintage, he must provide a fancy unguent in exchange. The sophisticated banter about the proposed exchange of wine for nard carries social as well as philosophical significance. The playful attribution to the addressee of the desire for a more expensive wine is a convention of invitational poetry, and Horace is consciously trading on sentiments expressed in a well-known epigram of Philodemus's.[35] Such badinage was the hallmark of the social intercourse of close literary friends; at the same time, by suggesting the *paupertas* of the poet-host, it prefigures the more general repudiation of materialism that is to follow (*studium lucri*, "the urge for a bargain").

The ode concludes with an elegant hortatory flourish that combines convivial prescription with pointed literary allusion (25–28):

> verum pone moras et studium lucri
> *nigrorum*que memor, dum licet, *ignium*

> misce stultitiam consiliis brevem:
> dulce est desipere in loco.

But set aside delay, and the urge for a bargain, and mindful of *the dark flames from the pyres*, mix, while you may, brief folly with your prudence. It is a pleasure to be unwise on occasion.

As some commentators have noted, the stilted phrase *nigrorum . . . ignium* imitates a memorable noun-epithet combination that Virgil twice uses in the *Aeneid* to refer to funeral pyres.[36] Both Virgilian narrative *loci*—a veiled threat of suicide by Dido in book 4 and the burial ceremony for the Trojan war dead in book 11—are freighted with melancholy, and Virgil's portmanteau phrase "dark fires" aptly evokes the gloomy penumbra of death. The interposition of a dark background at this point—the obligatory reminder of death— is given special weight by the Virgilian image. The composer of grave epic is being tactfully urged by his friend and admirer to lay aside mournful themes (which, as we have seen from Philomela's song, are not exclusive to the epic genre) and to share, if only for a brief shining moment, in the carefree world of convivial *gaudia*. In the paradoxical cadence of the last two lines, the references to *stultitia* ("folly") and *desipere* ("be unwise") are, of course, amusingly ironic and tongue-in-cheek. The reader of the *Odes* is fully aware that lyric *sapientia*—the very opposite of *stultitia*—is what is actually being advocated, despite the playful self-deprecation and deference displayed in Horace's words. For the true practitioner of lyric values, *sapientia* includes the capacity to "pull out all the stops" when the occasion demands—even at the risk of appearing to the uninitiated to abandon it altogether (*de-sipere*). The key qualification here is in the expression *in loco* ("on occasion"), which conveys the Greek ideal: κατὰ καιρόν. Thus the closing apothegm of this *CD* poem succinctly reformulates and reaffirms a central philosophical precept of convivial wisdom in the *Carmina*.[37]

4

Modes of Praise and Dispraise

My analysis of the structure of convivial *carmina* has yielded a schema of recurrent motifs that acts as a vehicle for a set of related ideas. In turning to a consideration of certain strategies of encomium (as well as invective) employed by Horace in the *Odes*, I shall begin by observing some of the ways in which elements of the same schema are made to serve different, even at times contrasting, rhetorical purposes.[1]

MODES OF PRAISE

LAUS TIBURIS: HORACE TO PLANCUS
(*C.* 1.7)

My starting point will be *Laudabunt alii* (*C.* 1.7), an ode whose latter half I have previously discussed in illustration of the technique of generic remodeling. In revisiting the Teucer ode at this point in my investigation, I shall be focussing on the entire opening segment (lines 1–14). The argument that unfolds in these lines is both dense and central to Horace's lyric program. A careful exegesis of the passage confirms the insight of those interpreters who, like Pasquali, have insisted on the organic coherence between the two halves of the poem. A reproduction of the text of lines 1–14 will facilitate the inquiry.

> Laudabunt alii claram Rhodon aut Mytilenen
>   aut Epheson bimarisve Corinthi
> moenia vel Baccho Thebas vel Apolline Delphos
>   insignis aut Thessala Tempe:
> sunt quibus unum opus est intactae Palladis urbem
>   carmine perpetuo celebrare et
> undique decerptam fronti praeponere olivam:
>   plurimus in Iunonis honorem

> aptum dicet equis Argos ditisque Mycenas:
>   me nec tam patiens Lacedaemon
> nec tam Larisae percussit campus opimae,
>   quam domus Albuneae resonantis
> et praeceps Anio ac Tiburni lucus et uda
>   mobilibus pomaria rivis.

Some will sing the praises of glorious Rhodes, or Mytilene, or Ephesus, or the walls of Corinth-that-spans-two-seas, or Thebes made illustrious by Bacchus or Delphi by Apollo, or the vale of Tempe in Thessaly. There are some whose sole project is to celebrate the city of virgin Pallas Athene in continuous song and to place upon their foreheads an olive wreath indiscriminately plucked. Many a bard in honor of Juno will sing of "horse-rearing Argos" and "opulent Mycenae." For my part, neither tenacious Sparta nor the plain of affluent Larisa has smitten me so deeply as the home of echoing Albunea, and the steep-sloped Anio, and the grove of Tiburnus, and the apple-orchards moistened by coursing rivulets.

From a purely formal perspective—a necessary first step in rhetorical analysis—these lines are framed by the familiar device of the priamel, deployed in the service of what I have been calling "generic disavowal."[2] Other unnamed bards (*alii* of line 1) with their preferred themes are paraded as foil for the lyric minstrel, whose peculiar choice thereby gains both relief and resonance. The very first word of the poem—*laudabunt*—announces that the generic foil is to consist of praise poetry, and the "voluntative" cast of the future tense here indicates that the discourse of disavowal is initially to be conducted at a level of gnomic generality.

The ensuing catalogue of discarded themes (the banal encomia composed by "others") is, as always in the sophisticated priamels of Horace, loaded in such a way as to furnish the speaker with rich material for constructing self-serving antitheses and for defining his own artistic outlook. The specific epithets allocated to each of the cities and places in the catalogue of themes (e.g., *claram, insignis*) are, we may note in passing, specimens of disavowed encomiastic diction; just as the mention of particular gods in conjunction with certain places (*Baccho Thebas; Apolline Delphos*) mimics a hackneyed encomiastic topos—the god adds lustre to the *sedes*. One feature of the ordering of the included specimens is especially significant: Horace has subdivided his catalogue into three groups of diminishing length, introduced respectively by (a) *laudabunt alii* (line 1), (b) *sunt quibus* (line 5), and (c) *plurimus* (line 8). The final subgroup (c) receives added saliency because it stands immediately before the "pronominal cap" that reveals the speaker's own choice (Bundy, 5). The resounding *me* is in stark opposition to the preceding *plurimus*, thus demarcating the one from the many—a demarcation that is, of course, a major rationale for the priamel form as a whole.

Subdivision (c) also contains allusions to, and imitations of, Homeric diction that are part and parcel of the evolving argument. Although the standard commentaries duly record that the Latin epithets applied to Argos and Mycenae are virtual paraphrases of Homeric noun-epithet formulas, the full implications of these paraphrases have not been adequately delineated.[3] What rhetorical goal does the poet gain by interjecting specimen epithets from the *Iliad* at this juncture of the ode? The answer lies, at least partially, in the poetics of generic differentiation. Not only are prestigious subjects of encomia being disavowed, but also those preferred by prestigious poets—in fact, by the most prestigious of them all, Homer. The transparent appropriation of Homeric grandiloquence as a climax to the generic foil is therefore highly remunerative; for the lyric voice gains both validity and authority from such a flattering juxtaposition.

I have discussed one conspicuous way in which the catalogue is loaded—the copying of Homeric formulaic language in a context of lyric utterance. No less charged is the content of certain phrases that the poet uses to characterize the types of song he is eliminating as candidates for his own *carmen*. The most important of these is the much-discussed expression *carmen perpetuum* (line 6), which describes a monotonous encomium of the city of Athens. It is by now a widely accepted view that the words are a rendition of a Callimachean phrase used in reference to the kind of lengthy poem the Hellenistic poet represented himself as being inadequate to produce.[4] Since disavowals, from my vantage point, are by definition programmatic, it is not surprising that a Callimachean polarity has been carefully planted in Horace's elaborate prooemium. By implication, then, the present ode, which embodies the virtues of the concise, densely packed lyric, is favorably compared with the protracted encomium in a more heroic mode. As E. J. Kenney has shown in his exemplary analysis of Ovid's proem to the *Metamorphoses*—a proem that ostentatiously cites the term *carmen perpetuum* from *C.* 1.7—Augustan poets are capable of extraordinary economy in their frequent variations on the conventional apparatus of the *recusatio*.[5] In this case it seems that Horatian inventiveness in the art of disavowal has contributed to the lexicon of critical terms in which the contemporary Augustan dialogue was framed. In the context of C. 1.7—a poem that follows closely in the collection on the heels of a *recusatio* set piece where Horace disclaims any ambition to be an *alter Homerus*[6]—the term *carmen perpetuum* acquires a faintly pejorative tone. The polar alternative to this type of *carmen*, the brief lyric, is not here presented in a modest, quasi-apologetic *aporia*, as in C. 1.6; rather, it is affirmed in ringing terms in contrast to the jaded themes of grander *laudes*.

The implicit self-praise in this version of the disavowal emerges even more clearly when we consider the metrical dimension. It is noteworthy that the so-called First Archilochian—the meter in which C. 1.7 is composed[7]—partly replicates heroic verse: a dactylic hexameter alternates with a dactylic tetrameter. In particular, the lyric hexameter verse in Horatian praxis generally "follows the pattern of the heroic hexameter" (Nisbet-Hubbard, xlv). In a poem that argues eloquently for the parity, if not the superiority, of lyric to other forms of encomiastic discourse, including the heroic, the artful manipulation of the epic hexameter is a tactic congruent with the overall strategy of the *carmen*. Like the appropriation of Homeric phraseology discussed earlier, it demonstrates the desire (and the ability) of the lyrist to "have his cake and eat it too."

If the *carmen perpetuum* is fundamentally denigrated on account of its prolixity (with the implied charge of surfeit), it is also seen as undesirable from another point of view: its triteness. What encomiastic topic could have been more jejune than the attractions of the city of Athens? Horace conveys the idea of the commonplace not only in the priamel form itself (which typically employs the commonplace as foil) but in the paramount metaphor of the wreath, which, as we have seen in chapter 2 above, often refers to crucial poetic principles. Since the composition of the *corona* is suggestive of thematic predilections, the question of what Horace signifies by the phrase "*undique decerptam* . . . *olivam*" (line 7) is of some pertinence.[8] If we take the words to mean "olive [= the theme of Athens] plucked here, there and everywhere," then the idea of monotony is compounded with the prior emphasis on indiscriminate length. In effect, the entire hexameter is a reformulation, in allegorical terms, of the ideas expressed in the preceding distich (*unum opus; carmine perpetuo*). The adverb *undique* is therefore crucial, insofar as it focusses attention on the misguided singer who persists in lauding the same *locus* regardless of his situation, instead of following the Pindaric prescription of concentrating on the present and the immediate.[9] I shall revert shortly to the matter of the lyric speaker's rival *locus* in connection with the subject of the ode's unity. For the moment, it is relevant to note that the spatial aspect of the wreath metaphor (*undique*) anticipates the Teucer paradigm in at least one important respect: when the unfortunate Teucer is about to leave the environs of Athens (Salamis), he dons a wreath conspicuously *not* of olive (the signature of Athens) but of poplar. His choice is exemplary of convivial lyric: it expresses what is philosophically *kairos* (*in loco*). There could be no greater antithesis to the inflexible composer of *laudes Athenarum* (who invariably culls the olive) than a symposiast who culls the proximate poplar.

Careful examination of the generic foil has prepared us to grasp the literary overtones of the *locus amoenus* that Horace sonorously constructs in lines 10–14. In interpreting its main features, we must be on guard against impoverishing its significance by reducing the description to the single dimension of geography. The concreteness of the toponyms (*Anio; domus Albuneae; Tiburni lucus*) easily lulls the reader into forgetting that Horace is speaking on two levels simultaneously: the geographic and the poetic. The environs of Tibur are not simply beloved haunts of Horace, but also *loci* generative of *melos*. As an encomiastic alternative to the places enumerated in the extensive foil, the *locus amoenus* of Tibur is, above all, the resonant theme that the Roman lyrist has chosen to celebrate in song.

A brief comparison of other passages in the *Odes* in which the naming of the Tibur region has a parallel effect may serve to clarify the conjuncture of place and theme, as well as the double signification of referents such as *lucus* and *nemus*. In the lengthy "authentication" passage in C. 3.4 (analyzed in chapter 2 above), the geographical catalogue is clearly concomitant with, and expressive of, poetic engagement (lines 21–24):

> *vester*, Camenae, *vester* in arduos
> tollor Sabinos, seu mihi frigidum

> Praeneste seu *Tibur supinum*
> seu liquidae placuere Baiae.

With you—yes, you—I rise to the Sabine heights, whether I am attracted by cool Praeneste or *sloping Tibur* or clear Baiae.

Here *Tibur supinum* is one of three named *loci* dear to Horace in his persona as bard possessed by the Muses. In the elaborate "disavowal" sequence in *C.* 4.2, where the Pindaric swan is opposed to the bee of Matinus, the grove (*nemus*) in which the poet laboriously gathers his lyric material is sited with equal precision (lines 29–32):

> grata carpentis thyma per laborem
> *plurimum circa nemus uvidique*
> *Tiburis ripas* operosa parvus
> carmina fingo.

gathering with much effort the pleasant thyme *around many a grove and the banks of the watery Tibur*, I, small artisan, produce well-crafted songs.

"The banks of watery Tibur" afford ample occasion for lyric productivity. The denomination of Tibur *qua* creative *locus* (a role underscored by assonance) is also the proud cap of the abbreviated priamel in the Melpomene ode (*C.* 4.3.10–13):[10]

> sed quae *Tibur* aquae *fertile* praefluunt
> et spissae nemorum comae
> fingent Aeolio carmine nobilem.

But the waters that flow by *fertile Tibur* and the dense growth of the groves shall make him illustrious for Aeolian song.

What these major references to Tibur in the context of a poetic vocation share is the use of an identical place-name as signifier not merely of a favorite spot in the most literal sense but of a privileged *locus amoenus* conducive to the Muses' activities—in fine, a *Dichterlandschaft* in the most profound sense (Troxler-Keller 1964, 91–96). In the context of the proem of *C.* 1.7, then, it is the *Tiburni locus* as preferred theme that Horace is celebrating in contradistinction to the *loci laudandi* of other bards.

The period in which the poet articulates his preference (lines 10–14) strikingly exploits a technique I have previously designated "incorporation." The verb *percutio* ("smite") is commonly employed in its literal sense in military contexts, and the violent image carries over into the figurative uses as well. In *Ep.* 11.1–2, for instance, Horace elects the participial form of the verb to characterize a "wound" inflicted by erotic passion on the speaker:

> Petti, nihil me sicut antea iuvat
> scribere versiculos amore *percussum*[11] gravi

> Pettius, I do not take pleasure as before in writing light verses, since I have been *smitten* by love's heavy blow.

In the above citation the libidinal blow suffered by the bard is so intense that it temporarily deflects him from poetic composition—at least from *versiculi* that fail to focus on the subject of *amor!* Whereas the *persona* of the epode is smitten by an *amor* that interferes with verse-making, the persona of the ode is smitten by the theme of Tibur. With respect to the generic disavowal in the Teucer ode, which foregrounds thematic inspiration, *percutio* figuratively incorporates an image from the rival domain of military exploits. Thus the alien discourse (heroic encomium) is annexed in order to enhance the anti-bellicose ambiance of *melos.*

Incorporation is not the only ruse at work in Horace's lexical maneuvers. If Nisbet and Hubbard are on target in glossing *percussit* as equivalent to the Greek ἐξέπληξεν (and the parallels they cite *ad loc.* make this gloss extremely persuasive, if not irrefutable), then Horace's choice of metaphor has strong literary "repercussions" (if I may extenuate the wordplay in my turn). An especially cogent parallel among those cited by Nisbet and Hubbard is a passage in the *Georgics* where Virgil appeals to the Muses for inspiration in his loftier thematic ambitions (2.475–77):

> Me vero primum dulces ante omnia Musae,
> quarum sacra fero *ingenti percussus amore,*
> accipiant caelique vias et sidera monstrent

> But first above all, may the sweet Muses, whose sacred emblems I bear, receive me, *smitten by a powerful love,* and show me the paths of the sky and the constellations.

The "powerful love" that here "smites" Virgil in his role as priest of the Muses is precisely a love for poetry as manifested in an access of creative energy for the task at hand or contemplated. It is worth noting that in the vocabulary of ancient literary criticism, the Greek noun ἔκπληξις cognate with ἐκπλήττω (= *percutio*, with an added connotation of astonishment) is often associated with the effects of a certain stylistic grandeur (Russell 1981, 133). Horace who, as the *Ars poetica* and the *Epistles* show, was well versed in the critical tradition that preceded him, may well be drawing on this semantic tributary as well. Be that as it may, the impact of the verb *percutio* in the cap of a literary priamel cannot be read as innocent in relation to an ongoing literary subtext. If the Roman *fidicen* is to compete seriously with the disavowed *laudatores*, then his claim, like that of his colleague Virgil, must rest, in part, on an authentic inspiration from the Muses. The moment of such authorization is dramatized in the figure of *me . . . percussit.*

The speaker's description of his beloved Tibur harbors allusions to a passage in a kletic poem by Sappho (2 LP, 5–8) that helps to validate his choice of theme:

> ἐν δ' ὕδωρ ψῦχρον κελάδει δι' ὕσδων
> μαλίνων, βρόδοισι δὲ παῖς ὁ χῶρος
> ἐσκίαστ', αἰθυσσομένων δὲ φύλλων
> κῶμα . . .

Within [the grove] cool water sounds through the apple branches, the entire place is shaded by roses, and from the quivering leaves a trancelike sleep . . .

Apple orchards, water, sound and shade are ingredients common to both Sapphic and Horatian groves. The shared profile, however much it owes to real places in Lesbos and Italy respectively, points to intertextual *labor* on Horace's part and to the melic tradition to which he is the Roman heir.[12]

Up to this juncture, I have looked, in separate discussions, at the substructure of the ode from both ends—the concluding exemplum of Teucer (lines 21–32) and the prooemial disavowal (lines 1–14). The remaining task is to demonstrate the organic unity of the poem as a whole by inspecting the intermediary segment (lines 15–21) that binds together opening and closing sections.

At the outset it is imperative to keep in mind a mode of organization that Horace shares with his Greek models, and with Pindar in particular—the paratactic presentation of motifs. Some medieval scribes, unable to grasp the unstated links in Horace's argument, proceeded to bifurcate the ode just after the description of the Tibur region.[13] In so doing, they failed to observe both the rhetorical scaffolding of the middle segment (lines 15–21) and its deliberate use of verbal cross-reference. The import of the scaffolding will not have been lost on the reader alert to *CD* structure; for Horace's convivial prescription is rooted in an insight concerning a necessary oscillation in the natural order (cf. chapter 3 above):

> albus ut obscuro deterget nubila caelo
>   saepe Notus *neque parturit imbris*
> *perpetuo,* sic tu sapiens finire memento
>   tristitiam vitaeque labores
> molli, Plance, mero, *seu* te fulgentia signis
>   castra tenent *seu* densa tenebit
> Tiburis umbra tui.

As Notus often turns to white and wipes away the clouds from a dark sky, *nor brings forth rain showers continuously,* so you in your wisdom remember to put an end to the sadness and the toils of life, Plancus, with a mellow unmixed wine, *whether* you are detained by the camp gleaming with standards *or* by the dense shade of your beloved Tibur.

As we saw at length in chapter 3, the *sapientia* enjoined on the addressee, Plancus, is based on the unblinkered acknowledgement of transmutation in nature and in human life. The portion of Horace's exhortation marked off by disjunctives (*seu . . . seu*) is, of course, a "complementary" in the formal linguistic sense I have indicated above—that is, the dichotomy *castra/Tiburis umbra* (cf. the familiar doublet *domi/militiae*) amounts to a global utterance: "wherever you may be." The "pragmatics"[14] of such complementaries should warn us against any rash inferences about the actual whereabouts of Plancus at the putative time of the ode's publication. The *convivium* is being proposed not as a solace for a unique occasion but as a general consolation for life's cares.

What, then, constitutes the underlying logical connection that is elided in Horace's paratactic skip from praise of Tibur to contemplation of the skies? The generic disavowal has culminated in a choice of theme that foregrounds melodious lyric; now, in an abrupt exhortation, the lyrist proceeds to express the kernel of the philosophy that very lyric is geared to celebrate. The convivial solution, in other words, is presented as the paradigmatic lyric weltanschauung. As if to tighten the ideational nexus between generic choice and philosophical orientation, the poet reiterates a key epithet from the disavowal in the alternation motif—*carmine perpetuo* on the poetic level corresponding to *imbris perpetuo* on the level of "scene."[15] This salient repetition is not in the least adventitious, for Horace's argument attains thereby a marvellous clarity that compensates for the paratactic elision. Just as the foil encomiast who goes on and on in monotonous laudation of Athens reveals his fundamental lack of decorum, so too the person devoid of *sapientia* (the implied antitype of the speaker and his addressee) shows no real cognizance of the alternation principle and mistakenly assumes that cloudy weather will continue in perpetuity. The composer of the *carmen perpetuum* converges, at the metaphysical level, with the mortal who denies change.

The priamel and the following *CD* schema are united by yet another motival bond: they both come to a head in separate annunciations of Tibur (cf. *Tiburni lucus,* 13, and *Tiburis umbra,* 21). The recapitulation of the toponymic motif combines with the duplication of the epithet *perpetuum* to undergird the conceptual bridge between opening and middle segments. This method of composition, which it is tempting to label "musicological," may be clarified even further by a tabular presentation of key correspondences both of lexemes and motifs:

carmine *perpetuo* (6)	imbris *perpetuo* (16–17)
uda . . . pomaria (13–14)	*uda* . . . tempora (22–23)
Tiburni lucus (13)	*Tiburis umbra* (21)
fronti praeponere olivam (7)	populea . . . vinxisse corona (23)
tristitiam vitaeque labores (18)	*tristis* . . . amicos (24) curas (31)
molli . . . mero (19)	vino (31)

The verbal and motival repetitions listed above substantiate the claim that all three segments of the ode are closely interconnected. Teucer, our "remodeled" hero from the domain of epic, provides a concrete representation of the convivial values enunciated earlier—values that, in turn, constitute the ultimate theme of a lyric *laudator loci.*

In retrospect, therefore, the deeper relationship between Teucer's closing speech and the prior election of Tibur as lyric *locus* comes more sharply into focus. Though a superficial reading of the ode might suggest a contradiction between the speaker's attachment to a unique place (Tibur) and Teucer's radical dislocation, the contradiction dissolves when we are made to realize that the *convivium*, as emblem of a mental outlook, is inherently *mobile;* the lyric *sapiens* may put his principles into practice *wherever* fortune places him. Thus the underlying message of the lyrist to Plancus in the complementary (at home / at war) is consonant with the admonitions of Teucer to his *amici*. Though alternately present and absent from the actual grove of Tibur, Plancus will come to recognize that, at a deeper level, he carries Tibur within him even when abroad in the form of lyric *sapientia*. In sum, *C*. 1.7 celebrates far more than a beautiful place. It is a self-serving, but no less magnificent, tribute to Horace's lyric virtuosity, and to the *CD* philosophy that nurtures and sustains it.

LAUS LUCRETILIS:
HORACE TO TYNDARIS (*C*. 1.17)

In the ode to Plancus, I traced the path by which preliminary praise of a place, Tibur, led on to a definition of a lyric ethos. Central to the process of definition, in our rhetorical analysis, is the articulation of the convivial ideal as a eulogistic topos. With a view to illuminating further the ancillary role of convivial motifs in the context of praise/blame, let us next examine a poem that also commences with a *laus loci* and goes on to construct an integral lyric universe: the ode to Tyndaris (*C*. 1.17).

The first three stanzas (lines 1–12) erect a schema that is progressively refined in succeeding lines:

> Velox amoenum saepe Lucretilem
> mutat Lycaeo Faunus et igneam
>   defendit aestatem capellis
>   usque meis pluviosque ventos.
>
> impune tutum per nemus arbutos
> quaerunt latentis et thyma deviae
>   olentis uxores mariti,
>   nec viridis metuunt colubras
>
> nec Martialis haeduliae[16] lupos,
> utcumque dulci, Tyndari, fistula

> valles et Usticae cubantis
> levia personuere saxa

Swift Faunus often exchanges Mount Lycaeus for pleasing Lucretilis, and defends my goats for the duration from fiery heat and
rainy winds. Unharmed through the safe grove, the wandering
spouses of the smelly mate look for hidden arbutus and thyme, nor
do the kids fear green vipers or martial wolves, whenever, Tyndaris,
the valleys and smooth rocks of sloping Ustica have resounded with
the sweet panpipe.

The initial stanza transposes a topos that is endemic in hymns, especially those of the kletic variety—the transfer of a divinity from
one favorite *sedes* (cult center) to another. Though the grammatical
form of Horace's sentences is declarative (whereas kletic hymns
typically operate with imperatives and exhortations), the underlying assumption common to both is that the theophany is a fait accompli.[17] In this instance, Faunus is described as exchanging Arcadia for the Sabine hills, site of the poet's villa. From the point of
view of a latent hymnal strategy it is very significant that the transfer is represented as *habitual* (cf. *saepe; usque*). Faunus-Pan, we
learn, is emphatically not making an epiphany that is sui generis;
rather the very frequency of the relocation is a testament to the
power of the Roman bard's rival *locus amoenus* (cf. Fraenkel, 204–5).

The god's visitations have beatific effects that are precisely enunciated: the alternate Italian *sedes* is protected from extremes of
weather, fiery heat and rainstorms (lines 2–3). The bucolic topography of the place is, of course, all of a piece with the predilections of the Arcadian Pan in his mask as Faunus. Equally in tune
with the pastoral ambiance is the topos of a magically induced *pax
animalium*—a motif that has its ultimate source in descriptions of
the legendary Golden Age.[18] In Horace's seductive "version of the
pastoral," the she-goats may graze and wander safely (*deviae; tutum*) without fear of snakes or wolves. There is transparent humor
in the circumlocution *olentis uxores mariti* ("spouses of the smelly
mate"), which combines turgid style with earthy content, as well as
in the exclusion of wolves on the part of a god who has left behind
a "wolfish" mountain peak (Lykaon from *lykos*).[19] The humorous
tonality does not undercut the fundamental point that the protection afforded by Faunus-Pan is diffused throughout the whole

natural habitat, and that a principal means of that diffusion is the sound of the premier bucolic instrument, the panpipe (*fistula*). As Fraenkel has shrewdly perceived, the claim here made on behalf of Faunus *qua* musician redounds, at bottom, to the credit of the host minstrel, Horace (Fraenkel, 206). The grammar of the third strophe leaves the identity of the performer (and thus the scaffolding) unclear. Is the song emanating from the visiting Faunus, from the resident poet, or from the latter's female companion and musician, Tyndaris? The indeterminacy is perhaps deliberate; for the suggestion that the players are interchangeable helps to extend the fiction of a harmonious community united in competence and performance.

There is more at stake, however, than the competence of Faunus and his gifted devotees. The clear implication of the temporal conjunction *utcumque* is that the very security enjoyed by the community is crucially dependent on music—that is, poetry. The moderate weather, suspension of predatory attacks, absence of anxiety— all these are manifest "whenever" the music of the panpipe is heard in the land. The *locus amoenus* of Lucretilis, then, is not merely a straightforward geographical entity, but also a magical place intermittently revitalized, in a figurative sense, by the power of song. The sound of the *dulcis fistula* no less than the physical features (*nemus; thyma*) is an essential component in the lyric artifact.[20] Like his fellow-poet and friend Virgil, whose *Eclogues* were an admired precedent (see chapter 3 above apropos of C. 4.12), Horace subscribes to the audacious fiction of an interdependence of nature and music in the context of teaching the woods to "play back" (*resonare*) the name Amaryllis:

> tu, Tityre, lentus in umbra
> formosam *resonare* doces Amaryllida silvas
> (*Ecl.* 1.4–5)

> you, Tityrus, relaxing in the shade, teach the woods to play back "bonny Amaryllis."

so Horace makes his Sabine environs deeply resonant (*personuere*) with melodies that are transmitted on the instrument of Arcadian Pan. The name Tyndaris, like Amaryllis, is carefully inserted into a texture of vowel sounds that enhances its intrinsic musicality (*utcumque dulci, Tyndari, fistula*). The felicitous expression *Usticae cu-*

bantis ("sloping Ustica") recalls the similar image of a recumbent Tibur (*Tibur supinum*) in a context that, as we have seen, also seeks to define the superior "resonance" of the melic voice (cf. C. 1.7.12, *Albuneae resonantis*).

The full ramifications of this vocal intercourse between humans and natural surroundings are brought out in the general statement that opens the next stanza: "di me tuentur, dis pietas mea / et musa cordi est" ("the gods protect me, my integrity and muse are dear to the gods"). As in the parallel case of asyndetic sequencing of motifs in C. 1.7, the move from description of particular place to generalization need not be construed as caprice on Horace's part. Since the sounds that pervade Ustica are a direct consequence of the co-presence of Faunus the musician-god and human pipers, the bold assertion of the Muses' deep attachment to the speaker serves to refine the latter's role in the whole configuration. The initial sentence of the third stanza strictly relates to the preceding, then, as general to particular. The gods' (Faunus's and the Muses') protection of the poet is the latent "proposition" of which the divine epiphany and its repercussions are the immediate "proof."

As I have remarked in chapter 2 above in respect to other lyric arguments, poetry and *pietas* are conceptually conjoined in the *Carmina*. The quality of *pietas* is not a separately conceived ethical state, but rather an integral attitude of devotion to the divine craft. The figure whose *pietas* is dear to the gods is therefore none other than the *Musophilos*, and the particular collocation *pietas et musa* is tantamount to a hendiadys in Horace's conception. In the light of this conjunction, it is plausible to interpret the following pleonastically phrased affirmation of *copia* to refer not only to abundance of harvested fruit (*les richesses champêtres* of Dacier 1727 *ad loc.*) but also to abundance of lyric production (14–16):

> hinc[21] tibi copia
> manabit ad plenum benigno
> ruris honorum opulenta cornu

From this source a rich profusion of country blessings will pour forth for your benefit in full spate from a generous horn of plenty.

If we concede two levels of reference in Horace's redundancy, then the term *ruris honorum* is probably meant to include the *honos*[22] of a copious outpouring (cf. *manabit*) of bucolic song.

Having adumbrated the *copia* in broad strokes of the brush, Horace proceeds to fill in the picture with vivid details of Tyndaris's future idyllic existence at the Sabine *locus*. Like other members of the bucolic community, the *amica* will be protected from excessive heat; but most important of all, she will be a prime participant in the activity that is the very touchstone of the community: she will compose *carmina* (17–20):

> hic in reducta valle Caniculae
> vitabis aestus et *fide Teia*
> *dices* laborantis in uno
> Penelopen vitreamque Circen.

> Here in a secluded valley you will avoid the heat of the Dog Star, and *on the lyre of Anacreon you will sing* of those who labored over the same man: Penelope and glittering Circe.

The type of composition she will contribute is spelled out with some precision. Anacreontic lyric (*fide Teia*) devoted to erotic themes will be her preferred genre. To appreciate the minutiae of her program, however, we need to pay close attention to the generic remodeling it reflects. Penelope and Circe are to be transposed from the heroic high ground of Homer's *Odyssey* and, by a kind of Alexandrian *reductio*, the distinction between the two women is to collapse into the low valley of an erotic rivalry. In this amusingly irreverent remodeling, faithful spouse and temptress are juxtaposed on the same plane (*laborantis in uno*, "those who labored over the same man").[23] In sum, the female singer whose very name "Tyndaris" assimilates a notorious epic patronymic (Helen of Troy was commonly so designated) will not balk at accommodating well-known figures from Homer's world into her lyric cosmos, *mutatis mutandis*. The generic interplay (Homeric *epos* / Anacreontic *melos*) is carefully nuanced, as so often in the *Odes*, and Horace's convivial partner is there to sponsor his own erotic-lyric agenda.

An essential aspect of that agenda is the convivial ideal, the focus of contrapuntal elaboration in the final two strophes (21–28):

> hic innocentis pocula Lesbii
> duces sub umbra, nec Semeleius
> cum Marte confundet Thyoneus
> proelia, nec metues protervum

> suspecta Cyrum, ne male dispari
> incontinentis iniciat manus
> et scindat haerentem coronam
> crinibus immeritamque vestem.

Here you shall drink beneath the shade goblets of harmless Lesbian wine; nor will Bacchus, son of Semele, mix it up in battles with Mars; nor will you, under suspicion, have to fear that bully Cyrus, lest he should cast upon you his unchecked, violent hands, and tear apart the wreath clinging to your hair and your undeserving raiment.

The rhetorical design of this closure is the well-tried device of the foil. The *positive* bucolic symposium (cf. the emblematic *sub umbra*) is first epitomized in a few pregnant words; then, in glaring contrast to this image of tranquillity, a *negative* symposium—one radically perverted by violence from within—is portrayed in vivid detail. The antithetical pairing of the symposia allows the speaker to manipulate a favorite motif for the dual purpose of both praise and censure. Praise, of course, is the preponderant goal of the poem as a whole, despite the powerful negative image that closes it. The censured symposium, in other words, helps to define the values of the ideal put forward as a decorous cap to the *laus Lucretilis*. In the negative portrayal, there is, we may note, an "invasion" from the opposite sphere of war (*Marte; proelia*). The opposition *amor/bellum* is implicitly upheld through this graphic example of its violation. On the level of emotions, there is a comparable invasion of fear and suspicion (*metues; suspecta*)—emotions regularly excluded in the protected ambiance of the Sabine magic *locus*. The disorderly behavior that erupts in the imaginary countersymposium is fraught with symbolic import.[24] The violence done to Tyndaris's wreath and raiment is an incisive warning of the consequences of transgressing the rule of *mediocritas*—a point Horace conveys more explicitly in the following poem by means of a negative mythological exemplum (*C.* 1.18.7–9):

> ac ne quis modici transiliat munera Liberi,
> Centaurea monet cum Lapithis rixa super mero
> debellata . . .

And lest anyone transgress the precious bounds of Bacchus who observes limit, he should be warned by the brawl between Centaurs and Lapiths, which was fought out over unmixed wine . . .

What more potent allegory for a degenerate *convivium* is conceivable than the ripping apart (*scindat*) of its major emblem, the *corona* itself? In the violent closing vignette of the Tyndaris ode, the value system that underlies the Horatian lyric ethos receives one of its most trenchant formulations.

SPIRITUS TENUIS: THE INTEGRATION OF LIFE AND ART (*C.* 2.16)

The ideal of a harmony between life and art, between *mensa tenuis* ("frugal table") and *spiritus tenuis* ("frugal inspiration") (Mette 1961) is the rhetorical *telos* of *C.* 2.16 (*Otium divos*).[25] In aligning an ethical outlook with an aesthetic orientation, Horace seeks to vindicate an integrated vision of a *bios*, which he presents, in the final strophe, as a personal synthesis. The main accent of the ode is on the ethical boundaries that determine a mature lyric praxis. As a first approximation to Horace's mode of representing this vision, let us elucidate the formal organization of the first four strophes.

I–IV

Otium divos rogat in patenti
prensus Aegaeo, simul atra nubes
condidit lunam neque certa fulgent
    sidera nautis;

otium bello furiosa Thrace,   5
otium Medi pharetra decori,
Grosphe, non gemmis neque purpura ve-
    nale neque auro.

non enim gazae neque consularis
summovet lictor miseros tumultus   10
mentis et curas laqueata circum
    tecta volantis.

vivitur parvo bene, cui paternum
splendet in mensa tenui salinum
nec levis somnos timor aut cupido   15
    sordidus aufert.

Peace is the seaman's request from the gods, when he is caught in a storm in the open Aegean sea, as soon as a black cloud has hidden the moon and the stars do not shine as stable guides for sailors. Peace is the request of Thrace, when wars are raging; peace the request of Medes adorned with quivers, O Grosphus—peace that cannot be purchased with gems, with purple finery or with gold. For neither treasures, nor the consular lictor can remove the wretched disturbances of the mind, and the cares that fly around panelled ceilings. That person lives well on little whose inherited salt dish gleams on a frugal table, and whose smooth sleep is not preempted by fear or base greed.

Recognition of the priamel form in these lines is vital to a comprehension of the poem's total anatomy. Each of the first three strophes constitutes a conventional item of foil in a "vocational priamel" that comes to a cap in the fourth strophe. Sailor (I), soldier (II), and politician (III) are successively put on stage as a device for setting off the wise man who observes frugality (IV). The cap is not concretely personalized at this stage, but takes the impersonal form of a *sententia*. Horace's technique is, once again, "schema and refinement," for the anticipated personal cap with its resounding *me* is artfully postponed to the final stanza of the reprise.

The separate items in the subdivided foil deserve at least a cursory inspection. The sailor who is caught in a storm and prays desperately for *otium* belongs to the proverbial type of the *mercator* (though the actual designation is elided in this passage). Horace's memorable sketch of this foil figure in the programmatic priamel of C. 1.1.15–18 exposes the purely contingent and opportunistic basis of the desire for *otium* on the part of the *nauta-mercator*:

> luctantem Icariis fluctibus Africum
> *mercator* metuens *otium* et oppidi
> *laudat rura* sui; mox reficit ratis
> quassas, indocilis pauperiem pati.

> *The trader*, when he fears the struggle between the south wind and the Icarian waves, *praises peace and the countryside* near his hometown; in a short while, however, he refits his battered vessels—a man that cannot be taught to put up with modest means.

In both priamel passages, it is clear that the *mercator* is by no means motivated by a quest for *otium* per se; rather he urgently desires (and praises!) something that he calls *otium* only when he is faced with the grim prospect of a setback (note *simul*). What drives him, instead, is the obsessional pursuit of riches; and concomitant with his obsession is an incapacity to lead a frugal life (*pauperiem pati*). The denigration of materialistic greed is often an associated motif of the Horatian priamel of vocations, where it is usually embedded in the foil. In passing, we may note that the merchant-sailor is abruptly brought to his *laus otii* (if I may so style it) by the confrontation with a malign change (the storm at sea). We are left with the suspicion that for him *otium* may mean no more than the "calm" that he hopes will replace the storm and allow him to resume his profit-making activities.[26] The second foil figure, the *miles*, is introduced not as an individual token, but as a plurality (*Thrace; Medi*). Despite the plural cast, however, the speaker does manage to give a personal edge to the portrayal by insinuating a wordplay on the addressee's name, Grosphus, which, as Nisbet and Hubbard have emphasized (*ad* 17), signifies "javelin." The witty wordplay helps to situate Grosphus metaphorically in the camp of the militaristic "other"—along with warlike nations such as Thracians and Persians. The addressee also enters into the poem's typology through his link with the subjoined leitmotif of excessive wealth (Pöschl 1970, 142 n. 35). The two conventional figures of *nauta* and *miles* are further articulated by means of a latent complementary—sea/land—which, as we have seen, is a universalizing device dear to our poet.

In a negative formulation (*non enim gazae*, 9), wealth resurfaces as a motive force behind the next counterfigure in the sequence, the successful politician. In this third example of "otherness," the speaker concentrates his implicit censure on the wealthy magistrate's failure to overcome mental anxiety (*miseros tumultus mentis; curas*).

My review of the tripartite foil of the priamel points to the conclusion that the *otium* motif is properly to be viewed as part of the scaffolding the poet uses to build the larger argument. Although *otium* is a common request in mankind's prayers to the gods, it is conceived in manifestly diverse ways by diverse types of people (sailor, soldier, and politician being shorthand for "the rest of mankind"). The main effect of the anaphora of *otium*, then, is ironic: we intuitively place conceptual quotation marks over the word, because we are aware that true *otium* is the preserve of those who know how to "live well" (*vivitur bene*, 13).

The fourth strophe brings the priamel phase of the ode to rest on a broad gnomic plateau, rather than on a narrow, isolated peak (*vivitur parvo bene*). The defining relative clause, *cui . . . aufert* (13–16), provides a graphic, though partial view of the ideal *bios*. Horace will complete and supplement this view in the closing verses. In the intervening stanzas, however, it is the purely ethical aspect of the ideal that now receives the limelight. It is instructive to observe the imagery in which that ideal is epitomized: the inherited salt dish resplendent upon the modest board. As so often in the *Carmina*, a convivial setting encodes philosophical enlightenment, and *mensa tenuis* becomes an emblem for the wise man of modest means who conducts his life in accordance with its principles.

The next strophe deploys a reprise that eventually comes to a head in mythological exempla:

V–VIII

> quid brevi fortes iaculamur aevo
> multa? quid terras alio calentis
> sole mutamus? patriae quis exsul
>   se quoque fugit?   20
> scandit aeratas vitiosa navis
> Cura nec turmas equitum relinquit,
> ocior cervis et agente nimbos
>   ocior Euro.[27]
> laetus in praesens animus quod ultra est   25
> oderit curare et amara lento
> temperet risu; nihil est ab omni
>   parte beatum.
> abstulit clarum cita mors Achillem,
> longa Tithonum minuit senectus   30
> et mihi forsan, tibi quod negarit,
>   porriget hora.

Why do we take valiant aim at so many targets in our brief time of life? Why do we change our country for lands warmed by an alien sun? What exile from his homeland escaped also himself? Vile Anxiety climbs on board the bronze-girded ships, and does not abandon the squadrons of cavalry, more swift than stags, more swift than the East Wind as he drives the clouds. A mind that is happy in the present despises concern about what is to come, and moderates bitter circumstances with a tranquil smile; nothing is happy in all respects. A swift death carried off the famous Achilles; unlimited old age wasted away Tithonus; and the hour perchance will proffer to me what it has denied to you.

The reprise begins by annexing the imagery in which a major partition of the priamel was laid out: the soldier's existence. The annexation operates on the figurative plane. The verb *iaculamur* ("take aim"—often used of javelin-throwing) has a double cross-reference to the addressee's symbolic name (an obvious continuation of the wordplay) and to the entire rejected life-style of the soldier. The first person plural is transparently disingenuous, however, because, with the modifier *fortes* emphasizing the martial domain, the speaker egregiously "incorporates" that alien modality of endeavor in order to neutralize and dismiss it. The rhetorical question, therefore, highlights the futile striving of the majority of mankind ("we"), while the military metaphor brackets and distances that futile striving as belonging to others. The collocation *fortes iaculamur* is framed, in typical Horatian fashion, by a phrase that starkly delimits the ontological terrain, so to speak, of the human: *brevi . . . aevo*. With these two well-placed salvos, the poet concentrates the motif of mortality and thereby punctures the ambitions of the metaphorical javelin-thrower.

The remaining two related rhetorical questions (lines 18–20) point to a very important philosophical insight that Horace expresses on several occasions in different poetic genres, including the *Satires* and *Epistles*.[28] Nowhere is the ideological unity of the Horatian *corpus* more evident than in the variations on the maxim "Patriae quis exsul se quoque fugit?" ("What exile from his homeland escaped also himself?"). As a close parallel to our passage, commentators aptly adduce the end of the epistle to Bullatius, in which the precept receives a less compact formulation:

> nam si ratio et prudentia curas,
> non locus effusi late maris arbiter aufert,
> caelum non animum mutant qui trans mare currunt.
> strenua nos exercet inertia: navibus atque
> quadrigis petimus bene vivere. quod petis hic est,
> est Ulubris, animus si te non deficit aequus.
>
> (*Epist.* 1.11.25–30)

For if anxieties are removed by reason and wisdom, and not by a site that dominates an extensive stretch of ocean, then those who run away across the sea change only their climate, not their mental outlook. We are in the toils of an idle exertion: by traveling in ships or in chariots, we aim to find the good life. What you are aiming after is right here: it is Ulubrae, so long as you do not lack an even mind.

In addition to the epigrammatic *sententia* in line 27 (*caelum . . . currunt*), there are several motifs in *Epist.* 1.11 that are shared with

C. 2.16. For example, the complementary land/sea in *navibus atque quadrigis* (not always so recognized) is used to globalize human striving (*petimus*) for the good life (*bene vivere*); the *rational* pursuit of equanimity (*animus . . . aequus*) is the approved avenue for the removal of cares (*curas . . . aufert*).

In the lyric poetry, no less than in the *Epistles* and *Satires*, we find the same idea of an interior stability expressed in a more picturesque form. The Teucer paradigm, for instance, inscribes the precept that external *locus* is ultimately irrelevant to inner happiness (*C.* 1.7.25–32). The exiled sympotic figure there overcomes vicissitude (*fortuna*) by his mental resources, which he takes with him wherever he goes. The gnomic questions of *C.* 2.16, 17 ff., then, are consistent with the Horatian lyric stance at its deepest philosophical level. Whether or not Horace adopted this notion from Epicurean doctrine by way of Lucretius,[29] it is undeniable that he regarded it as a cornerstone of his ethical credo. In reference to the evolution of the *Otium divos,* the *sententia* on the need for self-knowledge (for this is what is implied, at bottom, in the critique of futile self-escape) seems to have a resumptive function parallel to that of the military metaphor of line 17. In the figure of the *patriae exsul,* might we not discern the shadow of the political exile? If so, Horace may be discreetly recalling the conventional type of the politician (successful in 9–10; victim of misfortune in 19–20). Be that as it may, the three rhetorical questions of stanza V "refine" the modes of existence schematized in the priamel by delving into the metaphysical grounds for others' frustrated striving after an elusive *otium.* The frustration that accompanies mankind's *strenua inertia* (in the phraseology of the epistle) results from a double failure to take cognizance of one's *breve aevum* (a failure of perception) and to come to terms with one's identity (a failure of insight).

The following strophe continues to refine the implications of the priamel by returning to the military token for the differentiated "other." Though some philologists have mistakenly interpreted the *aeratas navis* of line 21 as private triremes belonging to the rich, it is virtually certain that *navis/equitum* is yet another instance of a complementary (sea/land) whose function is to reveal the actions of personified *cura* as ubiquitous. The ships, then, are battleships, not yachts (cf. *C.* 1.6.3). The topic of the stanza may be expressed *grosso modo* as follows: the warrior cannot escape *cura,* no matter where his arena of battle may lie. In other words, the military trope has here assumed the synecdochic role that was originally assigned to the priamel as a whole. As soldier, sailor, and politician have together stood for the rest of mankind, so now the soldier has become shorthand, in the *reprise*, for all those alien life-styles that the speaker wishes to discriminate from his own. This summational function is underscored by the word *cura* itself, which makes its first appearance in the ode in reference to the sleeplessness of the wealthy man ("curas laqueata circum / tecta volantis," 11).

If the items of the opening foil are reintroduced in various imagistic transformations (*iaculamur; Cura*), so does the cap itself, which, as we saw, first received an impersonal form in *vivitur parvo bene*. Stanza VI with its relief portrait of the serene *animus* is fundamentally an elaboration of stanza IV, in which we were given our initial glimpse of the *mensa tenuis*. In the amplified image of the *sapiens* that occupies the sixth stanza, we begin to see more sharply what is the genesis of *vitiosa cura* in others, and, by contrast, how the *laetus animus* successfully keeps it at bay (*oderit curare*). By focussing on the present (*in praesens*) and excluding the future (*quod ultra est*), the sage can construct and live by an ethos that takes vicissitude in its stride. Once again, it is the full acknowledgement of vicissitude and all its ramifications that constitutes the epistemological bedrock of Horatian *sapientia*: "nihil est ab omni parte beatum" ("nothing is happy in all respects"). The image of the smile that tempers misfortune inscribes an idea that goes back to Horace's model, Archilochus, for whom the good life also depended on an adjustment to the master principle of alternation (see chapter 3 above).

Though the apothegm on the limits of felicity uses a spatial metaphor ("nihil est *ab omni parte* beatum"), it is actually the temporal axis that, in the immediate sequel, establishes its general validity. The entire orientation of stanza VIII, which illustrates the apothegm, is towards time (cf. *hora*, 32), which operates to vary the individual life-span. A closely analogous gnome occurs in *C.* 2.5.13–15:

> currit enim ferox
> aetas et illi quos tibi dempserit
> apponet annos

For intractable time runs on, and will add to her the years it has subtracted from you.

The exemplification of the apothegm in *C.* 2.16 is fourfold, involving two pairs of human actors: (a) Achilles and Tithonus and (b) speaker and addressee (*mihi/tibi*). The first pair is culled from the domain of heroic legend and located in the distant past; the second, on the other hand, is from the poem's discursive "scaffolding" and projects an imaginary future for the lyrist and Grosphus. The two members in each subset (heroes and ordinary mortals) are polarized in reference to life-spans (mythical and hypothetical), and the chiasmus accentuates the polarity: {Achilles (short)—Tithonus (long)} {speaker (long)—addressee (short)}. If we assume that the *exempla*, both legendary and personal, are logically supportive of the gnome, then it follows that death (*mors*)—the ultimate limit of felicity—is the crucial measure of the good life; for it provides the only criterion by which we can judge, in retrospect, the *quality* of a total *bios*. In the Achilles/Tithonus opposition, the criterion is somewhat enigmatically formulated. Tithonus, after all, did not actually "die" in the literal sense; but the ostensible paradox dwindles into insignificance once we realize that *longa senectus* is, in this context, the equivalent of *mors*. *Longa*, as several scholars have noted (see chapter 3 above), is an Horatian synonym for *aeterna*, and as a qualifier of *senectus* it acquires a powerfully ironic meaning. The only other place in the *Carmina* where the hero Tithonus is mentioned is enlightening in this regard. In *C.* 1.28.7–8 (the Archytas ode), he is coupled with Tantalus in the category of blessed heroes who nonetheless suffered death!

> occidit et Pelopis genitor, conviva deorum,
> Tithonusque remotus in auras

> [Tantalus] father of Pelops also died, though a guest at gods' banquets; and Tithonus was carried off into the air.

Despite Tithonus's quasi-immortality, then, the poet conceives his *longa senectus* as a kind of life-in-death and therefore, for rhetorical purposes, tantamount to death itself. Thus the polarity *cita mors / longa senectus* stresses contrasting durations of the heroes' respective life-spans—durations that are matched in the hypothetical life-spans of contemporary speaker and addressee. Within the ode's total argument, the central fact of mortality ("even Achilles and Tithonus, no ordinary mortals like you and me, had to die") provides the substratum for the achievement of an *otium* that is devoid of *cura*.

The topic of the relative duration of man's *aevum* is governed, at bottom, by the antinomy of quantity versus quality. Beatitude, it transpires, is an interior, not an external, state and as such is independent of length of life. In the wealthy, disavowed *bios* attributed to Grosphus in stanza IX, numerical hyperboles are salient (*centum*; *bis*), whereas in the poetic alternative (stanza X) there is no such coefficient.

IX–X

te greges centum Siculaeque circum
mugiunt vaccae, tibi tollit hinnitum
apta quadrigis equa, te bis Afro
    murice tinctae   35
vestiunt lanae: *mihi* parva rura et
spiritum Graiae tenuem Camenae
Parca non mendax dedit et malignum
    spernere vulgus.   40

Around you moo a hundred herds of Sicilian cows; for you the mare fit for four-horse chariots raises its neighing; you are clothed in wool that has been twice dyed in African purple. *For my part*, a Destiny that does not lie has given me a modest estate, and the frugal inspiration of a Greek Camena [Muse], and disdain for a begrudging crowd.

In these two final strophes, the discrimination between self and non-self is focussed more narrowly on the contrast between speaker, as representative of *paupertas*, and addressee, as representative of *divitiae*. As is customary in the *Odes*, concrete vignettes clinch the major points developed earlier in the poem. In this instance, two vignettes, epitomizing the life-styles of addressee and poet respectively, are elaborately counterpoised (cf. above apropos of C. 4.2.53–60). The discrimination is multi-layered, comprehending several "oppositions": noise/quiet (cf. *mugiunt*; *hinnitum*), quantity/quality, matter/spirit, many/one.

No less effective than the dense layering of the antithesis is the recapitulation, both overt and subtle, of ideas, motifs, and key lexemes. The more nuanced of these reintegrations concerns the sub-

ject matter of the priamel. The mention of expensive clothing material and purple dyes retraces the reference to *otium* as *neque purpura
venale*, and with it the leitmotif of the disavowal of wealth (stanza
II). The phrase *apta quadrigis equa* is also recapitulative, albeit in a
more roundabout way: the "mare fit for four-horsed chariots" unmistakably conjures up athletic contests (see Nisbet-Hubbard *ad
loc.*). The athlete, we remember, is a stock type in vocational priamels, and Horace conspicuously includes the Olympic victor in
his inaugural master-priamel in C. 1.1.[30] By insinuating the prospect of athletic success into his humorous portrayal of Grosphus's
menagerie, he obliquely invokes a standard foil term—one that he
has omitted to deploy in his opening review of man's pursuits. The
intimated athletic contest, therefore, becomes a kind of abbreviation or code for all the rejected avenues to *otium* that the first
strophes have put into prominence. The *bios* of Grosphus, then,
while it introduces new details of the super-rich *modus vivendi*, is
amplified by resonances from the priamel.

The vision of an alternative *bios* that terminates the poem has
been aptly described as a *kallimacheische Kunstideal*.[31] The epithets
parvus and *tenuis*, it is by now generally recognized, are close to
technical jargon for the aesthetic program of the *genus tenue* (Mette
1961), and I need not expatiate on the documentation compiled by
a host of modern philologists on this score. What is especially illuminating in the present context, however, is the studied use of
verbal repetition as a device to integrate the philosophical and the
artistic modes of life. Thus *parva*, which in the finale modifies the
site of lyric (*rura*), fuses with the capping definition of the good life
("*vivitur parvo* bene") in line 13; while the adjective *tenuis*, which
encodes the stylistic level of the genre ("spiritum Graiae *tenuem*
Camenae") is shared with the antecedent motif of *simplicitas* (frugality) and its convivial emblem, the *mensa tenuis* (line 14). Reiteration of key words as a means of organic integration of a *carmen* is,
as I have stressed, not uncommon in the collection, but the ultimate strophe of the *Otium divos* contains one of the most transparent examples of the compositional technique.

In the light of the ode's programmatic climax, the closing phrase,
malignum spernere vulgus, is best read in terms of a literary, rather
than a social, disposition (cf. Nisbet-Hubbard *ad loc.*). The decision
to avoid the crowd is a variation on a Callimachean topos that is

classically expressed in the *Aetia* prologue as well as in a famous epigram.[32] The forceful adjective *malignum*, as applied to the *vulgus*, adds complexity to the topos, for it carries the further implication of hostile criticism. As antonym to *benignus*, *malignus* suggests a grudging, ungenerous attitude toward praiseworthy achievements (*phthonos:* envy). The motif of *phthonos*, in turn, owes as much to Pindaric models as it does to Callimachean *recusatio* discourse.[33] Having just defined his poetic affinities (*Graia Camena*), Horace is here thinking of the reception of his unique lyric oeuvre; hence his *malignum volgus* is, like Pindar's *phthoneroi* or Callimachus's "Telchines," conventional foil for the melic *laudator*. *Phthonos*, then, as concretized in the *malignum volgus*, sets in relief the poet's affirmation of his enduring merit. In this regard *Parca non mendax*—a personified Destiny (Moira) that reveals its veracity over time[34]—is a crucial element in the claim of the closing antistrophe, since it eventually gives the lie to *phthonos* and guarantees poetic immortality.

My partial account of the economy of the *Otium divos* has brought to the fore what might be called the underlying encomiastic agenda: praise of the poet's own integrated *bios*. Self-praise, and the accompanying discriminations between self and non-self, are not often as overt in modern European lyric as they were in Augustan verse conventions, but definitions of one's chosen poetic path are almost invariably self-serving. Horace's achievement in *C*. 2.16 consists in his having created a resplendent vision of an intellect that, *pace* W. B. Yeats, is not "forced to choose / Perfection of the life, or of the work."[35]

MODES OF DISPRAISE

My exposition of three poems of praise (*C*. 1.7; 1.17; 2.16) has sought to illumine the collateral role of sympotic motifs in the articulation of the ideal *bios*. In my treatment of the antithetical climax of *Velox amoenum*, I also had occasion to note how a "negative" symposium—one subverted by violence from within—helps the poet to impart contour to his *laus loci*. In the second part of this chapter, I shall turn my attention to three odes whose primary rhetorical goal is *detraction*. In the process, I plan to elucidate Horace's *indirect* use of the symposium (in both positive and negative images) as a "subtext." This mode of blame depends, for its most telling effects, on emblematic evocations of a contrasted *CD* philosophy that is implicitly regarded as lacking in the *detractandus* (if I may be permitted, *faute de mieux,* so cumbersome a locution).[36]

HIEMIS SODALIS: EXCLUSION FROM THE *CONVIVIUM* (C. 1.25)

Parcius iunctas quatiunt fenestras
iactibus crebris iuvenes protervi,
nec tibi somnos adimunt, amatque
    ianua limen,

quae prius multum facilis movebat   5
cardines; audis minus et minus iam
"me tuo longas pereunte noctes,
    Lydia, dormis?"

invicem moechos anus arrogantis
flebis in solo levis angiportu,   10
Thracio bacchante magis sub inter-
    lunia vento,

cum tibi flagrans amor et libido,
quae solet matres furiare equorum
saeviet circa iecur ulcerosum,   15
    non sine questu

laeta quod pubes hedera virenti
gaudeat pulla magis atque myrto,
aridas frondis hiemis sodali
    dedicet Euro.[37]   20

More rarely now do the petulant young men rattle your jointly fastened windows with frequent missiles; nor do they deprive you of your sleep; and your door loves to hold on to your threshold—your door that previously moved so readily on its hinges. Less and less now do you hear the words: "While I, who am yours, am perishing throughout the long nights, do you, Lydia, sleep?" In your turn, old and devalued, you will lament in a deserted alleyway the superciliousness of paramours; while the Thracian wind steps up its Bacchic orgies with the advent of moonless skies; meanwhile a blazing passion and desire, such as normally drives mares to madness, will run riot in your ulcerous liver, causing you to complain that joyful youth takes greater pleasure in green ivy and dark myrtle, and dedicates dry leaves to the East Wind, winter's drinking-companion.

Before I proceed to trace the presence of convivial tropes in the *Parcius iunctas,* a preliminary scrutiny of its main rhetorical objective will prove expedient. The vilification of Lydia, brutally candid though it may be, is by no means as simplistic or univocal as it is sometimes represented in the critical tradition. The aging *hetaira* is faulted for neither indiscriminate wantonness, on the one hand, nor unyielding coldness, on the other.[38] The text is unequivocal about her ample love-life—no more so than in the transferred image of the clinging door (cf. *amat*) that was formerly loose (lines 5–9). What gives a certain edge, in the first instance, to the speaker's censure of Lydia is not her sexuality per se (though this is crucial in shaping her eventual misfortune) but the fact that it is selective: she has consistently repudiated or neglected this would-be *amator* in favor of others. Part of the particular motivation for the detraction, we may assume, is to warn the addressee against the consequences of her "arrogance." The *Schadenfreude* that colors the warning is manifestly self-regarding and serves to soothe the pain of rejection. So much is marginally implicit in the elliptical narrative of the ode. Despite the seemingly vindictive note in the defamation, however, it would be a mistake, in my view, to overlook the universal dimension of Horace's critique of Lydia's pathological life-course. The addressee's failure, I plan to show, is not merely a sort of vulgar *hubris* (*arrogantia*, narrowly conceived), but a more comprehensive failure of *insight* in Horatian terms. To appreciate the full scope of her failure, we need to recover, beneath the almost "iambographic" aura of the surface, some of the ethical subtext that provides a rationale for the speaker's censure.

The scaffolding of the ode is perspicuous and undisputed: it is constructed within the *cadre* of the *amator exclusus*.[39] That framework is two-tiered and symmetrical as far as the *amator* is concerned. The arrogant female lover who has "excluded" others in the past is imagined as suffering the identical fate in the future— that of the *amator exclusa*. The interchange of role is described in the third stanza, in which the term *arrogantis* is ascribed to the youthful *moechi* who now repudiate an amorous Lydia (the presumption being that she, like Chloe in *C.* 3.26.12, was formerly *arrogans* herself).

There is more to Lydia's fate, however, than ironic role reversal or neat symmetry. The word *invicem* that sets in motion the central strophe is pivotal for the underlying argument of the poem. As we have seen, *vicem* in the *Odes* frequently functions as a motif signal within the *CD* complex. In the full *CD* context *vicem* signifies the alternation principle in nature, which bears an important message for the human observer. What is signaled in the present context, by contrast, is not natural *alternation* (cyclical; reversible) but human *alteration* (linear; irreversible). The speaker's point is not simply the banal truth of physical decline, but, more on target, the insight that spiritual decline is by no means an inevitable concomitant of ageing. Lydia's failure to "age gracefully" is the psychological, as well as logical, consequence of her prior failure to anticipate, and come to terms with, her gradual loss of physical appeal. Her experience of change would, the poet implies, have been less traumatic if she had accepted its inevitability. At a deeper level, her myopia is rooted in the illusion I have earlier characterized as *spes longa*—the tacit denial of her own mortality. Her efforts to negate time by ignoring it come to grief in spectacular fashion in the form of a libido that increases in proportion to her bodily degeneration. If Commager is right in his incisive remarks on this poem, the term *interlunia* in lines 11–12 (marked by word division between lines) points ironically to *temporal* periodization—in a word, to the very aspect of reality that Lydia has fondly hoped to erase (Commager, 258). From this perspective, her wretched plight is a consequence of metaphysical blindness.

Horace's prognosis of an unhappy old age for Lydia is as unsparing as it is precise: racked by a libidinal drive (*amor et libido*) that rages out of control, she can only weep in abject frustration and dishonor (*levis*) in a deserted alleyway, exposed to the fury of the Thracian North Wind. The hyperbolic comparison of her sexual desire to that of a mare in heat adds a note of the grotesque to the vivid portrayal of a *turpis senecta* (the phrase is from C. 1.31.19). The whole projection of a sleepless, aging *amator*, though basically repulsive and alienating, gains in depth and universality from intertextual rapprochement with a famous poem of Ibycus (5 *PMG*, lines 6–13):

> ἐμοὶ δ᾽ ἔρος
> οὐδεμίαν κατάκοιτος ὥραν.
> †τε† ὑπὸ στεροπᾶς φλέγων
> Θρηίκιος Βορέας
> ἀίσσων παρὰ Κύπριδος ἀζαλέ-
> αις μανίαισιν ἐρεμνὸς ἀθαμβὴς
> ἐγκρατέως πεδόθεν †φυλάσσει†
> ἡμετέρας φρένας

For me, however, Desire does not rest at any season. [Like] the Thracian North Wind blazing with lightning, it shoots down from Cyprian [Aphrodite], dark, fearless, with desiccating madness, and from bottom to top it overwhelms my heart.

The parallels in imagery and motif between the two descriptions of unrequited *eros* deserve a detailed illustration:

	Ibycus	Horace
Thracian wind	Θρηίκιος Βορέας	Thracio . . . vento
blazing love	ὑπὸ στεροπᾶς φλέγων	flagrans amor et libido
madness	μανίαισιν	furiare; saeviet
unseasonableness	οὐδεμίαν κα- τάκοιτος ὥραν	hiemis sodali
desiccation	ἀζαλέαις [μανίαισιν]	aridas frondes

The persona (presumably aging) of the Ibycus fragment is in the grip of a passion that is "untimely, irregular and violent" (Bowra 1961, 262). Since the Archaic Greek intertext is purportedly self-descriptive (it exposes the feelings of the speaker), whereas Horace's is descriptive of the addressee, the plurality of echoes in the latter accomplishes a complex purpose within the overall framework of a censorious discourse. Though the sufferings of both Greek love-poet and superannuated *hetaira* are degrading, the imagistic kinship between the two texts serves to lessen the distance between Horace's *detractanda* and ourselves. Lydia's plight may be self-induced, but it is far from unique, and our acknowledgment of its commonality should encourage us to qualify the *communis opinio* regarding the ode's lack of empathy for the addressee. We know that Lydia will never attain the serene acceptance implied in Yeats's "bodily decrepitude is wisdom"[40] but her failure to do so appears, through the veil of the Ibycus allusion, to be as much pathetic as repulsive.

The ulterior significance of Lydia's fall is refracted through the carefully intricate metaphors of the ode's ultimate stanza. The floral metaphors have a dual referentiality—to the human body (cf. "That time of year thou mayest in me behold" in Shakespeare's

Sonnet 73), and to the sympotic convention of the *corona*. The interweaving of the two frames of reference is material to the speaker's mode of dispraise, for Lydia is thereby disqualified not merely from erotic partnership, but also, and no less crucially, from the *convivial* sodality. The green leaves that the young men select are presumably to be employed in the construction of wreaths, the emblem of the symposium. This plausible assumption about the poem's latent scaffolding is confirmed by the iconographic meaning (often overlooked) of the *sets* of leaves chosen— ivy (*hedera*) and myrtle (*myrtus*). The former is closely associated with the wine-god, Bacchus, the latter with the love-goddess, Venus. These choices for *coronae* are patently overdetermined, inasmuch as they are exquisitely germane to the convivial existence and its chief divine patrons. They also speak to the addressee's psychic predicament, which combines unsated desire (*amor et libido*) with a rage (*furiare*) that matches the Bacchic fury of the wind (*bacchante*). The sympotic framing of the addressee's exclusion is also intimated in the word *sodali*, which, as applied to the rejected Lydia, underscores her ostracism from the circle of accepted *sodales* (Horace's regular term for the companions at table). In fine, the scope of Lydia's exclusion transcends the "elegiac" reversal at the threshold to include alienation from the social site of the lyric—the *convivium*.

The convivial subtext that I have traced in the pattern of imagery is not wholly confined to the exfoliation in the final lines. There is also an element of ring composition in the close, since the opening picture of *iuvenes protervi* ("petulant young men") beating on windows in a riotous mob is typical of the social custom of the *comissatio* (Greek: κῶμος)—the wild revelry that is often an adjunct to the symposium. The drunken revelers, who would normally themselves be wreathed, would often lay *coronae* at the lovers' door. At this level of poetic economy, the *laeta pubes* ("joyful youth") of the concluding vignette joins up with the *iuvenes protervi* of the beginning. The implied social setting for both—the *convivium*—is foil to Lydia's isolated, companionless existence (cf. *solo . . . angiportu*).

If my reading of Lydia's dual exclusion is valid, then the speaker's final anathema takes on a metonymic pertinence ("aridas frondis hiemis sodali / dedicet Euro": "[and dedicate] dry leaves to the East Wind, winter's drinking-companion"). In an expression that has an almost ritual flavor, Lydia is formally "dedicated" (*dedicet*) to Eurus as "winter's companion," not only because she is in the winter of her life (as opposed to the young men who are in their spring), but because she has treated her own youth as if it were eternal—a metaphysical myopia that the lyric voice consistently condemns. Her true *sodalis*, therefore, is the season associated with impending death—the very circumstance she has implicitly negated by her prior conduct. Behind her wretched plight, then, is the ethical immaturity Horace criticizes in many *CD* odes—the failure to come to terms with one's mortality. This philosophical deficit is ironically related to her earlier unresponsiveness to the figurative death of others (cf. *pereunte*).

I have hinted, in passing, at an intergeneric dimension (elegiac versus lyric) in Lydia's peripety and exclusion. This facet of the poem's latent script is best elucidated by a comparison between the two citations—one direct, the other indirect—that are featured in the duplicated sketch of the *exclusus amator*. The direct citation (lines 7–8) purveys the lament of the young *inamorato* Lydia has rejected:

> "me tuo longas pereunte noctes,
>   Lydia, dormis?"

"While I, who am yours, am perishing throughout the long nights, do you, Lydia, sleep?"

This embedded sample of a paraclausithyron[41] is, though brief, a fabric of clichés. If we set aside the meter, the pregnant sample is very much in the spirit and diction of the *querela* of the elegiac *amator* as we know it from the Augustan practitioners of erotic elegy. The corresponding *questus* (line 16) of the reversed Lydia is clothed in similar catchwords (cf. *flebis*, 10) that indicate the speaker's awareness of the overtones of the *exclusus amator* motif in contemporary *flebiles modi* (see chapter 1 above). In spite of the similarity, however, Lydia's complaint, the contents of which are reported in indirect clauses, is distinctly complicated by the inclusion of integrated tropes that evoke the sympotic ambiance. Furthermore, it reflects the belated insight into time and *kairos* that the addressee has previously lacked. In this supremely ironic sense, the closing antiphonic *questus* of the censured *hetaira* paradoxically embodies a glimpse of the "positive" *convivium* (*laeta; gaudeat*) from which she has peremptorily been debarred.

As a pendant to my diagnosis of Lydia, let us briefly consider two analogous cases in the *Odes* of blameworthy lovers of advanced age—C. 3.15 and C. 4.13. In the former invective, the *detractor* lays stress on the unseasonableness of the addressee's *amor* (1–10):

> Uxor pauperis Ibyci,
> tandem nequitiae fige modum tuae
>   famosisque laboribus:
> maturo proprior *desine* funeri
>   *inter ludere virgines*
> et stellis nebulam spargere candidis.
>   *non,* si quid Pholoen satis,
> et te, Chlori, *decet:* filia rectius
>   expugnat iuvenum domos,
> pulso Thyias uti concita tympano.

O spouse of Ibycus, a man of modest means, impose a limit at long last on your wantonness and your scandalous routines: as you draw closer to a seasonable demise, *cease to cavort among the young women,* and to cast a cloud over the bright stars. *Not everything that suits* Pholoe in some measure also *suits* you, Chloris: your daughter more appropriately assaults the dwellings of young men, like a bacchant goaded to frenzy by the beat of the tympanum.

In further specifying what is inappropriate behavior for the amorous *uxor,* Horace once again appeals to emblematic features of the symposium (music, wreaths, wine-drinking) (13–16):

> te lanae prope nobilem
> tonsae Luceriam, non *citharae* decent
>   nec *flos* purpureus *rosae*
>   nec *poti* vetulam faece tenus *cadi.*

What suits you, an old woman, is wool shorn in the vicinity of renowned Luceria, not *the lyre,* nor the bright *bloom of the rose,* nor *the wine jars drained* to the dregs.

Though the *detractanda,* Chloris, is not here conceived as an *hetaira* in terms of her social status, it is clear that her incongruous behavior is comparable to that of Lydia, and her ultimate penalty as imagined by the speaker ought to be her exclusion from symposia, in which she continues to violate *modus*.

A similar contravention of the principle of *kairos* is the basis for the virulent denigration of Lyce in C. 4.13:

> Audivere, Lyce, di mea vota, di
> audivere, Lyce: fis anus, et tamen
>   vis formosa videri
>   *ludis*que et bibis impudens
>
> et *cantu tremulo pota* Cupidinem   5
> lentum sollicitas. ille *virentis* et
>   doctae psallere Chiae
>   pulchris excubat in genis.
>
> importunus enim transvolat *aridas*
> quercus et refugit te, quia luridi   10
>   dentes te, quia rugae
>   turpant et capitis nives.
>
> nec Coae referunt iam tibi purpurae
> nec cari lapides tempora quae semel
>   notis condita fastis   15
>   inclusit volucris dies.

The gods, O Lyce, have heard my prayers; they have heard them, O Lyce: you are becoming an old woman, and nevertheless you want to be regarded as a beauty; *you cavort* and drink without shame; and, *in your cups,* you try to arouse a reluctant Desire with your *tremulous singing.* That god, however, stays awake on the beautiful cheeks of Chia, who is *in the bloom of youth* and is skilled at playing the lyre. For he unceremoniously flies by *dry* oaks, and steers clear of you, because yellow teeth, and wrinkles, and your snowy head render you unsightly. Neither purple raiments from Cos, nor expensive gems can bring back those times that the winged day has once stored away and locked up in its infamous annals.

This later *carmen* not only resumes several of the motifs from *Parcius iunctas,* but also repeats some of its key words and metaphors, such as *virentis* (6, of the young) and *aridas* (9, of the old). In addition, the unseasonable cavorting of the aging *hetaira* Lyce [42] in the company of ardent youth (cf. *iuvenes fervidi,* 26) recalls the indecorous antics of Chloris in *Uxor pauperis Ibyci* (cf. *ludis: ludere; cantu tremulo: citharae; pota: poti . . . faece tenus cadi*). The underlying consistency in the depictions supports the interpretive stance that regards the individual *puellae* in the *Odes* as representative of moral and psychological types.[43] A common denominator in the separate detractions is a philosophical critique of the type of conduct that ignores time, and, by extension, seeks to deny the implications of *mors aequa*.

SEMPER VACUAM: DENIAL OF CHANGE IN THE PYRRHA ODE (C. 1.5)

The brief ode addressed to Pyrrha (C. 1.5) has drawn a disproportionately large number of scholarly moths to its flame, whether the compulsion to reach its lucent core has involved translation or exegesis. Quite apart from its intrinsic merits (elegance in form, coherence in imagery), its placement in the sequence of "parade odes" inaugurating the *tribiblos* invites speculation about its paradigmatic significance. As the first erotic lyric in the collection, its programmatic status is an almost necessary presupposition (cf. Pöschl 1970, 20). In the discussion to follow, I shall adumbrate the implied critique of the immature *amator* whom the speaker refers to anonymously as *puer*. The behavioral shortcomings of the *puer* are, I hope to make clear, profoundly akin to those I have diagnosed in other *detractandi* so far considered.

I–IV

Quis multa gracilis te puer in rosa
perfusus liquidis urget odoribus
   grato, Pyrrha, sub antro?
    cui flavam religas comam,

simplex munditiis? heu quotiens fidem   5
mutatosque deos flebit et aspera
   nigris aequora ventis
    emirabitur insolens,

qui nunc te fruitur credulus aurea,
qui semper vacuam, semper amabilem   10
   sperat, nescius aurae
    fallacis! miseri, quibus

intemptata nites. me tabula sacer
votiva paries indicat uvida
   suspendisse potenti   15
    vestimenta maris deo.

What svelte young lover, dripping with liquid perfumes, is putting pressure on you, O Pyrrha, amidst so many roses under the canopy of a cosy grotto? For whom are you fixing in a bun your flaming hair with chic simplicity? Alas, how often shall he come to lament your infidelity and the change in divine favor and, in his inexperience, be completely surprised by seas that have turned rough with darkling gales—he who now enjoys your golden aura; who hopes you will be always available, always there for him to love, he blissfully unaware of the deceiving breeze. Unfortunate are they who have no experience of your glitter. For my part, the sacred wall with its votive tablet indicates that I have hung up my dripping raiments in dedication to the divinity who controls the sea.

The two middle strophes (II and III) depict the emotional attitude and sentiments of the *puer* in complementary panels. In the first, the lover's *future* infelicity is foreshadowed (*heu . . . insolens*); in the second, by contrast, his *present* euphoria is represented (*qui . . . fallacis*). The latter panel, which functions as a refinement of the opening strophe, discloses the ultimate basis of the speaker's disparagement of the youth. As the pronounced reiteration of *semper* (line 10) is meant to bring home, the *puer* is prey to the fatal delusion (or expectation) that his present felicity is irreversible. Such delusion, we learn, is fed by a misplaced hope (cf. the verb *sperat* in initial position in verse 11). The relative clauses marked by anaphora (9–12) characterize the youth as vulnerable not merely to Pyrrha's fickleness (predictable in a *hetaira*) but to his own puerile fantasies. With the key words *semper* and *sperat*, an important *Grundmotiv* of Horace's *Carmina* here receives memorable formulation in an erotic context. The *spes* that in the immediately preceding CD ode, addressed to Sestius (*C.* 1.4), expresses a longing for immortality (*spem . . . longam*, 15) now has its counterpart in the domain of *amor* in the boy's naive wish for unbroken felicity. The rhetorical intent of the poem, then, is disapprobation, not of the beautiful *hetaira*, but rather of the immature lover.

Naive wishes, in turn, have their ulterior origin in a conceptual fallacy regarding mutability. Implicit in the *spes longa* attitude, as we have seen at some length above, is the denial of the phenomenon of alternation. The *puer* is ironically represented as a "slow learner" in this respect, for the burden of the word *quotiens* (5) is to insinuate that he is doomed to experience Pyrrha's inconstancy on repeated occasions. The phrase *fidem mutatosque deos* is, as several have remarked, grammatically compressed—*fides* has been transmuted into its opposite.[44] The controlling metaphor through which the idea of transmutation is conveyed is virtually a type example for Horace: it is the storm at sea, vividly adumbrated in the words *aspera / nigris aequora ventis.* The sudden alternation, calm to storm, here stands as a trope for erotic misfortune, and the unprepared *amator* can only express astonishment and disbelief at the prospect of rough seas. In this incisive sketch of a certain kind of lover, then, the speaker constructs a paradigm for the philosophically flawed person who is condemned, by his failure of insight, to experience a predictable change as catastrophic—and to do so repeatedly![45] The Pyrrha ode converges, at the level of an ethical critique, with those convivial odes that postulate the acceptance of mutability as the foundation for a serene existence.

The tension between distancing and rapprochement, divergence and convergence of older and younger *amatores* is especially apparent when one looks at the binary structure of the temporal planes that dominate the four strophic partitions:

I	II
Present	Future (*puer:* storm)
III	IV
Present	Past (poet: shipwreck)
(felicity)	(infelicity)

In the reprise that commences with the third strophe, the older speaker's past seems to converge with the younger lover's future as narratives of infelicity (figurative storm at sea and shipwreck). In foreshadowing this point of convergence, the gnomic transition, "miseri, quibus intemptata nites" ("unfortunate are they who have no experience of your glitter," 12–13), has the dual effect of dismissing the "foil" (the *puer* who is ignorant of the hazards) and uniting all of Pyrrha's lovers, old and young, in the inclusive category of *miseri.* In view of the fact that *miser* is a common signifier of "love-sick" in the Latin erotic code, Horace's contemporary audience undoubtedly grasped the ambivalent nature of the misery faced by those fortunate/unfortunate enough to be exposed to Pyrrha's radiance. After the generalization about the *miseri,* we are made aware that the speaker, unlike certain others, has gained insight lacking in the *puer*, who will no doubt continue to be surprised by future erotic gales (*quotiens . . . emirabitur*). As a mode of dispraise, then, *C.* 1.5. evinces a high degree of sophistication: empathy and disapproval are both present in Horace's depiction of the perils of mutable love relationships.

From a generic perspective, the *puer* who wishes to negate change embodies a stereotype from the rival domain of elegiac amatory discourse. The telltale *flebit*, the monotonous *semper*, the epithets signifying gullibility and ignorance (*credulus*, 9; *nescius*, 11)—all these point to the type of *amator* whom we see represented, *ad nauseam*, perhaps, in the pages of Catullus, Tibullus, and Propertius. The lyric persona is, of course, concerned to differentiate himself from such an unsophisticated view of something as complex as *amor*, and the disjunction between older speaker (self) and *puer* (other) as *amatores* is formally inscribed in the final strophe. There the speaker's valediction to love is the subject of a votive tablet hung up on the wall of a shrine. The very pictorial dedication that inscribes the poet's escape from past danger is, however, in part paradoxical, in that it reestablishes a limited bond between Pyrrha's lovers even while it sets the lyrist irrevocably apart from the current short-sighted *detractandus*.

It is precisely within the framework of change as denied or acknowledged by human actors that the concluding reference to the *deus* is to be apprehended. There has been some philological controversy over the sex of the unnamed divinity—is it the male Neptune or the female Venus to whom Horace dedicates the representation of his escape from amatory shipwreck?[46] The controversy over the particular deity has distracted attention from the poem's total argument, which is brought to a close by the word *deo*. To recuperate it, we need to remind ourselves that the sea, in this poem, is, among other *significata*, the arena of change, and the god whose sphere of influence or *dynamis* is defined as *potenti maris* is, in the context of the ode, primarily the master/mistress of alternation. The gender and particular identity of the divinity who controls the changing sea of love pales into insignificance beside the god-induced spectacle of change itself. Once again the commentators have vainly striven to narrow a picture that the poet has sought to enlarge. The final word of the ode redirects our attention to the *mu-*

tatos deos of line 6, and thereby to the theme of a mutability that is out of man's hands. As the poet puts it in the Convivial parallel case: "permitte divis cetera, qui simul / stravere ventos aequore fervido / deproeliantis, nec cupressi / nec veteres agitantur orni" ("leave the rest to the gods; for as soon as they have straightened out the winds that do battle over the seething sea, then neither cypresses nor ancient ash trees continue to be driven about": C. 1.9.9–12). Having come to terms with his own change of fortune vis-à-vis Pyrrha, the speaker, who has learnt, and generalized, from his rude immersion, consecrates his sea-soaked garments to the divinity responsible for his abrupt vicissitude.

The maturity of the speaker and the immaturity of the *puer* acquire deeper significance when they are viewed against the faint but distinguishable background of a convivial *cadre*. Though the presumptive setting of the Pyrrha ode cannot be absolutely determined, there are several indications in the text that a convivial scaffolding is appropriate to the circumstances described. A point-by-point analysis of typical features in the description will bear out the assumption.

multa . . . in rosa (line 1)

There is a plethora of roses, but what precisely do they evoke? The jury is still out on the vexed issue of whether we are meant to imagine a rose-strewn ground or rose garlands. If *coronae* are involved, the preposition *in* is problematic, so at least it has been maintained,[47] unless Horace is indulging in gross hyperbole at the boy's expense. In my judgment, the two images—roses strewn around and roses in wreaths—are by no means mutually exclusive, and we do not have an either/or determination to make in respect to the location of the roses. Despite the fact that a literal reading of *in* conjures up a bed of roses, we must also give due weight to the consideration that roses were often strewn around at *convivia* in which the participants, according to hoary custom, simultaneously wore garlands on their heads. A convivial setting, therefore, readily accommodates both alternatives.

A cursory survey of all contexts for the rose motif within the scope of the *Odes* is enlightening in more than one respect. A rose, it transpires, is not simply a rose as far as Horace's floral imagery is concerned. It is striking, in the first place, that in all seven other instances in which roses are featured in the *tribiblos*, the setting is explicitly convivial.[48] Within this master context, certain collateral ideas recur in association with the rose, such as the evanescence of youth and extravagance in accoutrements. Let us briefly review the relevant passages.

Roses are linked with an extravagant banquet in at least one ode from each of the first three books. In C. 1.36, the poet proposes an especially wild celebration to mark the return of a *sodalis*, Numida. Among the items he enjoins as imperative to such an occasion are roses (11–16):

> neu promptae modus amphorae,
> neu morem in Salium sit requies pedum,
>   neu multi Damalis meri
> Bassum Threicia vincat amystide,
>   *neu desint epulis rosae*
> *neu vivax apium neu breve lilium.*

Let there be no limit to the ready wine jar, nor rest for feet dancing a Salian beat, nor defeat for Bassus at the hands of that heavy drinker Damalis in the Thracian drinking bout. *Let there not be lacking to our banquet either roses, or fresh green celery-leaves, or the briefly blooming lily.*

We may note, in passing, that though the *rosae* do not have their own epithet, the juxtaposition with "*vivax* apium" and "*breve* lilium" contextualizes the topic of evanescence. In the programmatic finale to book 1 (*Persicos odi*), which I have discussed at length in chapter 2 above, roses not in season are excluded from the "simple" myrtle wreath (*simplici*) that the poet contrasts with the elaborate *corona* desired by the *puer*. There is a clear imputation of overindulgence in the boy's choice of the rose.

Extravagance bordering on the outrageous is marked, in the rollicking carousal of C. 3.19, by the liberal scattering of roses (18–22):

> *insanire iuvat*: cur Berecentiae
>   cessant flamina tibiae?
> cur pendet tacita fistula cum lyra?
>   *parcentis ego dexteras*
> *odi: sparge rosas*

To lose one's mind is sheer pleasure: why do the blasts from the Berecyntian flutes die down? Why does the panpipe hang idly along with the silent lyre? *I despise hands that stint: shower the roses.*

The party envisaged above is at the other extreme from the restrained ambience of the *Persicos odi.* What is eschewed (*odi*) in one context is demanded in the other—the rose with its symbolic connotations of prodigality. On the other hand, in the elaborate invitation ode to Maecenas, *Tyrrhena regum progenies* (C. 3.29), Horace, though he claims *paupertas* and *simplicitas* and disavows extravagance, does not hesitate to offer his wealthy friend precious roses as an inducement to leave Rome (1–5):

> tibi
> non ante verso lene merum cado
> *cum flore,* Maecenas, *rosarum* et
> pressa tuis balanus capillis
> iamdudum apud me est.

for you there has long since been sitting at my house a mellow vintage in a jar not yet sampled, *along with the bloom of roses,* Maecenas, and exotic perfumes extracted for your hair.

Several Convivial odes intertwine roses with the theme of transience. In the *detractio* of Ibycus's wife, Chloris, that I have glanced at in the preceding section, the aging woman is pilloried because of her debauched conduct at parties (C. 3.15.14–16):

> non citharae decent
> *nec flos purpureus rosae*
> nec poti vetulam faece tenus cadi.

not the lyre, *nor the bright bloom of the rose,* nor the wine jars drained to the dregs.

As an emblem of passing time, the bright rose is incongruous on the brow of the declining *uxor.* Horace's treatment of the emblem, however, is complex. What is inappropriate for this *detractanda* may be entirely appropriate for the *sodales* who are urged to feast *en plein air* in the ode to Hirpinus (C. 2.11.13–16):

> cur non sub alta vel platano vel hac
> pinu iacentes sic temere et *rosa*

> *canos odorati capillos,*
> dum licet, Assyriaque nardo
> potamus uncti?

Why do we not drink, while we may, as we lie beneath the tall plane tree or this pine, without ceremony, *our white hair scented with roses,* and ourselves anointed with Syrian nard?

The singular *rosa* is collective, but it conveys something of the emblematic significance of the notoriously evanescent bloom entwined in the prematurely gray hair of the speaker.

As the final example of this review of the rose motif, the outdoor *convivium* in another ode from book 2 (*C. 2.3*) brings together several of the elements we see compactly assembled in the opening strophe of the Pyrrha ode—shade, unguents, roses, and youthfulness (9–16):

> quo pinus ingens albaque populus
> *umbram* hospitalem consociare amant
> ramis? quid obliquo laborat
> lympha fugax trepidare rivo?
>
> huc vina et *unguenta* et nimium brevis
> *flores* amoenae ferre iube *rosae,*
> dum res et *aetas* et sororum
> fila trium patiuntur atra.

Why do the huge pine and the white poplar love to join in creating a welcome *shade* with their branches? Why does the fleeing water labor under stress in the slanting stream? To this spot order wine to be brought, and *perfumes,* and the too-brief *flowers of the lovely rose,* as long as circumstances and *age* and the dark threads of the three sisters permit.

The scenario described in C. 1.5, my point of departure, does not explicitly include wine-drinking; yet it is in all other respects consistent with the emblematic status of the rose throughout the Convivial odes. As my synopsis of all later occurrences of the motif in the *tribiblos* confirms, a non-convivial scaffolding for the poem would be anomalous to the paradigm. What the assumption of such a scaffolding contributes to our understanding is to deepen our perception of the incongruous spectacle of too earnest a *puer* in a context that demands a *carpe diem* attitude. The critique of the *puer* therewith assumes an ironic tonality. The adjective *multa,* employed in hyperbaton, obviously evokes extravagance, and the embedding of the *puer* in a plethora of roses may subtly suggest the ancillary motif of the evanescence of youth.

perfusus liquidis . . . odoribus (line 2)

If an abundance of roses seems by itself to be inadequate grounds for imagining a sympotic backdrop, the use of unguents should sway the skeptic. Annointment with unguents was, of course, de rigueur at symposia. While it does not follow *logically* that since all symposiasts are perfumed, all perfumed figures are symposiasts, the actual association of ointment and banquet is so pervasive in the *Odes* that the former is virtually an index of the latter. In this particular instance, there is an added nuance to the anointment: the young hopeful who now enjoys Pyrrha's favor has gone "overboard"—if I may anticipate his symbolic fate—with his application of perfumes (*perfusus*). Like the profusion of roses, the profusion of unguents is a mark of inappropriate excess, of a lack of *modus* betraying poor judgment. As Pyrrha's contrasting *simplicitas* in matters cosmetic is meant to underscore, his excess is, in view of the situation and the intended recipient, profoundly misplaced. The nature of his participation in a standard convivial convention, then, discloses his lack of sophistication.

cui flavam religas comam (line 4)

Other details of Horace's canvas corroborate the inferences I have drawn from roses and perfumes. Pyrrha, like her female congeners in the *Odes*, is a beautiful *hetaira*. In this regard even her famous hairdo—the tresses bound back into a bun—is not unique, but rather a gesture true to type. We have only to compare the cosmetics of a girl named Lyde who is summoned to a drinking party (C. 2.11.21–24):

> quis devium scortum eliciet domo
> Lyden? eburna dic age cum lyra
> maturet in comptum Lacaenae
> more *comas religata nodum*.[49]

Who will entice that sly wench Lyde from her quarters? Come, tell her to hurry on over with her ivory lyre, *her hair fixed up*, in Spartan simplicity, *into a chic bun*?

Pyrrha's *religatio* is a normal act of the courtesan's repertoire, and part of the irony in Horace's portrayal lies in the innuendo that the *puer* fancies that it is done specially for him (*"cui* flavam religas comam?"*: *"for whom* are you fixing in a bun your flaming hair?").

The accumulation of circumstantial indices (roses, unguents, *hetaira*, hairdo) favors the view that Pyrrha's juvenile partner has been placed in an unfamiliar, if not alien, environment—that of *hetairae* and ephemeral joys, ironic detachment and resignation to vicissitude. The convivial subtext I have uncovered helps to articulate the impression of basic incongruity. Out of place and bemused (*insolens*) in such a world, he becomes the object of amused obloquy on the part of the lyric persona, chiefly on account of his irrational desire to negate change—a desire that, for Horace, is on the far side of a dividing line between insight and folly.

From Dispraise to Praise: The Transfiguration of the Vanquished (C. 1.37)

The penultimate ode of book 1—conventionally labeled the Cleopatra ode—has posed an enigma with respect to the dynamics of praise and dispraise. The main paradox centers on the dual portrayal of Cleopatra: she is dramatically transformed, in the course of the poem, from object of dispraise to object of praise, from *detractanda* to *laudanda*. The surprising volte-face in the attitude of the speaker from disapproval to admiration has unleashed a good deal of controversy regarding the poem's ideological raison d'être. In particular, questions surrounding the victor's image seem to demand answers that are apparently irreconcilable with a uniformly encomiastic posture. What place does praise of a dreaded adversary have in the context of a victory celebration? Is the marked shift from censure to praise of the foreign queen motivated by some hidden propaganda motive, and is it consistent with an underlying intent to eulogize Octavian? In my ensuing interpretation of the ode, I propose to account for the paradoxical conversion of the queen in terms conducive to a coherent encomiastic program. In addition, I hope to demonstrate that the very nature of the conversion speaks to the poet's most cherished philosophical convictions as expressed elsewhere in the *Odes*.

Nunc est bibendum, nunc pede libero
pulsanda tellus, nunc Saliaribus
    ornare pulvinar deorum
        tempus erat dapibus, sodales.

antehac nefas depromere Caecubum   5
cellis avitis, dum Capitolio
    regina dementis ruinas
        funus et imperio parabat

contaminato cum grege turpium
morbo virorum, quidlibet impotens   10
    sperare fortunaque dulci
        ebria. sed minuit furorem

vix una sospes navis ab ignibus,
mentemque lymphatam Mareotico
    redegit in veros timores   15
        Caesar ab Italia volantem

remis adurgens, accipiter velut
mollis columbas aut leporem citus
    venator in campis nivalis
        Haemoniae, daret ut catenis   20

fatale monstrum; quae generosius
perire quaerens nec muliebriter
    expavit ensem nec latentis
        classe cita reparavit oras;

ausa et iacentem visere regiam   25
vultu sereno, fortis et asperas
    tractare serpentis, ut atrum
        corpore combiberet venenum,

deliberata morte ferocior,
saevis Liburnis scilicet invidens   30
    privata deduci superbo
        non humilis mulier triumpho.

Now it is time to drink, time to beat upon the earth with free-footed dancing, high time to adorn the gods' festal couches with banquets on a Salian scale, my friends. Before now it was taboo to bring out the Caecuban vintage from ancestral wine cellars, as long as a queen was hatching senseless plots of death and destruction against Capitol and empire, along with her infested troop of disease-ridden profligates—a queen powerless to control her unlimited hope, and drunk on fortune's sweet liquor. But her madness lessened when barely a single ship was rescued from the flames, and her senses, diluted with Mareotic wine, were restored to the world of real fears by Caesar, who pursued her with his oars as she flew away from Italy, like a hawk pursuing the gentle dove, or a swift hunter the hare in the plains of snowy Thessaly, intending to put in chains that prodigy of doom. She, however, in her quest for a more noble death, evinced no womanly fear of the sword, nor did she make for secret shores with her swift fleet; she ventured to look upon her ruined palace with a serene countenance, even so bold as to handle venomous snakes, in order to drink up with her whole body the dark poison: all the more formidable once she had determined to die and disdaining, no doubt, to be conveyed as a private citizen by means of Liburnian warships in a proud triumphal procession—no mean woman!

The transfiguration of Cleopatra unfolds in three well-articulated narrative episodes that reflect crucial phases in her mental state: (*a*) lines 6–12 (*dum . . . ebria*); (*b*) lines 12–21 (*sed . . . monstrum*); and (*c*) lines 21–32 (*quae . . . triumpho*). My analysis will focus on each episode in turn with a view to exposing the encomiastic infrastructure of the whole. Despite the prominence accorded to Cleopatra in the narrative, the oblique rhetorical agenda is praise of the ruler whose name appears at the precise midpoint of the poem: Caesar (line 16).

(*a*) *fortuna dulci ebria*

In the first narrative segment, the *convivium* motif is used to define the scope of the queen's initial aberration. True to his strategy of erecting elaborate foils to the ideals he wishes to vindicate, Horace juxtaposes two polarized *convivia* within the compass of the first three stanzas. The positive *convivium*, in which a select group of *sodales* will participate,[50] is to be unrestrained, even ecstatic, as befits the importance of the occasion. The characterization of the projected feast as Salian is, of course, in line with Horace's common practice of using proper names as tokens for ideas—in this case, the idea of sumptuousness.[51] Lavishness of dishes is to be matched by excessive drinking (underscored by the Alcaean "motto"),[52] choice vintages (Caecuban), and uninhibited dancing (*pede libero*). The lack of moderation is here advertised as appropriate to, even demanded by, the occasion (the Latin gerundives *bibendum* and *pulsanda* being more forceful than the Greek χρῆ).

The perverted *convivium*, on the other hand, brings together not a select group of discerning *sodales*, but an indiscriminate herd (*grex*), who are pointedly portrayed as pathological (*contaminato . . .*

turpium morbo). Their leader is a *regina* who, in a transferred epithet, is designated as demented (*dementis ruinas*, 7; cf. *furorem*, 12; *mentem lymphatam*, 14). Mental aberration, then, is the hallmark of the negative *convivium*. The speaker is fairly explicit about the nature and dimension of this aberration. A careful diagnosis is central to the understanding of the ode's latent scale of values.

When Horace refines his description of Cleopatra's *dementia* by saying she is "powerless to control hope" (*quidlibet impotens sperare*), he is doing more than indicting a specific historical personage. History, as interpreted and mediated by the poet, here intersects with a larger philosophical critique of character. Nowhere is Aristotle's famous comparison between poetry and history (quoted as the epigraph on page 1) more accurate than in the Augustan poet's particularization of Cleopatra's folly on the eve of Actium; for writ large in that particular exemplum is the general failure of perception that I have been tracing in Horatian lyric under the rubric of *spes longa*. It is no accident that a poem that foregrounds convivial motifs should couch its disapprobation of an exemplary figure in terms of an ethical failure frequently decried in the *Carmina*—the inability of the unenlightened to set limits to *spes*. Cleopatra's notable failure, then, links up with the common tendency of the immature to entertain unrealistic expectations, including, of course, the expectation of immortality. The linkage between the queen's *dementia* and the standard convivial foil becomes even more transparent when we consider the ramifications of the cleverly placed metaphor *fortunaque dulci ebria* (11–12). Unlike the lyric symposiast, Cleopatra is *inappropriately* "inebriated" and the malign source of her inebriation is the warped expectation that *fortuna*, which is currently *dulcis*, will remain irreversible. Implicit, however, in the very conception of *fortuna* is mutability itself, so there is deep irony in a drunkenness that dissolves or denies the ineluctable law of vicissitude. The particular diagnosis of Cleopatra's madness is therefore perfectly consonant with Horace's general indictment of persons who are philosophically adrift.

A corollary aspect of the poet's brief against the queen in her degenerate phase (narrative *a*) has to do with the concept of *kairos*. Time and timing are crucial to the notion of decorum, and the speaker carefully highlights this by his repeated emphasis on the scheduling of the celebration: *nunc; tempus erat;*[53] *antehac; dum*

(1–6). The poet and his companions know how to *defer* the celebration until the appropriate time, so that the choice of the sympotic moment seems virtually preordained by divine dispensation (there is a religious connotation in the notion of a prior taboo: *antehac nefas*). The tacit inference the reader draws from the contrasted celebration of the Egyptians is that it is premature and untimely as well as philosophically misguided. Since it is founded on a false premise (*spes longa*) that is profoundly opposed to the outlook of the *sapiens*, it can only generate a form of ineffectual "inebriation." In contrast to the "imbibing" of a Horace or an Alcaeus, which claims to reduce anxiety because it is ultimately grounded in the reality of death, the decadent drinking of the downgraded "other" leads to increased anxiety and a flight from reality. In this sense, Commager's acute observation that the *convivium* is "the Ode's articulating image" is precisely on target (Commager, 91, 94).

(b) fatale monstrum

Phase (*a*) of the narrative sequence terminates in the pejorative epithet *ebria*, which also marks the lowest point in the queen's spiritual existence. The succeeding phase, which comes to a ringing climax in the expression *fatale monstrum*, is characterized by an abatement of her *dementia* and thus represents a turning-point in the narrative. The words *sed minuit furorem* introduce an intermediate stage (*b*) in the transformation of Cleopatra's identity. Madness (*furor = dementia*) and its accompanying euphoria do not vanish abruptly, rather they go through a decrescendo (*minuit*) as she is gradually made to confront a fearful reality ("*veros* timores").

What is the reality that she has previously sought to avoid and that she is now obliged to face? Though the poet does not explicitly state it, it is patent that the specter of her imminent death is what induces "true fear" in the mind of the now sober queen. The agent of this confrontation with a bitter fortune that compels her to come to terms with her mortal destiny is none other than the *laudandus*, Caesar, whose name resoundingly appears at the beginning of line 16. If we recall that, within the moral universe of Horatian lyric, acceptance of death is the *sine qua non* of a healthy existence, we are in a better position to see Cleopatra's conversion in proper perspective. A change of fortune, which has been aptly compared to the reversals typical of tragic drama, has brought about an Aristotelian peripety and with it a belated acquisition of insight (cf. Leeman [1965] 1985). What needs to be stressed in this peripety, however, is the *content* of the newly acquired insight. Succinctly put, it is identical with the fundamental insight that grounds Horatian *sapientia*—the unqualified acknowledgement, emotional as well as intellectual, of one's mortality.

From this angle of vision, Cleopatra's "moment of truth" is interconnected, in a non-trivial way, with the philosophical substratum of the ideal *convivium*. The rehabilitation of the degraded symposiast, moreover, is seen to rest not on a romantic whim on the part of a capricious poet, but on a eulogistic platform that projects Octavian in the role of transformer and the queen of Egypt in the role of enlightened opponent. Since the latter's enlightenment is entirely owing to her adversarial relationship to Caesar, her transfiguration thereby implicitly redounds to his credit.

The ennoblement of the vanquished takes place on several levels, not the least of which is the stylistic. The entire ode is composed in the grand manner, which some scholars have correctly viewed as an imitation of Pindaric discourse.[54] In addition to the "Pindarizing" narrative structure and manner, an epic coloration is injected into the poem in the segment that describes the pursuit of Cleopatra by Octavian. As the standard commentaries have amply documented, the simile that compares pursuer and pursued to hawk and dove has a Homeric provenance that is not without significance for the status of the belligerents in Horace's theater. The borrowed simile brings the pursuit of Cleopatra into intertextual play with the famous scene of the pursuit of Hector by Achilles in the *Iliad* (22.139–42). One obvious effect of the allusion, as Pöschl (1970) and others have pointed out, is to assimilate Octavian to the heroic figure of Achilles. No less important for the speaker's encomiastic strategy, however, is the corresponding (implicit) ennoblement of the adversary, Cleopatra. The similes upgrade both pursuer and pursued: the vanquished shares willy-nilly in the elevated ambiance of the victor.[55]

What, it is reasonable to inquire, does the proclaimed *laudator Caesaris* gain from a symmetrical elevation of the antagonists, especially in light of his former *derogation* of the queen in the *dementia* phase of the narrative? The answer is neither obscure nor over-

subtle. As warrior, the victor can only increase in stature and re-
nown if his opponent is portrayed as worthy of his prowess. From
this vantage point, the heroization of the queen is *logically* exigent
at the rhetorical level. It becomes nothing less than a poetic masterstroke when that heroization is presented, not merely as logically
compelling, but as a necessary consequence of the victor's trans-
forming presence. The full implications of the transfiguration can
now be restated even more trenchantly. In the conversion narrative
of Horace's ode, the degenerate becomes regenerate through the
agency of the *laudandus,* and the praise of the vanquished has the
effect of redoubling the praise of the victor.

The intermediate narrative phase (pursuit) ends with a cryptic
locution that has been universally admired for its epigrammatic
force—*fatale monstrum.* This intriguing phrase has been interpreted
in many different ways, both malign and benign. The substantive
monstrum, in particular, has suggested to some that Cleopatra is
here reduced to something less than human. If my general account
of Horace's gradual ennoblement of Caesar's adversary is valid,
then we should ascribe a neutral, or at least a non-pejorative, connotation to *monstrum* in this particular narrative context. The appellation, by this reading, makes Cleopatra not subhuman, but, inversely, transhuman. As a "portent" (the original denotation of
monstrum),[56] she acquires something of a numinous character, and
the modifier *fatale* points to her exalted role as an instrument of
destiny. In a word, the climactic designation *fatale monstrum* en-
dows the already heroized figure of Cleopatra with an additional,
quasi-impersonal and preternatural aura. As such, she begins to
approximate the cosmic status of some of the adversarial figures
that appear in the mythical Titanomachia—*monstra* who are no
mean opponents of the Olympian gods and whose subjugation is
a prerequisite for a civilized order.[57]

(c) *non humilis mulier*

However numinous the queen may appear to have become as a
result of her change into a *monstrum,* she still retains her all-too-
human susceptibility to *mors aequa.* Her suicide, which at one level
may be viewed as her attempt to control the timing and manner of
her demise, occupies the concluding phase (c) of the narrative. The

transition from pursuit (*b*) to suicide (*c*) is formally engineered by
devices that are conventional in Pindaric narration. Thus the employment of the relative pronoun to introduce the figure who will
be the focus of the ensuing anecdote parallels standard Pindaric
praxis in relation to mythical exempla (Bundy, 8). The formal function of Horace's *quae* is even more pronounced in context because
of its grammatical relation to its antecedent in a *constructio ad sen-
sum* (*monstrum; quae*). Also Pindaric, perhaps, is the simultaneous
deployment of a transitional signpost first identified as such by
Bundy—the *thauma* ("marvel") motif. If something of the notion of
the miraculous may adhere to the word *monstrum* (as Virgil's quasi-
formulaic epic phrase *mirabile monstrum* tends to suggest),[58] the
narrator may be signaling the end of the pursuit segment with a
climactic marvel that has a superhuman origin (cf. *fatale*) (Bundy,
3). In short, quite apart from their actual or supposed connotations
as characterizations of Cleopatra, the words *monstrum* and *quae*
may also constitute formal counters in a narrative tactic that the Roman poet absorbed from his great Greek predecessor. The adoption of Pindaric conventions at this juncture helps to bracket the
next and final stage of the narrative as containing matter analogous
to legendary, heroic paradigm. By these means the suicide episode
is imbued with the quality of a myth *in statu nascendi.*

Certain facets of Cleopatra's mythic exploits—if I may refer to
the denouement of the ode in these heroic terms—expand and
ramify the theme of a transfiguration. Salient among these is her
metaphorical manliness, which the narrator brings into prominence with the clause "*nec muliebriter* expavit ensem." The topos of
her courage as contradictory to her identity *qua* female does more
than attest to the routine chauvinism of late Republican society.
Rhetorically, it accomplishes the purpose of further upgrading
Rome's antagonist by encoding her transcendence of fear in terms
of gender transgression (Augustus's opponent is no ordinary
woman but a masculine female). A newly acquired fearlessness (cf.
veros timores and *nec . . . expavit*) is attributed to a female figure
whose very femininity is erased or denied at that point in the story
where she becomes an exemplum of a kind of ethical *aretē.* The
transsexual persona, figuratively speaking, is part and parcel of
the overall strategy to convert the queen into a worthy adversary of
the *laudandus,* Caesar. As such, she exhibits the *audacia* (cf. *ausa*

est) and serenity (cf. *voltu sereno*) required by her role as regenerate royalty who stages her own death drama in noble terms.

In the semiotics of her metaphorical transformation, Cleopatra is redefined not only as male but also as a brave warrior.[59] The latter incarnation is connoted by the epithets *fortis* and *ferox,* which are ascribed to her in the death scene (lines 26, 29). To be sure, the action she is represented as committing—suicide by snake venom[60]—does not take place on the battlefield; but the narrator imparts a bellicose shading to her conduct and attitude, especially in the final stanza, where she is styled "deliberata morte *ferocior,"* and where the ships of her victorious adversary are dubbed *saevis* (line 30). As "male warrior" she can, with greater cultural credibility, be permitted to deprive Octavian of one feather in his capacious cap without thereby subverting the latter's primary glory as proud *triumphator.*

The justly famous expression *non humilis mulier* ("no mean woman") that crowns the last line of the ode is paradoxical in a way that corroborates the main argument of the narrative as a whole. On the one hand, the word *mulier* seems to reinstate a female identity that has been previously taken away (or at least downgraded) in the adverbial phrase *nec muliebriter.* The reinstatement of womanhood, however, is accompanied by the litotes *non humilis* (= *generosa*), which suggests that the queen has fully recuperated the status of *generositas*—the very status that she had sought to regain in the first place by surmounting her "womanly" fear ("quae generosius perire *quaerens* nec muliebriter . . ."). The appositional phrase *non humilis mulier,* then, operates as a self-fulfilling prophecy on two levels, internal and external. Internally, it provides the *telos* that Cleopatra has aimed to bring about by suicide (she reestablishes her nobility);[61] externally, it functions as a performative insofar as it helps to shape for posterity the very Cleopatra legend of which Horace's splendid ode is a primary source. The poet's encomium assures the *kleos* of Cleopatra.[62]

The closing word of the ode, *triumpho,* brings us back, ringwise, to the opening prescription in which the speaker and his *sodales* are urged to celebrate the fall of the queen. Is there an organic connection between the elaborate Cleopatra narrative and the inaugural theme of conviviality—besides the superficial one that the death provides the official pretext for the party? The answer, I believe, is unequivocally in the affirmative. Horace's complex portrayal of a transfigured adversary is a sophisticated fusion of convivial and encomiastic motifs. While the ennoblement of Cleopatra serves to promote Octavian in the indirect ways I have demonstrated, her demise also gives depth and meaning to the *convivium*, which, after all, has its metaphysical justification in the very notion of ineluctable death. Cleopatra's fate serves, inter alia, to remind lesser mortals of the non-discriminatory nature of *mors* (even queens and tyrants must die).

In his unforgettable portrayal of the queen's act of suicide, the poet wittily insinuates a convivial metaphor:

> fortis et asperas
> tractare serpentis, ut atrum
> corpore *combiberet* venenum

even so bold as to handle venomous snakes, *in order to drink up* with her whole body the dark poison

This conspicuous use of the drinking trope—"the Ode's articulating image"—runs the risk of an irony that borders on the macabre (cf. Commager, 91). By investing Cleopatra's action in this figurative garb, however, Horace subtly pays his subject the ultimate compliment in poetic transfiguration: the nobility of her end is symbolized for all time in a gesture that "incorporates" sympotic activity.

Epilogue

> The reason I have decomposed sonata form into a set of dif-
> ferent forms is not to saddle us with a more complex tax-
> onomy, but to make possible a more flexible approach to
> history. We must beware of taking any of these forms as a
> kind of real presence behind the individual examples.
>
> Charles Rosen, *Sonata Forms*

The itinerary of *Polyhymnia* has encompassed some major rhetorical sites (modes) in the ample and multi-layered terrain of the *Carmina*. Since my visits (and, in some cases, revisits) to these sites
have involved both close inspections and more distanced viewings,
any final attempt on my part to contrive a panoramic view of the
area I have traversed would be, in the nature of the case, both self-
defeating and redundant. In place of a summarizing conclusion,
then, I shall briefly reformulate a few of the principles that have
guided my interpretations, while casting retrospective glances here
and there at earlier formulations.

A study devoted to rhetorical analysis in the widest sense of the
term deserves to be clarified by a compact priamel of its own. All
discursive choices, whether inscribed in critical or literary texts, ipso
facto exclude. By choosing to focus on select rhetorical strategies, I
have deliberately and inevitably set aside, as peripheral to my main
enterprise, many competing perspectives derived from strictly extraliterary contexts—political, social, historical, biographical. Other
scholars of the *Odes* have made successful excursions, some bold,
others tentative, into domains that lie beyond the boundaries of my
project (cf. Pöschl 1956; Johnson 1967; Habinek 1986; Murray 1985;
Woodman and West 1984). Such efforts to bring extrinsic contexts
into play in the explication of Horatian lyric have proved most productive, in my view, when they implicitly pay heed to strictures
best articulated by the late Sir Ronald Syme, who in two of his
more recent works carefully reminded his readers of the hazards of

using literary texts—including Horace's *Odes*—for the purpose of historical and social documentation (Syme 1986, 382–402; 1978). In a very important sense, therefore, the strong claim that sustains my account of Horatian lyric—that paradigmatic analysis of lyric motifs is a prerequisite to an adequate linear reading of individual odes—is not intended to be totalistic. The rhetorical level of analysis is best regarded as potentially complementary to, rather than a substitute for, other axes of interpretation (cf. Abrams 1953, 3–29). Without diluting the strength of this qualification, however, I have maintained throughout my exegeses that unless the underlying codes shaping the lyric discourse are taken into account, inferences about the poet's relationship to the real world are likely to be ill-founded (see chapter 2 above on the credibility of autobiographical *mythos*). How many hoary handbooks of Latin literature, I have often mused, have invented lost epic poems on the basis of a literal reading (or rather misreading) of the rhetorical foils of generic disavowals?

It is axiomatic that persuasion is the ulterior motive of rhetoric. The individual readings I have conducted have paid as much attention to the "what" as to the "how" of Horatian lyric argument. A leitmotif of the foregoing chapters has been the philosophical outlook immanent in the text—the system of values that the lyric speaker promotes (with a degree of consistency that is far from trivial). Whether he is subtly assimilating generically alien matter and manner (see chapter 1) or overtly manipulating the conventions of encomium and invection (see chapter 4), the lyric singer frequently reaffirms an ethos that may be concisely summed up in the deceptively simple term *conviviality*.

The repeated advocacy of this convivial ethos, I need hardly re-emphasize, is far more complex (and certainly less complacent) than it may sometimes appear in a superficial reading: it is deeply rooted in an epistemological subtext that is material to the lyric argument—whether that argument is highly condensed and figurative (see chapter 2 on the *Persicos odi*) or subject to extended elaboration (see chapter 3 on the *Tyrrhena regum*). In his "Two Essays concerning the Symbolic Representation of Time," the anthropologist Edmund Leach proposes a general dichotomy, in the way time is traditionally conceptualized in various cultures, between "repetitive" and "non-repetitive" models (E. R. Leach 1961, 125). This posited dichotomy becomes, in his exposition, the basis for the interesting hypothesis that

> all other aspects of time, duration for example or historical sequence, are fairly simple derivatives from these two basic experiences:
> (a) that certain phenomena of nature repeat themselves
> (b) that life change is irreversible.

Whether or not Leach's antithetical models can be proved to have universal validity, they are strikingly congruent with the motival syndrome I have described in chapter 3 above as scene and insight (where the former corresponds to oscillation [repetition] in nature, the latter to irreversibility [non-repetition] in human life). In developing the paradigm of *sapientia* in the figure of the mature symposiast, Horace makes the reader inescapably cognizant of the gap between these competing models. As we saw in the analysis of the nexus of convivial motifs in chapter 3, the *carpe diem* injunction is projected in part as a means of recognizing and, simultaneously, of bridging this existential gap: in the face of nature's reversibility and oscillation, the *sapiens*, by fully accepting his own irreversibility, undertakes to defy time by a gesture that valorizes the present at the expense of both past and future.

The kind of enlightened hedonism that is the ethical basis of the convivial gesture has many points of convergence with the "new hedonism" of Epicurus (De Witt 1954; Pöschl 1961). There is an undeniable basic affinity between the Epicurean desire to eliminate the fear of death by a rigorously materialist account of the universe and the Horatian (and traditional) lyric project of a full engagement in the present that is unencumbered by anxiety over a future beyond one's control. As an attempt to locate the philosophy that undergirds the lyric stance of the *Odes* within its contemporary intellectual milieu, the Epicurean label, if interpreted in a generously broad sense, has some measure of validity. Insofar as it suggests adherence to a school or orthodox credo, however, the label is potentially misleading. "Vixere fortes ante Agamemnona / multi" ("There were many brave men before Agamemnon": *C.* 4.9.25–26). Long before the vogue of a vulgar Epicureanism (figured and, in a sense, travestied in Horace's burlesque self-reference to a "pig from Epicurus's flock": *Epist.* 1.4.16), the Greek lyrists of the Archaic period, who were the poet's main poetic models, had refined an ethic that revalued the life-moment against a scene of vicissitude. Horace's reworking and further refinement of this pristine generic stance is arguably as much beholden to Archilochus's reflections on the "rhythm" of existence and to Alcaeus's sympotic argument as it is to historically more recent ethical premises and dogmas emanating from the Epicurean garden.

Throughout my presentation of the *Odes*, I have sought to document the sophisticated means by which the speaking subject—the lyric self—is constructed in the discourse, often against the backdrop of generic others (epic, elegiac, or iambic). The diversity of subsidiary lyric scaffoldings I have examined in various poems may appear to substantiate a contradictory impression—that of a plurality of lyric selves that, by implication, attest to the disintegration of a presumed univocal subject. My different contention, however, has been that such scaffoldings, though varied, tend to support cognitive edifices that provide coherence to the artistic persona.

As I have stated at more than one pivotal juncture in this study, the modes that serve as organizing principles (assimilation, authentication, consolation, praise and dispraise) are not intended to evoke taxonomic subgenres (see the cautionary words I have adopted as the epigraph to this chapter [Rosen 1988, vii–viii]). While consciously avoiding the sclerosis of rigid taxonomies, however, I have sought, by my regroupings and juxtapositions of poems, to validate a view of Horace's poetics that puts the issue of generic boundaries at the discursive center-stage. Of all the prerogatives claimed by the lyrist with the implicit connivance of the reader, that of generic versatility is among the most crucial. The reader who accepts the role of collusion demanded, for instance, in the poet's rhetorical aside to posterity, *credite posteri!* also accepts, and helps to legitimate, the transgression of boundaries that the speaker has already accomplished (see chapter 2 above). The self-conscious inscription of such acts of transgression in the text itself is best illustrated from the coda to the ode to Pollio (C. 2.1.37–40):

> Sed ne relictis, Musa procax, iocis
> Ceae retractes munera neniae
>   mecum Dionaeo sub antro
>   quaere modos leviore plectro.

But lest, O wanton Muse, you abandon playful topics and reproduce the poetic gifts of Cean [Simonidean] dirge, seek with me beneath Dione's grotto measures plucked with a lighter pick.

After nine strophes of an ode that engages in the "sincerest form of flattery"—quasi-involuntary imitation of the addressee's grandiloquent matter and manner—the very speaker who has already stretched lyric norms in the poem encodes his audacious transgression in a closing apostrophe that both restores light lyric and defends the transgeneric fait accompli. This witty reaffirmation of the lyric speaker's ultimate license to roam beyond the artificial thresholds of conventional genres and to return safely with the reader's secured assent may serve as a fitting note on which to close this investigation. The Muse whom Horace invokes in his inaugural poem under the Greek name Polyhymnia (she of many songs) stands, by my choice of title, as a comprehensive token for the Roman bard's ability to accommodate a variety of styles and generic dispositions without losing his sense of remaining an authentic composer of lyric song.

Notes

1. See the extensive treatment of the subject in Race 1982.

2. The sketch of an isolated drinker indulging himself in daylight near a fountain is tantalizingly ambiguous: on the one hand, drinking is an essential component of the ideal convivial life (eventually included in the "cap" of the priamel); on the other hand, it requires a social context—at least a gathering of like-minded *sodales*). Horace's sophistication consists in adding complexity to a set of foil terms that are usually either neutral or derogatory in toto.

3. For the Greek biographic tradition, consult Lefkowitz 1981. In the particular case of Horace, even apparently unimpeachable autobiographical passages in the *Satires* must be treated with circumspection (cf. Harrison 1987).

4. In this convention, the addressee is usually single and named. A notable exception is *Ep.* 13.3 where the circle of unnamed *amici* are harangued—an anomaly that spurred the great Housman to invent a friend of the poet named Amicius (cf. p. 260 n. 1 below).

5. On the other hand, an addressee name like Thaliarchus (*C.* 1.9) is patently fictitious, tailor-made to suit the sympotic context.

6. Consult Kristeva 1984, 59–61, where the vulgar sense is carefully distinguished from the technical (*inter-textuality:* the "transposition" of one sign system into another).

7. There is, in the nature of the case, irreconcilable dissension among scholars about the order of composition of various individual odes and epodes. Compounding the problem is the lack of philological consensus regarding general criteria for positing relative and absolute chronologies. The synchronic approach obviates the necessity for assuming other than gross relative chronologies for books of odes.

8. For a useful characterization of this aspect of Pindaric criticism, see Shankman 1988, with references therein cited.

9. Attempted reconstruction of conventions "from the inside out" suggests the careful alignment and synchronic analysis of motifs (the method of Bundy). An alternative method ("from the outside in") seeks to apply preexistent schemata and formulas gleaned from rhetorical handbooks to the poems (the method of Cairns 1972).

CHAPTER 1

1. Horace imitates the proem to *P.* 6 (especially lines 10–18) at *C.* 3.30. Cf. also Pindar fr. 177e (Snell). On the Hesiodic "Precepts of Cheiron," see M. L. West 1978, 23.

2. The words occur at the diaeresis that divides the iambelegus into two halves. The elegiac portion contains the word *puer*, which creates the effect of a diminuendo.

3. E.g., the phrase *subtemine Parcae* is to be compared with Catullus 64.327 (the refrain sung by the Parcae).

4. Heinsius had proposed *flavi*, which was rejected by both Bentley and Housman. The latter supported the conjecture *ravi* (Housman, 104–5). The sole grounds for emendation is the blatant clash with the Homeric epithet, *megas*.

5. Treu (1968, 82–112) has some pertinent observations on the limits of Homeric landscape description.

6. In this regard, the verbs *contraxit* and *deducunt* in the opening lines of the epode may acquire, in retrospect, philosophical-aesthetic connotations. *Deducere*, in particular, has resonances, in Horace and the Augustans, with literary predilections for non-elevated genres (*deductum* = *tenue:* see Conington and Nettleship 1898 *ad* Virgil *Ecl.* 6.5).

7. Pacuvius's play *Teucer*, for example, was extremely popular, particularly in the Ciceronian age. See the testimonia to fr. 380 (Warmington); Nisbet-Hubbard *ad* line 25.

8. For Teucer's claim to Trojan ancestry, see Virgil *Aen.* 1.625–26.

9. My classification of the poem as erotic lyric is not incompatible with Cairns's suggestion that the presumptive setting is sympotic (see Cairns 1977, 131).

10. The usually alert Commager here lapses momentarily when he regards the poet's advice in this ode as a "curious inversion of his own beliefs" on Horace's part, since the poem, as Pasquali has eloquently shown, is tongue-in-cheek from beginning to end (Commager, 305; Pasquali, 489–95). In the closing lines of the poem, the speaker is revealed as a far from disinterested member of an erotic triangle!

11. Pasquali, 492–93, discusses Alexandrian sources for detailed physiognomic descriptions of Homeric heroines. For abundant documentation of blond beauties in ancient literature, consult Pease 1935 *ad* Virgil *Aen.* 4.590. Cairns (1977, 133–34) makes the subtle point that Achilles' blondness is unique among the three heroes mentioned. In Homer, *xanthos* is used to describe other prominent figures such as Menelaus and Odysseus (see Pease *loc. cit.*).

12. I side with those commentators who construe the adverb *prius* with *insolentem* rather than with the main verb. For a discussion of the alternatives, consult Nisbet-Hubbard *ad loc. Insolens* may also connote "unaccustomed," as at *C.* 1.5.8, where a blond Pyrrha (cf. *flavam . . . comam*) enthralls an inexperienced young lover.

13. See LSJ s.v. τελαμών.

14. Ovid carries the trope to grotesque heights in his version of the Meleager story in *Met.* 8.445–525. For an extensive analysis of the tale, see Davis (1983a, 111–21). On the dialectical nature of the opposition of love and war, see ibid., 12–13. It is important to emphasize the tactical and purely relative nature of such oppositions. Horace is not above "contaminating" the two opposed spheres for humorous purposes—as, for example, in *Vixi puellas* (*C.* 3.26).

15. In this respect, our analysis has led us to a conclusion different from that of Cairns, for whom the assimilation takes place in the reverse direction—that is, Xanthias is upgraded (and put on a par with) Homeric heroes (see Cairns 1977, 134).

16. Though the ode is idiosyncratic in not containing a formal addressee, Horace may have intended it to be read as a sequel to the preceding (and no less enigmatic) poem, addressed to a *navis*. The idea of a linkage between these two adjacent odes has been re-proposed recently by Woodman (1980), who also argues in favor of W. S. Anderson's view that the ship in *C.* 1.14 is allegory for a woman (Anderson 1966). For an interpretation of the ship metaphor in *C.* 1.14 that depends on the premise of an underlying *recusatio*, see Zumwalt 1977–78; Davis 1989.

17. Cf. the strictures of Nisbet-Hubbard, 190. With similar consciousness of generic decorum, Nauck (*ad loc.*) cites Quintilian's assessment of Stesichorus: "epici carminis onera lyra sustinebat" ("with the lyre he bore the burden of epic song").

18. See the commentary of Wickham *ad loc.* In this respect Porphyrio gave disproportionate emphasis to Horace's putative debt to the lyric model of Bacchylides. On the possible influence of the latter's dithyramb involving a parainetic address of Cheiron, see Fraenkel, 66 n.6. For the text in question, consult Bacch. 27 (Snell-Maehler) (= *P Oxy* 2348 addendum).

19. The literal meaning of *carmina dividere* is an unresolved philological puzzle (see, e.g., Nisbet-Hubbard *ad loc.*). The expression may be interpreted to mean "share songs" in the sense of an amoebic exchange, in consonance with the picture we get in such odes as *C.* 1.17.17–20 (to Tyndaris) or *C.* 3.28.9–16 (to Lyde). This would assimilate Helen, the Tyndarid, to the standard *puellae* of Horace's love lyric—a move that further accentuates the irony in the portrayal of her lover as a lyre-player.

20. The occurrence of a trochee in the Aeolic base of the final line is at odds with Horace's usual practice of commencing with a spondee and has led some, since Lachmann, to hypothesize an early date for the ode (see Fraenkel, 191).

21. See Brink *ad Epist.* 2.1.257–59. The fact that the technical term *recusatio* is not ancient does not, of course, invalidate investigation of the actual form in all its variety.

22. Commentators have for the most part missed the point of the digression, which is an imitation of Pindar's use of the *thauma* motif in di-

gressions (cf. Bundy, 2–3). In the Latin text of this passage I depart from Wickham-Garrod in reading *Raetis* at line 17 (with Heinsius and Bentley, as against the *Raeti* of the MSS).

23. See Davis 1975, 81 n. 26.

24. For the evidence in support of the linkage of "Licymnia" with the speaker (rather than Maecenas), see Davis 1975.

25. Cf. Nisbet-Hubbard *ad C.* 1.6. The late Elroy Bundy referred to such pairs as "universalizing doublets." In modern linguistics they have been described under the heading of "complementaries": see Lyons 1968, 460; Palmer 1981, 94–97.

26. On the ramifications of the topos of Varius as an *alter Homerus*, see Davis 1987b.

27. The contrite pleader of *Ep.* 17.8–14 provides a corrective to this partial view of Achilles' stubbornness by portraying him as, precisely, capable of relenting, though obstinate: "movit nepotem Telephus Nereium. / . . . Unxere matres Iliae addictum feris / alitibus atque canibus homicidam Hectorem, / postquam relictis moenibus rex procidit / heu pervicacis ad pedes Achillei."

28. The impulse to deny the identity of the addressee as the poet Tibullus stems from trivial discrepancies, such as the fact that there is no *puella* code-named Glycera in the extant Tibullan corpus. The direct and indirect allusions in the ode to Tibullus's poetry, however, make the identification as probable as such things can be in the absence of external evidence.

29. Attempts to restrict the reference of the adverbial phrase *plus nimio* to the following *memor* are unlikely to succeed. The words apply equally well to the preceding verb, *doleas*.

30. See further Anderson, Parsons, and Nisbet 1979 apropos of the new Gallus fragment.

31. Cf. Virgil *Ecl.* 8.27–28. On the details of the Moschus parallel, see the discussion by Pasquali, 495–97.

32. Lycoris is cognate with many names in the *Carmina* that derive from *lykos*. As Nisbet and Hubbard point out, the nom de plume may be part of an elegiac convention that links the *puella* with the god Apollo, who of course has many cult epithets relating to *lykos* (cf. also Tibullus's Delia; Propertius's Cynthia).

33. On the social status of the name (which is attested for *meretrices*), see Bentley; Nisbet-Hubbard *ad loc.*

34. The danger of an attractive neighbor is also a motif in Moschos's "chain of love" (cf. n. 31 above).

35. Though the epithet *duram*, in apposition to *te*, is imagined as uttered by the ardent suitor and *vocare* consequently means "call" rather than "call upon," the ritualistic character of the phrase preceding the epithet is guaranteed by such hymnal parallels as *C.* 1.32.16 (*mihi vocanti*); and *C.* 1.30.2 (*vocantis te*).

36. Wickham tries to palliate the force of *adhuc* by contrasting it with

hactenus; Pasquali, however, perceives the obvious irony in even a purely temporal adverb: "Orazio pare voglia acquietare la donna sulla fedeltà dell'amante, ma le parole di consolazione finiscono in un *adhuc* di cattivo augurio: *frustra . . . integer;* sino a quando?" (Pasquali, 466).

37. Archilochus 19 W.

38. Cf. *C.* 1.23 (*Vitas inuleo*), where the name is also used of a young girl. Recall that Tibullus in *C.* 1.33 was apprehensive about being outshone by a younger rival (see pp. 39–40 above).

39. *Il.* 6.1.155 ff.; *N.* 4.57–62 (Snell). Some commentators aptly compare Horace's *mille vafer modis* (line 12) with Pindar's words on the guile of Hippolyta: δολίαις τέχναισιν (lines 57–58). There is, I submit, a complementary approximation to a Pindaric metaphor that, to my knowledge, has gone unnoticed: the phrase *maturare necem* (in the Bellerophon myth: line 16) imitating the botanical image of φύτευέ οἱ θάνατον (in the Acastus myth: line 59).

40. Consult Pasquali, 465, who cites, inter alia, Prop. 2.32.41, where heroic myths become *tantum stuprorum examen* ("so great a flock of paramours").

41. Cf. Hebrus in the Neobule ode, *C.* 3.12.6–12, where, in addition to bearing an exotic *Flußname*, the attractive male is described in language that closely duplicates the depiction of Enipeus (he is preeminent in athletics, including the obligatory swim in the Tiber, and is even compared in equestrian skill with Bellerophon!).

42. Some commentators allude to Augustan *sodalicia* in relation to Enipeus's athletic pursuits, but such passages as Tibullus 1.4.11–12 and *C.* 3.12.7–12 indicate, to my mind, that we are as much in the world of literary cliché as of historical referentiality.

43. The tidy, almost baroque, orderliness of the ode is carried through also into the subdivision of the main segments, e.g., segment (a) is partitioned into two halves by *non* and *nec* and into quarters by the *aut* in line 2 and the corresponding *aut* in line 6. Syndikus (p. 395) makes the imaginative suggestion that the structural order with its clearly defined boundaries is meant to contrast with the disorderliness of most elegiac effusions.

44. The verb *viduantur* may be imported from Virgil *Georgics* 4.518, where a wintry landscape forms a backdrop of pathetic fallacy for Orpheus's prolonged mourning—a detail that anticipates the more pointed allusion in the third stanza to Virgil's tale of woe. As is well known, the opening lines of *C.* 1.9 constitute a motto derived from Alcaeus 338 LP.

45. The topographical features in the examples here and in the final stanzas exhibit a curious concern for *poikilia;* hence the varied sequence: *agros; mare; oris; querceta; Niphatem* (mountain: see Nisbet-Hubbard *ad loc.*); *flumen; campis.* Note further that the first two items, *mare* and *agros,* form a complementary (on which see n. 25 above). The adjectives *hispidos* and *inaequales* are proleptic, as Nauck saw in the case of the former.

46. On Valgius's putative generic range in general, consult Schanz-Hosius, 172–73; Nisbet-Hubbard *ad loc.* The fact that the author of the

panegyric to Messalla proposes him as a potential epic bard says very little, in my opinion, about his actual range of production, given the frequency of the motif of the surrogate *laudator*. For an informative discussion of Valgius's distichs in relation to bucolic poetry as well as to neoteric epigoni, see Rostagni 1961, 405–27; Alfonsi 1943. Valgius's neoteric tastes are evident from the fragments (see Morel-Buechner, 135–36). For a bucolic version of (literary) *amores*, see the lines attributed by Virgil to Gallus at *Ecl.* 10.53–54: "tenerisque meos incidere amores / arboribus; crescent illae, crescetis, *amores*".

47. Mystes is attested in inscriptions as a servile name. See Nisbet-Hubbard *ad loc.*

48. See LSJ s.v. μύστης.

49. Detienne 1974 gives a persuasive ethnographic explanation of the motifs in Virgil's account.

50. *Ademptum* is probably to be understood as a euphemism for "dead"—a meaning that sits well with the allusions to the Orpheus myth (cf. also *C.* 2.4.10; Catullus 101.6; Nisbet-Hubbard *ad loc.*). The meaning "lost to a rival" was suggested by Quinn (1963), and ably defended by Anderson (1968), who also demolished once and for all the erroneous view (originating with Porphyrio) that the poem is to be classified as a *consolatio*.

51. See C. Valgius Rufus fr. 2 (Morel-Buechner); Alfonsi 1943, 243.

52. *Georgics* 3.1–48 (esp. 30–33); on which see Nisbet-Hubbard, 137.

53. The final cola of the ode, "intraque *praescriptum* Gelonos / *exiguis* equitare campis" are brilliantly economical in their double reference to literary and military-political topics. *Praescribere* is thickly associated with poetic activity: cf. Virgil *Ecl.* 6.11; Propertius 3.3.31 (where the parallel with Horace's metaphorical usage is precise); Ps-Tibullus 3.7.177–80 (in the context of Valgius's putative epic talents!): "non ego sum satis ad tantae praeconia laudis / ipse mihi non se *praescribat* carmina Phoebus. / est tibi, qui possit magnis se accingere rebus, / *Valgius*: aeterno proprior non alter Homero."

54. The modifier *lasciva*—a synonym of *procax* (playful)—focusses attention on the character of the Muse that the poet has been neglecting (cf. *lascivos amores* [C. 2.11.7]; *Musa procax* [C. 2.1.37]).

55. The *animus* that he readily gives over is the Latin equivalent of the Greek *thymos* (cf. Ovid's *fert animus* at *Met.* 1); as such, it is identical with the poet's will or inclination to reopen closed *amores*.

56. Cf. *C.* 3.7, where the context is also amatory.

57. On the expression in line 8, cf. Sappho 31.7–8 LP, imitated by Catullus 51.6–7.

58. Contamination is also the witty point of Ovid's *Militat omnis amans* (*Amores* 1.9).

59. Cf. Wickham *ad loc.*: "The lute implies that his love-songs are over as well as his loves."

60. See Williams 1969, 132–33. Bentley's famous emendation of *arcus* to *securesque* destroys the metaphor (the bow of Cupid) in favor of a too-literal

account of the fictive situation. A similar neglect of the figurative cast of the renunciation is apparent in Housman's efforts to improve on Bentley (Housman, 3–4).

61. See Fraenkel, 410–11, and cf. Kiessling-Heinze, 386; on the *recusatio* aspect of the poem, see Wimmel 1960, 268–71.

62. Even the circumspect Wickham, who is normally skeptical with respect to other female names, draws the line at Cinara on the grounds of "the personal feelings that seem to accompany its mention and . . . its recurrence among the reminiscences of the poet's life in the Epistle" (see Wickham, 376–77). A too-literal acceptance of Ligurinus informs the views of Shackleton Bailey (1982, 67–75).

63. *Rust.* 10.235–41: "Hispida ponatur cinara, quae dulcis Iaccho / Potanti veniat. . . ."

64. The word *liguritio* signifies "fondness for dainties." Consult L&S s.v. *liguritio;* Ernout-Meillet s.v. *lingo.*

65. Cf. *C.* 1.13.5–8; *Epp.* 11.8–10 and 14.1–8; Sappho 31 LP. The Sapphic echoes are subtly interpreted by Putnam 1986, 39–42.

66. Cf. Catullus's *lingua sed torpet* (51.9) in imitation of Sappho 31.9 LP.

67. Even the pose of the ex-*amator* is not new: already in the earlier *Quis multa gracilis* (*C.* 1.5), the wise, experienced speaker distances himself from a *puer* in a framework of ostensible renunciation.

68. See *Epist.* 1.19.23; 2.2.59 (on which see the exegesis of Brink).

69. The so-called First Pythiambic strophe (dactylic hexameter coupled with iambic dimeter) used by Archilochus, e.g., 193 W.

70. Archilochus 193 W; Sappho 31 LP.

71. Thus Shorey and Laing 1919 *ad loc.* Cf. discussion of *flebiles modi*, pp. 50–60 above).

72. Cf. "neque uno contenta" with Catullus 68.135: "uno non est contenta Catullo." Note that *Ep.* 11 shows the poet indulging unashamedly in a distraught "elegiac" mode. The opening plea is, in essence, quite similar to the *inertia* of *Ep.* 14: "Petti, nihil me sicut antea iuvat / scribere versiculos amore percussum gravi, / amore, qui me praeter omnis expetit / mollibus in pueris aut in puellis urere." Unlike most commentators, I understand *versiculos* as a narrower reference to the *Epodes*, rather than to poetry in general.

73. On the iconography of vases ostensibly depicting the poet Anacreon, see Frontisi-Ducroux and Lissarrague 1983, an illuminating study that argues for their generic, rather than particular, signification. I owe this reference to an astute and erudite former colleague, the late Jack Winkler.

74. Cf. Cairns 1978, 549–50. The orthodox position has been vigorously challenged by Nisbet-Hubbard, 203.

75. MacKay 1962; Nisbet-Hubbard *loc. cit.*

76. Brink *ad Ars poetica* 79; cf. Davis 1987a apropos of the hypothetical disavowal of *iambi* in the *Integer vitae.* On the stock character of Archilochus's opponents, such as "Lycambes," and their thinly veiled symbolic

meaning, see Dover 1964, 181–212; West 1974, 25–27; Nagy 1979, 243–52.

77. See the penetrating discussion of the connotations of the verb *recantare* in Daube 1974.

78. *Pap. Colon.* inv. 7511, lines 7–8. Cf. Marcovich 1975 *ad* line 7 for documentation of the topos. For other possible allusions to the Cologne epode in Horace (primarily in the *Epodes* rather than in the *Odes*), see Henrichs 1980, 16–17, with literature cited therein.

CHAPTER 2

1. If such coincidence were demonstrable by evidence extrinsic to the poem, it would not necessarily be relevant to the analysis of the rhetoric. The need for caution, if not a healthy agnosticism, in such matters is cogently argued by Griffith 1983 in relation to Hesiod's pastoral *bios*. Even Horace's autobiographical experiences as recounted in *S.* 1.4. are mediated through a literary prism (see E. W. Leach 1971).

2. *Pace* Kiessling and Heinze, who see modesty and discretion in the fact that Horace only states his presence in Elysium as a member of the audience. Modesty on the topic of poetic immortality is, however, a most un-Horatian virtue.

3. Commentators cite parallels in diction with *Ep.* 3 without fully exploring the literary ramifications of the self-imitation.

4. The most recent comprehensive study of the priamel is Race 1982; for seminal insights into the nuances of the form, see the earlier work of Bundy, passim.

5. The association of acceptance of mortality with a fundamental "lyric" stance is elaborated on pp. 155–60.

6. Cf. *C.* 1.17.13; 3.4.6–7; 1.24.11.

7. Horace, of course, would have had access to far more Lesbian melic verse than is available to us.

8. *Plenius* is a stylistic term; *queror*, as used by the Augustan poets, primarily connotes, in addition to an aggrieved tone, unrequited love and the *genus tenue*.

9. The stated preference for intimate as opposed to public themes is, however, a topos of the *recusatio* (generic disavowal); cf. such motifs as "quid Tiridaten terreat, unice securus" (*C.* 1.26.5–6). The controversy over the referent of *illis* is, in my judgment, somewhat misguided. The stanza is obviously summational and *illis* may refer to both types of *melos*—the whole (bifurcated) gamut of Lesbian lyric. Of course, grammatically the demonstrative should point to the more remote of the two (the former: Sappho); but as we have been contending, Horace is not judging a poetry contest but reformulating the tradition for his own purposes.

10. *Recreare* is a laudatory term in such a context, as is proved by its use in reference to the effect of the Muses' song on the *princeps* in *C.* 3.4.37–40. The motif of the lyric audience that includes Cerberus and certain un-

derworld *impii* (Ixion, Tityos, Danaids) occurs also in the hymn to Mercury, *C.* 3.11.13–24.

11. Alcaeus 428 LP; Anacreon 202 (Gentili).

12. Cp. Nisbet-Hubbard *ad* line 9. The purely humorous aspect of Horace's treatment derives, at least partially, from Aristophanes' frequent denigration of the *rhipsaspis* in several of his comedies (see Dover's commentary on *Clouds*, line 353).

13. I side with those who interpret the phrase *turpe solum tetigere mento* as portraying death, rather than supplication.

14. Cf. *fregi* (7): *fracta* (11); *celerem* (9): *celer* (13); *[sus]tulit* (14): *tulit* (16); *militiae* (2): *militia* (18); *coronatus* (7): *coronas* (24).

15. For the conception of the laurel as distinctive of bards, see Kambylis 1965, 18–23. Cf. also *C.* 4.2.9: *laurea donandus Apollinari* (apropos of Pindar). The distinction between tree and leafage (the fourth and second declensional forms of *laurus*) is, for the purposes of symbolic association, irrelevant.

16. If Zielinski's restoration of the name Hermes in Archilochus 95 W is accepted (consult the *app. crit.*, ibid., on line 4), Horace's salvation at the hands of Mercury has an archaic lyric (no less than quasi-Homeric) antecedent.

17. "*Brutum* antiqui *gravem* dicebant" (Festus 28.33: cf. Ernout-Meillet s.v. *brutus*).

18. Cf. Virgil *Ecl.* 6.5 (*deductum . . . carmen*). A thorough discussion of the connotations of the phrase in Augustan poetry is to be found in Eisenhut 1961. See the discussion above of *Ep.* 13, line 2 (*deducunt*).

19. The compatibility of warfare and makeshift symposium is also, in my judgment, the main point of the much controverted Archilochus 1 W (on which see Webster [1959] 1961, 30).

20. See Wickham's perceptive remark *ad C.* 1.1.32–4: "The two instruments are intended to include all varieties of lyric poetry." For the opposite (but related) motif of the commingling of the two types of instrument on special laudatory occasions, see *C.* 4.1.22–24; *Ep.* 9.5–6; Pindar *O.* 10.93–94.

21. Sappho 1 LP. Aphrodite's epiphany is there subtly represented in the "hypomnesis" (reminder portion) of the hymn (lines 5–24), which retells the past as generic blueprint for the present.

22. Rhetorically motivated theophanies of this kind are parodied in Aristophanes' *Clouds*, 291–95 (referred to by Syndikus, 53 n. 21).

23. Alcman's λίγηα is equivalent to the Latin *acris; acuta*. Bowra 1961, 29, discusses this fragment in relation to two others that invoke the Muse Calliope (14a; 27 *PMG*). Cf. Stesichorus 240 *PMG*.

24. I have reprinted the text as it appears in Wickham-Garrod, though the words *limen Apuliae* are almost certainly corrupt. Those modern philologists (including the most recent Teubner editors) who endorse the hoary MS reading *limina Pulliae* (where Pullia is incongruously supposed to be the name of Horace's nurse) are guilty of a fetishism that ignores thematic

and stylistic decorum (e.g., Borzsak 1984; Shackleton Bailey 1985). Cf. also the discussion of the passage in Fraenkel, 274–75.

25. On the literary-generic signification of the wolf in the symbolic universe of the *Integer vitae*, see Davis 1987a.

26. For the ambitious connotations of *animosus*, see C. 2.10.21.

27. The third incident involving near shipwreck is unmentioned elsewhere and is probably a rhetorical filler (see the literature thereon in Syndikus, 60, with n. 60).

28. For documentation of the topos, see Nisbet-Hubbard *ad* C. 2.6.1.

29. This facet is clear from the epithets Horace assigns to the geographical items: *ultimi; remotis; extremum.*

30. Cf. the globalizing function of the motif in C. 1.22.5–8 and 17–22.

31. Fraenkel, 199–201, vacillates somewhat between the two positions, but finally steers towards the believers. An Augustan parallel to Horace's vision is Virgil *Ecl.* 10.26, where the speaker claims to have seen Pan (*quem vidimus ipsi*).

32. In addition to the obvious Euripidean allusions noted by most commentators, cf. Pratinas 708 *PMG*, lines 3–5.

33. So (and rightly) Pöschl 1970, 167, with literature cited therein.

34. Cf. Commager, 326–28.

35. Kilpatrick 1969, 222–24, makes the interesting proposal of understanding *hunc sacrare* to mean *hunc honorem sacrare*. For poetic *honores* (*timai*), cf. Pindar *I.* 1.34; *N.* 9.10; *O.* 1.100–103; for an apt Horatian parallel, see Davis 1983b, 16, apropos of C. 3.2.18: *intaminatis . . . honoribus.*

36. There is a similar interchangeability of fountain and wreath in Lucretius 1.927–30—an acknowledged source for Horace's Lamia ode: "iuvat integros accedere *fontis* / atque haurire, iuvatque novos decerpere flores / insignemque meo capiti petere inde *coronam* / unde prius nulli velarint tempora musae" ("I take delight in approaching pure *fountains* and drinking from them; delight also in plucking fresh flowers and seeking an illustrious *wreath* for my head from a place whence the Muses have never before garlanded the temples of any person"). In this light the epithet *novis*, as applied to *fidibus*, probably does not, as some have supposed, imply that Horace is here carrying out a novel experiment in Alcaics, rather that he is celebrating a "fresh" theme in eulogizing Lamia.

37. On voluntative futures—a much-overlooked feature of ancient rhetorical practice—see Slater 1969; Davis 1983b, 24. Kilpatrick 1969, taking the future literally, sees the Lamia ode as containing a promise fulfilled in the following poem, C. 1.27.

38. In the phrase *in mare Creticum*, Horace may also be alluding to the well-worn heroic topos of the storm at sea, since the epithet *Cretan* is stereotypically employed to signify "proverbially stormy sea" (cf. Wickham *ad loc.*).

39. Cf. also C. 3.19.1–8; Callimachus *Aetia* 15–16 (Pfeiffer) (dismissing Massagetae and Medes); Nisbet-Hubbard *ad* C. 1.38.1. For a possible parallel in Alcaeus (the evidence is inconclusive), see Treu 1949.

40. Tedium is suggested by the anaphoric repetition of *quis . . . quid.*

41. In line 6 I read *cura* with Bentley—an emendation that has not gained the acceptance it merits. See further Nisbet-Hubbard *ad loc.;* Fraenkel, 297 n. 4.

42. See R. Reitzenstein 1963, 15–17; Nisbet-Hubbard, 422–23; for the contrary position (in favor of symbolism), see, e.g., Fraenkel, 297–99; Syndikus, 340–42.

43. On the other hand, Brink *ad loc.* reads the crown as given in compensation for poetic merit.

44. See documentation in Gow-Page, *HE,* 2: 593–97, apropos of *Anth. Pal.* 4.1; also Nisbet-Hubbard *ad C.* 1.26.7 (*flores*); Keller-Holder *ad* line 8 (*coronam*).

45. E.g., Philodemus: *Anth. Pal.* 11.35 (= Gow-Page, *GP* 3302–9); Nicaenetus 6 (Powell); cf. Hendrickson 1918, 32–41; Cairns 1979, 18–21.

46. Both Commager, 117–18, and Fraenkel, 299, rightly regard Horace's vociferous disavowal of elaborate poems as ironic and (partly, at least) insincere.

47. Sappho 55 LP, 2–3; see Kambylis 1965, 174.

48. Hendrickson 1918, 39, apropos of *C.* 1.38.

49. See references in note 42 above.

50. Cf. *Dionaeo sub antro* (*C.* 2.1.39); *sub lauru mea* (*C.* 2.7.19); *sub umbra* (*C.* 1.17.22; 1.32.1).

51. For the distinction between *illocutionary* and *perlocutionary* (often confused), see Lyons 1977, 730–32.

52. Cf. Pindar *O.* 1.1 ff.; Sappho 96.6–9 LP; Alcman 1.319–43 *PMG.*

53. See the strictures of Richard Reitzenstein (1963, 89, n. 2). When Horace refers to a festival, this is usually an explicit part of the poem's scaffolding.

54. For the ethnographic significance of the kid's burgeoning horns ("outcrop of the life-substance"), consult Onians 1951, 237–39, who actually cites the ode in illustration.

55. Cf. Kambylis 1965, 23–30.

56. Fries 1983 contains a thorough analysis of Horace's catalogue in relation to the Alexandrian canon of Pindar's works.

57. See Syndikus, 302 nn. 38 and 39; Gow 1950 *ad* Theocr. 1.146.

58. Cf. Varro *Rust.* 3.16.4: *aptissimum . . . ad mellificium thymum.*

59. See Fränkel, 323 (with n. 38); for testimonia consult Simonides 88 *PMG;* further discussion in Oates 1932, 99–100.

60. Cf. *Epist.* 1.19.44, where the context suggests that the expression was a contemporary platitude.

61. Bentley's contention that *plurimum* is to be construed with *laborem* in the idiomatic sense of "dense" is, in my opinion, decisive.

62. E.g., *O.* 1.97–108; *P.* 1.46–50. On the variety and function of Pindaric "vaunts," see Race 1982, passim.

63. The text of line 49 is a notorious crux. *Terque* (Pauly's emendation, adopted by Wickham-Garrod) is not a completely satisfactory remedy for

the *teque* of the MSS. See *apparatus criticus* in the edition of Shackleton Bailey (1985).

64. Cf. Simonides 605 *PMG*; Syndikus, 308. The metaphor may also be drawing on the association of the Triumphator with Sol-Jupiter, on which see Versnel 1970, 63 and 295–96.

65. See Kiessling-Heinze *ad loc.* on the trochaic rhythm of the cited salutation.

66. Despite the discrepancy in syllabic quantity, *vitulus* may conceal a fanciful folk-etymological play on *vitulor*. See Ernout-Meillet: "être en fête à la suite d'une victoire" (with references cited).

67. For the topos of the small sacrifice as literary signifier, see Cairns 1979, 21, with references cited therein. Cf. Horace *C.* 2.17.32: "nos *humilem* feriemus agnam." Of course, a *vitulus* is not per se a humble offering, but it is so *relative* to the hecatomb of mature animals. In terms of stages of maturation in cattle as the Romans perceived it, the lexical sequence is: *vitulus* → *iuvencus* → *taurus* → *vetulus* (the authority is Varro *Rust.* 2.5.6).

68. See Servius *ad* Virgil *Georgics* 2.146.

69. Moschus 2.84–88. Cf. Homer *Il.* 23.454–55 (on which Moschus may be partly dependent); see chapter 1, n. 34, above on Horace's familiarity with other passages in Moschus.

70. Some modern poets have even chosen to retain and enlarge such standard classical emblems as the source; cf. Denise Levertov's poems "The Fountain" and "The Well" (Levertov 1961, 55 and 38–39).

CHAPTER 3

1. Because of an apparent discrepancy in respect to the number of addressees of the ode (line 3: *amici*; line 6: *tu*), several eminent textual critics from Bentley on have sought to homogenize Horace's vocatives through emendation. Housman's ingenious *Amici,* for instance, has recently been revived in the text of the Stuttgart Teubner (see Shackleton Bailey's *app. crit.* for other conjectures). Is there a cogent reason why Horace, in a paradigmatic *CD* poem addressed to nameless *sodales*, should not proceed to single out an individual banqueter as representative of the group—especially since the designated person is asked to perform the temporary role of *sommelier?*

2. The use of the death motif as stimulus to more intense engagement in life's pleasures is not, of course, confined to literature. For a striking ancient parallel from the visual arts, see Brendel [1934] 1980.

3. Gombrich 1960, esp. ch. 5, "Formula and Experience" (147 ff.).

4. *C.* 1.4.1; 4.7.3. I have elsewhere used the term *motif signal* to refer to a quasi-formulaic phrase that marks a recurrent motif (Davis 1968).

5. Alcaeus 338 LP.

6. Failure to recognize this crucial *CD* motif has led some of the standard commentators to confess bewilderment over the pertinence of the *qui*

clause (e.g., Nisbet-Hubbard: "this relatively unimportant manifestation of divine omnipotence"). The sequence of motifs is, in fact, closely paralleled in Archilochus 130 W (complete with alternation motif). The alternation is framed in Horace's variant by what Bundy called a "land-sea doublet" and what modern linguists call a "complementary"—on which see pp. 163–67.

7. This interpretation of *nunc* is airily dismissed by Fraenkel (225 n. 30). For a persuasive recent defense of *nunc* as referring to the time of speaking, see Vessey 1985, 36. Don Cameron in an unpublished article understands the verb *repetere* in the prescription of line 20 to denote "recall to mind"—a reading that imparts to the last two stanzas the perspective of a mature speaker recalling the past pleasures of youth as an antidote to present reminders of death.

8. I have placed a period after *diem* where Wickham-Garrod punctuates with a colon.

9. I have favored the MS variant *pius* over against *pater* (Wickham-Garrod).

10. Cf. the similar exclusion in C. 1.9.13–14; 3.8.27–28; Theognis 1047–48.

11. Cf. Alcaeus 347 and 338 LP (midsummer and midwinter respectively, employed as foil).

12. The MS variant *urit* is, in my view, more congruent, as a figure, with the ironies of the situation than *visit* (Wickham-Garrod and most editors). Vulcan's ardor is (from the vantage point of a *CD* model) conspicuously misdirected, flaming forge replacing libidinal fires. His spouse, Venus, makes no such transference.

13. See Searle 1969, 54–71; Lyons 1977, 725–53; Levinson 1983, 236–78.

14. Against Wickham-Garrod and the two recent Teubner editions, I side with those earlier editors who regard *fabulaeque* as a corruption.

15. Similar illocutionary force may well be present in Sappho 55 LP, where a list of blessings in the hereafter, from which the addressee is to be excluded, may have been intended as a warning rather than a straightforward dismissal.

16. E.g., Williams 1969, 104; Wickham *ad loc.*: "the purpose of this Ode can only be guessed." The recognition of the latent complementary helps to demystify the passage.

17. On the relevance of Peripatetic doctrine on this score consult Nisbet-Hubbard *ad loc*. As is well known, Horace's epithet *aurea* ("golden") is not an original Aristotelian locution.

18. Although the text is uncertain in lines 1–4, it is clear that the poet is addressing his *thumos* in line 1, and putting forward a strategy for transcending cares that seem ineluctable (see the discussion in Fränkel, 143).

19. The extent to which Horace's lyric, no less than his iambic, poetry is dependent on Archilochean antecedents needs to be more fully recognized by students of the *Odes*.

20. Cf. the unrestrained celebrations on the return of Numida (C. 1.36) and on the anniversary of the poet's escape from the tree (C. 3.8).

21. Cf. C. 1.27.1–4: "Natis in usum laetitiae scyphis / pugnare Thracum est: tollite barbarum / morem, verecundumque Bacchum / sanguineis prohibete rixis" ("To fight with wine cups created to serve our enjoyment is a Thracian habit: away with so rude a custom and defend Bacchus, who knows shame, from bloody brawls").

22. Cf. fr. 120 W: συγκεραυνωθείς (= *attonitus*).

23. Williams 1969 perceives the humor of the poet's assumed prerogative. On the banter regarding proportions of water to wine see the commentaries of Nauck and Orelli *ad loc.;* cf. also Page 1955, 309.

24. Pöschl 1970, 205.

25. The reading *Pater* (Wickham-Garrod: *pater*) follows Shackelton Bailey's Teubner text.

26. Hesiod *Erga* 582–88; Alcaeus 347 LP.

27. This archaic connotation (adopted by Horace) is attested by the grammarian Festus. The verb *involvo*, in turn, though routinely interpreted as referring to the act of "wrapping" oneself in a cloak, may also equally well apply to the book-roll (*volumen*, cognate with *volvo*). The latter nuance, if intended, would playfully preserve the etymological figure in *resigno*.

28. On the significance of the navigational trope in Horace and the Augustans, see Kambylis 1965, 149–55; Lieberg 1969; Davis 1989.

29. Those who persist in rejecting the identification of the addressee as the poet Virgil are forced to ignore or dismiss the intertextual evidence (consult the impressive list of allusions to Virgil's poetry compiled by Bowra 1928). For a succinct defense of the identification, see Perret 1964, 142–44.

30. Cf. Becker 1963; Syndikus, 400; Pasquali, 331–36. The point is not a trivial one: if this is a spring poem, then the connection with the *convivium* (prefigured in *sitim*) will appear both unexpected and inorganic (as it does in Williams 1968, 121–24).

31. Horace, like Virgil (*Ecl.* 6.78), probably follows the branch of the mythographic tradition that makes Philomela (not Procne) the mother of Itys, and the bird she becomes the nightingale (rather than the swallow).

32. According to a contemporary folk-etymology, the name Philomela is derived from *melos* (song) and *philein* (love). It is not implausible that both Horace and Virgil exploited the "melic" wordplay (the patent invalidity of the etymology in scientific terms is, of course, not a pertinent objection).

33. On the implications of the reference to a Virgilian Arcadia, see Bowra 1928, who also points out that neither Arcadia nor the Itys-Philomela myth is mentioned elsewhere in Horace.

34. Race 1978. Cf. Putnam 1986, 207–8. For the social dimension of invitational odes, see Murray 1985.

35. On the common topoi, see Race 1978, 184; Du Quesnay 1981, 90–97, with references cited therein.

36. *Aen.* 4.384 (*atris ignibus*); 11.186 (*ignibus atris*).

37. Cf. *Epist.* 1.5.14–15: "potare et spargere flores / incipiam, patiarque vel inconsultus haberi" ("I shall begin to quaff wine and scatter flowers, and let you regard me even as indiscreet").

CHAPTER 4

1. The rationale for considering praise and blame together is well established: they often share the same topical matrix (motifs of blame are often simply the inverse of those of praise). On the antiquity of the generic affiliation, see Nagy 1979, 222–42.

2. As Bundy demonstrated, the priamel is richly polymorphous (there are, after all, myriad ways of constructing a list!). On the pervasiveness of the device, see Race 1982. Santirocco (1986) is aware of the dual morphology of *C.* 1.7 (*recusatio* + priamel). In the perspective we have adopted here, *recusatio* and priamel both promote generic disavowal.

3. E.g., *Aptum . . . equis* [Argos] = ἱππόβοτον; *ditisque* [Mycenas] = πολυχρύσοιο (cf. Kiessling-Heinze *ad* line 9).

4. *Carmen perpetuum* presumably translates ἐν ἄεισμα διηνεκὲς (Call. *Aetia,* line 3 [Pfeiffer]). E. J. Kenney (1976) is extremely illuminating in this regard. Bundy 1972 should act as a brake against rash speculation about a historical polemic behind conventional stances such as these.

5. Despite the thoughtful qualifications of David Kovacs (1987), Kenney's observations on the parsimony of Ovid's proem to the *Metamorphoses* are still cogent (Kenney 1976).

6. On the topos of *alter Homerus* in *C.* 1.6, see Davis 1987b.

7. So also is the Archytas ode (*C.* 1.28), on which see the cogent and comprehensive analysis of Frischer 1984. Meter, by itself, does not, however, determine tone and manner. Horace's gross travesty in *Ep.* 12 deals with scurrilous "iambic" matter in the same rhythm! Stylistic decorum in antiquity is a regulative principle, not a constitutive rule (for the distinction see Searle 1969, 33–42).

8. Summaries of different interpretations are given in Wickham and Nisbet-Hubbard *ad loc.* Erasmus's justly famous emendation, *decerptae frondi,* has the advantage of restoring the notion of *preference* to *praeponere,* but at some cost to the figure of the *corona.*

9. On the dismissal of the distant in favor of the proximate, see Archilochus 19 W. Horace may also be decrying the vogue of sterile, epideictic encomia that treat subjects far removed from the experience of the *laudator.*

10. The priamel is there reduced to two conventional foil terms, articulated in negative clauses—athletic victor (subdivided into boxer and charioteer) and triumphing soldier (lines 3–9). The cap is, as usual, the poet: *Aeolio carmine nobilem* (line 12).

11. Horace may be consciously imitating the description of the trans-
fixed lover in Archilochus 193 W:

δύστηνος ἔγκειμαι πόθωι,
ἄψυχος, χαλεπῆισι θεῶν ὀδύνηισιν ἕκητι
πεπαρμένος δι' ὀστέων.

Abject I lie with desire, lifeless, pierced through the bones with grievous
pains inflicted by the gods.

The first line of the same epode may also refer to another Archilochean
passage, 215 W:

καί μ' οὔτ' ἰάμβων οὔτε τερπωλέων μέλει.

I have no heart either for iambic verses or for pleasures.

12. Commentators also compare the sentiments expressed in Archilochus 22 W:

οὐ γάρ τι καλὸς χῶρος οὐδ' ἐφίμερος
οὐδ' ἐρατός, οἶος ἀμφὶ Σίριος ῥοάς.

For there is no land as beautiful or desirable or lovely as that by the
streams of the Siris.

13. Borszák 1984 (*app. crit. ad* line 15) documents MS authority for the
bifurcation. Even Porphyrio, a commentator not distinguished for his
sagacity, balks at dividing the ode, though on the grounds that the addressee was from the Tibur region ("Plancus enim inde [sc. Tibure] fuit
oriundus").

14. I employ the term *pragmatics* in the technical sense current in modern linguistic theory. An overview of the movement and its major tenets is
succinctly provided by Leech 1983.

15. The MS variant *perpetuos* would not, if preferred, affect the repetition, since the adjective is to be construed adverbially.

16. The reading *Haediliae* (proper name) was rightly condemned by
Bentley, but like the equally ludicrous *Pullia* at *C.* 3.4.10, it is occasionally
revived by modern editors intent on trivializing the *Carmina*.

17. In Sappho's hymn to Aphrodite (1 LP) previous theophanies of the
goddess are implied in the hypomnesis (reminder) segment. The Akka-
dian "Hymn to Ishtar" (translated in Pritchard 1955, 383) engineers a divine fait accompli in its closing "request" segment.

18. Cf. Virgil *Ecl.* 4.22.

19. On the further significance of the wolf in relation to the *locus* of
lyric, see Davis 1987a.

20. A symbolic signification for these features cannot, of course, be
ruled out in view of passages like 3.4.5–8. Consult Troxler-Keller 1964,
40–47, under the subheading "Musenhain—*nemus.*"

21. I have adopted this MS variant in preference to *hic*.

22. *Honores* connote poetic accolades in the ode to Lamia (*C.* 1.26.10: "nil sine me / prosunt *honores*").

23. The suggestion here put forward of a "remodeled" Penelope is in conflict with the common view that Horace is upholding the pristine Homeric antithesis between the two female characters (cf. Kiessling-Heinze *ad* line 20).

24. For a reading that takes a more ironic view of the speaker's motivation, see Pucci 1975.

25. A brief, but densely informative, article by H. J. Mette (1961) is devoted to this theme in the *Odes*.

26. This sense of *otium* occurs at *C.* 1.15.3.

27. Pöschl 1970 has, in my judgment, thoroughly demolished the jejune hypothesis of an interpolated *Cura*-strophe.

28. *S.* 2.7.111–15 (through the mouthpiece of Davus); *Epist.* 1.11.25–30 (addressed to Bullatius).

29. The substantive Lucretian parallels are detailed and discussed in Pöschl 1970 and Nisbet-Hubbard *ad loc.*

30. See also *Epist.* 1.11.28–29 (quoted above, p. 209): "*navibus atque / quadrigis* petimus bene vivere."

31. So Klingner 1964, 451, in a passage citing with approval the insight of Wehrli.

32. Call. *Ep.* 28; *Aetia*, lines 25–28 (Pfeiffer).

33. See the "Index of Greek Words" in Bundy under the entry φθόνος. Further illumination of the motif is to be found in Race 1987, 133–36; Miller 1982.

34. Cf. *verae Parcae* at Horace *Carm. saec.* line 25.

35. From the poem "The Choice" (Yeats [1933] 1956), 242; Gigon 1977 reveals some of the intellectual sophistication in Horace's lyric vision. The thought trajectory of the *Otium divos* is closely analogous to that of *Quid dedicatum* (*C.* 1.31).

36. To my knowledge, there is no generally accepted pair of terms within the critical discourse on invective that would correspond to *laudator* and *laudandus* (the pair made current by Bundy's *Studia Pindarica*). The utility of the pair *detractor* and *detractandus* for our analyses lies in the implicit recognition of the conventional and representative aspects of most ancient *detractiones*.

37. *Euro*, which I have adopted, is the very plausible Renaissance emendation of the MSS *Hebro*. The conceit in *hiemis sodali* has an intriguing parallel in *C.* 4.12.1, where the zephyrs are dubbed "veris *comites.*"

38. Cf. Syndikus, 246, refuting Orelli (*ad loc.*).

39. Consult Nisbet-Hubbard *ad loc.* Copley 1956, the *locus classicus*, ascribes a puritanical flavor to Horace's denigration that is plainly anachronistic (pp. 58–60).

40. See the poem "After Long Silence" (Yeats [1933] 1956, 260, line 7).

41. Horace produces a complete version of the genre in *C.* 3.10 (*Extremum Tanain*). It is noteworthy that the lyric *exclusus* there undercuts his

abject attitude at the close by asserting that he will not be prostrate forever: "*non* hoc *semper* erit liminis aut aquae / caelestis patiens latus."

42. This vitriolic ode forms a thematic pendant to the *querela* of C. 3.10 (also directed at a woman named Lyce), on which see note 41 above. If indeed the *detractanda* is the same (as the coincidence of name and theme suggests), then we have another example of the triumph of the *exclusus* who lives to see his former tormentor become an *exclusa* in her turn.

43. The ethical criterion here appears to predominate over the purely social. The spouse of Ibycus, presumably a *matrona*, is in the same behavioral category as the courtesans, Lyce and Lydia. All three are faulted, not for sexual mores per se, but for ignoring or denying the *modus* of age.

44. The expression *fidem / mutatosque deos* has been plausibly read as a zeugma (*fidem mutatam . . .*).

45. The replicated lament, with its implied corollary of replicated misfortune, is the speaker's way of disclosing the obtuseness of the *detractandus*—a point passed over by Bentley, who objected to *insolens* because it *logically* contradicts *quotiens* and therefore rejection would cease to be unfamiliar after the first incidence, the *puer* becoming thereby *expertus* and then *assuetus*.

46. Since *deus* may be common gender, emendation is, from a strictly grammatical point of view, unnecessary even for those who support the identity of the divinity as Venus—an observation that I owe to my former colleague Michael Wigodsky.

47. E.g., Nisbet-Hubbard *ad loc.*: "[but] Pyrrha and her friends are not wearing garlands (as some imagine), but lying on the petals (as *multa* shows)."

48. Interestingly enough, the only other occurrence of the word *rosa* in the entire Horatian *corpus* is in *Odes* 4.10.3, where the rose bloom is a metaphor for the evanescent youth and beauty of the addressee, Ligurinus. The ode is a *querela* and reflects several *loci communes* discussed above in connection with the excluded lover.

49. Bentley's emendation, *incomptam . . . comam . . . nodo*, is both ingenious and eminently logical, but if accepted, would remove the suggestion of *munditiae* in the word *comptum*. Part of the point of the cosmetic topos, I believe, is to contrast simplicity and neatness of appearance with duplicity of behavior.

50. Horace here envisages a private symposium of his *sodales* that coincides with the public celebration mentioned in the historical sources (cf. Syndikus, 333; Pöschl 1970, 76–78). As several scholars have pointed out, a *lectisternium* (suggested in *ornare pulvinar deorum*) is not to be confused with a *supplicatio*.

51. A fastidiously particularistic reading of *Saliaribus . . . dapibus* is offered by Hardie (1976, 133–34) who imagines the ode as uttered by a chorus representing the *collegium* of Salian priests! The proverbial association of "Salian" with "sumptuous" is manifest in C. 1.36.12; 4.1.28.

52. The Alcaeus tag (332 LP) foregrounds the excessiveness of the commended drinking spree:

νῦν χρῆ μεθύσθην καί τινα πὲρ βίαν
πώνην, ἐπεὶ δὴ κάτθανε Μύρσιλος, . . .

Now it is time for one to get drunk and do some powerful drinking, since Myrsilos is dead . . .

53. Wickham *ad loc.* provides a sound exposition of the idiomatic use of the imperfect in this phrase.

54. Cf. Hardie 1976; Fraenkel, 158 ff.

55. The fact that the similes feature animals has misled some readers into supposing that the effect may be intended to be derogatory—a supposition confounded by a glance at the Homeric prototypes, which clearly do not detract from the warriors.

56. Fraenkel's clarification is worth quoting: "Here *monstrum*, in this case a *monstrum* brought about by Rome's *fata*, probably contains less of what we hear in monster and more of what a Greek heard in τέρας, a Roman in *portentum* or *prodigium*, something outside the norm of nature, something at which we look with wonder and often with horror." Cf. Verdière 1968, 9.

57. Even if we concede with Nisbet-Hubbard *ad loc.* that Cleopatra may also be approximated to a "monster" (in the semantics of the English cognate), she nonetheless remains larger than life. We need only recall the cosmic status of the Olympians' adversaries in the mythical battles against Titans and Giants—*monstra* whose subjugation is a prerequisite for a civilized order. The analogy between mythic *monstra* and historical opponents of Caesar Augustus is made explicit in the lengthy encomium of 3.4.

58. Virgil utilizes this repeated phrase to close the hexameter five times in the *Aeneid* (2.680; 3.26; 8.81; 9.120; 10.637) and once in the *Georgics* (4.554). On the possible connotation of "wonder" inhering in *monstrum*, see the citation of Fraenkel (note 56 above).

59. This aspect of her transformation reflects her total displacement of the unmentionable soldier, Antonius, in Horace's narration.

60. Since the rearing cobra had sacral meaning in the iconology of Egyptian theocracy, the very form of Cleopatra's suicide implies ennoblement.

61. The Horatian portrait of a transmuted Cleopatra has an intriguing afterlife in Renaissance art. Michelangelo's two drawings of the death scene reflect contrasting conceptions of her emotional condition: in the published version (Florence, Casa Buonarroti inv. 2F *recto*), he depicts her imbibing the venom with composure; in a recently recovered alternate sketch, however, her expression is distraught and fearful, with open mouth signifying a shriek of pain. Whatever may prove to be the ultimate source(s) of the iconography of both versions, the mutation offers a parallel with Horace's narrative representation. Despite sporadic skepticism in

learned quarters about the authenticity of the published drawing, the attribution to Michelangelo is now generally accepted (see Hirst 1988, 116–17). The earlier version has only very recently been recovered from the *verso*, where it remained in partial obscurity until Florentine conservators were making preparations for the exhibit "Michelangelo Draftsman," which opened at the National Gallery, Washington, D.C., in 1988 (for further details see Kimmelman 1988).

62. Although the name Cleopatra is deleted from Horace's ode, it is no less "conspicuous by its absence." With *generosius* and *non humilis*, the *laudator* may be engaging in etymological wordplay (*kleos*, glory; *patra*, clan). The nobility that the queen regenerates—the Ptolemaic lineage—is, of course, not Egyptian but Macedonian in origin.

References

The following list comprises all works cited in the text and notes except those works already itemized in the list of abbreviations.

Abrams, Meyer H. 1953. *The Mirror and the Lamp: Romantic Theory and the Critical Tradition*. New York: Oxford University Press.

Alfonsi, L. 1943. "Studi di poesia Augustea (1): Su Valgio Rufo," *Aevum* 17, 242–46.

Anderson, R. D., P. J. Parsons, and R. G. M. Nisbet. 1979. "Elegiacs by Gallus from Qaṣr Ibrîm." *Journal of Roman Studies* 69, 125–55.

Anderson, William S. 1966. "Horace *Carm.* 1.14: What Kind of Ship?" *Classical Philology* 61, 84–98.

———. 1968. "Two Odes of Horace's Book Two." *California Studies in Classical Antiquity* 1, 35–61.

Austin, John L. 1962. *How to Do Things with Words*. Ed. J. O. Urmson and Marina Sbisà. 2d ed. Cambridge, Mass.: Harvard University Press.

Bailey, D. R. Shackleton. 1982. *Profile of Horace*. Cambridge, Mass.: Harvard University Press.

———, ed. 1985. *Horatius Opera*. Stuttgart: Teubner.

Becker, Carl. 1963. *Das Spätwerk des Horaz*. Göttingen: Vandenhoeck & Ruprecht.

Borzsák, Stephanus, ed. 1984. *Q. Horati Flacci opera*. Leipzig: Teubner.

Bowra, Cecil Maurice. 1928. "Horace, *Odes* IV.12." *Classical Review* 42, 165–67.

———. 1961. *Greek Lyric Poetry*. Oxford: Oxford University Press.

Brendel, Otto. [1934] 1980. "Observations on the Allegory of the Pompeian Death's-Head Mosaic." In *The Visible Idea: Interpretations of Classical Art.* Translated by Maria Brendel. Washington, D.C.: Decatur House Press.

Bundy, Elroy L. 1972. "The 'Quarrel' between Kallimachos and Apollonios, Part 1: The Epilogue of Kallimachos' *Hymn to Apollo*." *California Studies in Classical Antiquity* 5.

Cairns, Francis. 1971. "Five 'Religious' Odes of Horace." *AJP* 92, 433–52.

———. 1972. *Generic Composition in Greek and Roman Poetry*. Edinburgh: Edinburgh University Press.

———. 1977. "Horace on Other People's Love Affairs (*Odes* I.27; II.4; I.8; III.12)." *Quaderni urbinati di cultura classica* 24, 121–47.

———. 1978. "The Genre Palinode and Three Horatian Examples: *Epode,* 17; *Odes,* 1, 16; *Odes,* 1, 34." *L'Antiquité Classique* 47, 546–52.

————. 1979. *Tibullus: A Hellenistic Poet at Rome*. New York: Cambridge University Press.

Conington, John, and Henry Nettleship, eds. 1898. *The Works of Virgil*. Vol. 1. 5th ed. Rev. F. Haverfield. London: George Bell & Sons.

Conte, Gian Biagio. 1986. *The Rhetoric of Imitation: Genre and Poetic Memory in Virgil and Other Latin Poets*. Translated by Charles Segal. Ithaca, N.Y.: Cornell University Press.

Copley, Frank O. 1956. *Exclusus Amator: A Study in Latin Love Poetry* (= *APA Philological Monographs* 17). Madison, Wis.: American Philological Association.

Dacier, André, ed. [1681] 1727. *Oeuvres d'Horace*. Vol. 1. 4th ed. Amsterdam: Wetstein.

Daube, David. 1974. "Withdrawal: Five Verbs." *California Studies in Classical Antiquity* 7, 93–112.

Davis, Gregson. 1968. "Studies in the Narrative Economy of Ovid's Metamorphoses." Ph.D. diss., University of California, Berkeley.

————. 1975. "The *Persona* of Licymnia: A Revaluation of Horace *Carm.* 2.12." *Philologus* 1.119, 70–83.

————. 1983a. *The Death of Procris: "Amor" and the Hunt in Ovid's Metamorphoses* (= *Instrumentum Litterarum* 2). Rome: Ateneo.

————. 1983b. "Silence and Decorum: Encomiastic Convention and the Epilogue of Horace *Carm.* 3.2." *Classical Antiquity* 2.1, 9–26.

————. 1987a. "*Carmina/Iambi*: The Literary-Generic Dimension of Horace's *Integer vitae* (*C.* 1,22)." *Quaderni urbinati di cultura classica*, n.s., 27.3, 67–78.

————. 1987b. "*Quis . . . digne scripserit?*: The *topos* of *alter Homerus* in Horace *C.* 1.6." *Phoenix* 41.3, 292–95.

————. 1989. "*Ingenii cumba*: Literary Aporia and the Rhetoric of Horace *C.* 1.14." *Rheinisches Museum* 132, 331–45.

Detienne, Marcel. 1974. "Orphée au miel." In *Faire de l'histoire*, ed. Jacques Le Goff and Pierre Nora, vol. 3, 56–75. Paris: Gallimard.

De Witt, Norman W. 1954. *Epicurus and His Philosophy*. Minneapolis: University of Minnesota Press.

Dover, Kenneth. 1964. "The Poetry of Archilochus." In *Archiloque* (= *Fondation Hardt Entretiens* 10), 181–212. Geneva: Fondation Hardt.

Du Quesnay, Ian M. 1981. "Vergil's First Eclogue." *Papers of the Liverpool Latin Seminar*, vol. 3 (= *ARCA Classical and Medieval Texts, Papers and Monographs* 7). Liverpool: Francis Cairns.

Eisenhut, Werner. 1961. "*Deducere carmen*. Ein Beitrag zum Problem der literarischen Beziehungen zwischen Horaz und Properz." In *Gedenkschrift für Georg Rohde* (= *Untersuchungen zur klassischen Philologie und Geschichte des Altertums* 4), 91–104. Tübingen: Max Niemeyer Verlag.

Festa, Nicola. 1940. "Asterie." *Rendiconti della classe di scienze morali e storiche dell'academia d'Italia* 7,1, 65–69.

Fraenkel, Eduard. 1932–33. *Das Pindargedicht des Horaz*. Sitzungsberichte der Heidelberger Akademie der Wissenschaften, Philosophisch-historische Klasse. 2. Abhandlung. Heidelberg: Karl Winter.

Fries, Richard. 1983. "The Catalogue of Pindaric Genres in Horace: *Carm.* 4.2." *Classical Antiquity* 2.1, 27–36.

Frischer, Bernard. 1984. "Horace and the Monuments: A New Interpretation of the Archytas Ode (*C.* 1.28)." *Harvard Studies in Classical Philology* 88, 73–102.

Frontisi-Ducroux, F., and F. Lissarrague. 1983. "De l'ambiguité à l'ambivalence." *Annali del seminario di studi del mondo classico* 5, 11–32.

Frost, Robert. 1969. *The Poetry of Robert Frost.* New York: Holt, Rinehart and Winston.

Giangrande, Giuseppe. 1968. "Sympotic Literature and Epigram." In *Epigramme grecque* (= Fondation Hardt Entretiens 14), 91–173. Geneva: Fondation Hardt.

Gigon, Olof. 1977. "Horaz und die Philosophie." In *Die antike Philosophie als Maßstab und Realität.* Zurich and Munich: Artemis.

Gombrich, Ernst H. 1960. *Art and Illusion: A Study in the Psychology of Pictorial Representation.* Princeton: Princeton University Press.

Gow, Andrew S. F. 1950. *Theocritus,* 2 vols. Cambridge: Cambridge University Press.

Griffith, Mark. 1983. "Personality in Hesiod." *Classical Antiquity* 2.1, 37–65.

Habinek, Thomas M. 1986. "The Marriageability of Maximus: Horace, Ode 4.1.13–20." *American Journal of Philology* 107, 407–16.

Hardie, A. 1976. "Horace Odes 1.37 and Pindar *Dith.* 2." *Papers of the Liverpool Latin Seminar* 1, 113–29.

Harrison, Geoffrey. 1987. "The Confessions of Lucilius (Horace *Sat.* 2.1.30–34): A Defense of Autobiographical Satire?" *Classical Antiquity* 6.1, 36–52.

Hendrickson, G. 1918. "An Epigram of Philodemus and Two Latin Congeners." *American Journal of Philology* 39, 28–43.

Henrichs, Albert. 1980. "Riper than a Pear: Parian Invective in Theokritos." *Zeitschrift für Papyrologie und Epigraphik* 39, 7–17.

Hirst, Michael. 1988. *Michelangelo and His Drawings.* New Haven: Yale University Press.

Jakobson, Roman. 1960. "Linguistics and Poetics." In *Style in Language*, ed. T. Seboek. Cambridge, Mass: MIT Press.

Johnson, W. Ralph. 1967. "A Queen, a Great Queen? Cleopatra and the Politics of Misrepresentation." *Arion* 6, 387–402.

Kambylis, Athanasios. 1965. *Die Dichterweihe und ihre Symbolik: Untersuchungen zu Hesiodos, Kallimachos, Properz und Ennius.* Heidelberg: Karl Winter.

Kenney, E. J. 1976. "Ovidius Prooemians." *Proceedings of the Cambridge Philological Society* 22, 46–53.

Kilpatrick, R. 1969. "Two Horatian Proems: *Carm.* 1.26 and 1.32." *Yale Classical Studies,* 216–29.

Kimmelman, Michael. 1988. "Newly Revealed Michelangelo to Be Shown." *New York Times,* Oct 5, c19.

Klingner, Friedrich. 1964. *Studien zur griechischen und römischen Literatur.* Zurich and Stuttgart: Artemis.

Kovacs, David. 1987. "Ovid, *Metamorphoses* 1.2." *Classical Quarterly* 37, 458–65.

Kristeva, Julia. 1984. *Revolution in Poetic Language.* Translated by Margaret Waller. New York: Columbia University Press.

Leach, Edmund R. 1961. "Two Essays concerning the Symbolic Representation of Time." In *Rethinking Anthropology.* London: Athlone Press.

Leach, Elinor W. 1971. "Horace's *pater optimus* and Terence's Demea: Autobiographical Fiction and Comedy in *Sermo,* 1.4." *American Journal of Philology* 92, 616–32.

Leech, Geoffrey N. 1983. *Principles of Pragmatics.* New York: Longman.

Leeman, Anton D. [1965] 1985. "Die dramatische Form der Cleopatra-Ode." In *Form und Sinn: Studien zur römischen Literatur (1854–1984).* Frankfurt am Main and New York: Peter Lang.

Lefkowitz, Mary R. 1981. *The Lives of the Greek Poets.* Baltimore: Johns Hopkins University Press.

Levertov, Denise. 1961. *The Jacob's Ladder.* New York: New Directions.

Levinson, Stephen C. 1983. *Pragmatics.* New York: Cambridge University Press.

Lieberg, Godo. 1965. "Die Bedeutung des Festes bei Horaz." In *Synusia: Festgabe für W. Schadewaldt,* ed. H. Flasher and K. Gaiser. Pfüllingen: Neske.

Lyons, John. 1968. *Introduction to Theoretical Linguistics.* London and New York: Cambridge University Press.

———. 1977. *Semantics.* Vol. 2. Cambridge: Cambridge University Press.

Mackay, L. A. 1962. "Odes 1, 16 and 17: *O matre pulchra . . . , Velox amoenum . . .*" *American Journal of Philology* 83, 298–300.

Marcovich, Miroslav. 1975. "A New Poem of Archilochus: *P. Colon.* inv. 7511." *Greek, Roman and Byzantine Studies* 16, 5–14.

Mette, Hans Joachim. 1961. "*Genus tenue* und *mensa tenuis* bei Horaz." *Museum Helveticum* 18, 136–39.

Miller, Andrew M. 1982. "*Phthonos* and *Parphasis:* The Argument of Nemean 8.19–34." *Greek, Roman and Byzantine Studies* 23, 111–20.

Murray, Oswyn. 1985. "Symposium and Genre in the Poetry of Horace." *Journal of Roman Studies* 75, 39–50.

Nagy, Gregory. 1979. *The Best of the Achaeans: Concepts of the Hero in Archaic Greek Poetry.* Baltimore: Johns Hopkins University Press.

Oates, Whitney J. 1932. "The Influence of Simonides of Ceos upon Horace." Ph.D. diss. Princeton University.

Olivier, Frank. 1917. *Les Epodes d'Horace.* Lausanne and Paris: Payot.

Onians, Richard B. 1951. *The Origins of European Thought about the Body, the Mind, the Soul, the World, Time, and Fate.* Cambridge: Cambridge University Press.

Page, Denys. 1955. *Sappho and Alcaeus: An Introduction to the Study of Ancient Lesbian Poetry*. Oxford: Oxford University Press.

Palmer, Frank R. 1981. *Semantics*. 2d ed. New York: Cambridge University Press.

Pease, Arthur S. 1935. *P. Vergili Maronis Aeneidos liber quartus*. Cambridge, Mass.: Harvard University Press.

Perret, Jacques. 1964. *Horace*. Translated by Bertha Humez. New York: New York University Press.

Pöschl, Viktor. 1956. *Horaz und die Politik*. Sitzungsberichte der Heidelberger Akademie der Wissenschaften, Philosophisch-historische Klasse. 4. Abhandlung. Heidelberg: Karl Winter.

———. 1961. *Die grosse Maecenasode des Horaz (c. 3.29)*. Sitzungsberichte der Heidelberger Akademie der Wissenschaften, Philosophisch-historische Klasse. 1. Abhandlung. Heidelberg: Karl Winter.

———. 1970. *Horazische Lyrik: Interpretationen*. Heidelberg: Karl Winter.

Pritchard, James B. 1955. *Ancient Near Eastern Texts Relating to the Old Testament*. Princeton: Princeton University Press.

Pucci, Pietro. 1975. "Horace's Banquet in Odes 1, 17." *Transactions of the American Philological Association* 105, 259–81.

Putnam, Michael J. 1986. *Artifices of Eternity: Horace's Fourth Book of Odes*. Ithaca, N.Y.: Cornell University Press.

Quinn, Kenneth. 1963. *Latin Explorations: Critical Studies in Latin Literature*. 2d impression, with corrections, 1969. London: Routledge & Kegan Paul.

Race, William H. 1972. "The 'Vaunt' in Pindar." Ph.D. diss. Stanford University.

———. 1978. "*Odes* 1.20: An Horatian *Recusatio*." *California Studies in Classic Antiquity* 11, 179–96.

———. 1982. *The Classical Priamel from Homer to Boethius* (= *Mnemosyne* suppl. 74). Leiden: Brill.

———. 1987. "Pindaric Encomium and Isokrates' *Evagoras*." *Transactions of the American Philological Association* 117, 131–55.

Reitzenstein, Erich. 1931. "Zur Stiltheorie des Kallimachos." In *Festschrift Richard Reitzenstein*, 23–69. Leipzig and Berlin: Teubner.

Reitzenstein, Richard. 1963. *Aufsätze zu Horaz. Abhandlungen und Vorträge aus den Jahren 1908–1925*. Darmstadt: Wissenschaftliche Buchgesellschaft.

Rosen, Charles. 1988. *Sonata Forms*. Rev. ed. New York: Norton.

Rostagni, Augusto. 1961. *Virgilio minore*. 2d ed., revised and enlarged. Rome: Storia e letteratura.

Russell, Donald A. 1981. *Criticism in Antiquity*. Berkeley and Los Angeles: University of California Press.

Santirocco, Matthew. 1986. *Unity and Design in Horace's Odes*. Chapel Hill: University of North Carolina Press.

Searle, John R. 1969. *Speech Acts: An Essay in the Philosophy of Language*. Cambridge: Cambridge University Press.

Shankman, Stephen. 1988. "The Pindaric Tradition and the Quest for Pure Poetry." *Comparative Literature* 40.3, 219–44.

Shorey, Paul, and Gordon Laing, eds. 1919. *Horace: Odes and Epodes.* Boston: B. H. Sanborn. Reprint. Pittsburgh: University of Pittsburgh Press, 1960.

Slater, W. J. 1969. "Futures in Pindar." *Classical Quarterly* 63, 19, 86–94.

Smith, Clement L., ed. 1931. *The Odes and Epodes of Horace.* 2d ed. Washington, D.C.: Catholic University Press.

Syme, Ronald. 1978. *History in Ovid.* New York: Oxford University Press.

———. 1986. *The Augustan Aristocracy.* Oxford: Clarendon Press.

Treu, Max. 1949. "Zu Alkaios 82D (32L) und Horaz C. 1.26." *Würzburger Jahrbücher* 4, 219–25.

———. [1955] 1968. *Von Homer zur Lyrik: Wandlungen des griechischen Weltbildes im Spiegel der Sprache* (= *Zetemata* 12). Munich: Beck.

Trimpi, Wesley. 1973. "The Meaning of Horace's *ut pictura poesis.*" *Journal of the Warburg and Courtauld Institutes* 36, 1–34.

Troxler-Keller, Irene. 1964. *Die Dichterlandschaft des Horaz.* Heidelberg: Karl Winter.

Trumpf, Jürgen. 1973. "Über das Trinken in der Poesie des Alkaios." *Zeitschrift für Papyrologie und Epigraphik* 12, 139–60.

Verdière, Raoul. 1968. "*Fatale Monstrum* (Horace, *Carm.* 1, 37, 21)." *Maia* 1.20, 7–9.

Versnel, H. S. 1970. *Triumphus: An Inquiry into the Origin, Development and Meaning of the Roman Triumph.* Leiden: Brill.

Vessey, D. W. T. 1985. "From Mountain to Lover's Tryst: Horace's Soracte Ode." *Journal of Roman Studies* 75, 26–38.

Webster, Thomas B. L. [1959] 1961. *Greek Art and Literature, 700–530 B.C.: The Beginnings of Modern Civilization.* New York: Praeger.

Wehrli, Fritz. 1946. "Der erhabene und der schlichte Stil in der poetisch-rhetorischen Theorie der Antike." In *Phyllobolia für Peter von der Mühll zum 60. Geburtstag am 1. August 1945,* by Olof Gigon et al. Basel: B. Schwabe.

Weinstock, Stefan. 1971. *Divus Julius.* Oxford: Clarendon Press.

West, David A. 1967. *Reading Horace.* Edinburgh: Edinburgh University Press.

West, Martin L. 1974. *Studies in Greek Elegy and Iambus.* New York: De Gruyter.

———, ed. 1978. *Hesiod: Works and Days.* Oxford: Oxford University Press.

West, Martin L., and Rheinhold Merkelbach, eds. 1983. *Hesiod: Fragmenta Selecta.* In *Hesiodi Theogonia, Opera et Dies, Scutum,* ed. F. Solmsen. New York: Oxford University Press.

Whitman, Cedric. 1958. *Homer and the Heroic Tradition.* Cambridge, Mass.: Harvard University Press.

Williams, Gordon. 1969. *The Third Book of Horace's Odes.* Oxford: Clarendon Press.

Wimmel, Walter. 1960. *Kallimachos in Rom: Die Nachfolge seines apologetischen Dichtens in der Augusterzeit.* Wiesbaden: Franz Steiner.

Woodman, Anthony J. 1980. "The Craft of Horace in Odes 1.14." *Classical Philology* 75, 60–67.

Woodman, Anthony J., and David West. 1984. *Poetry and Politics in the Age of Augustus.* New York: Cambridge University Press.

Yeats, William Butler. [1933] 1956. *Collected Poems.* Def. ed. London: Macmillan.

Zumwalt, Nancy. 1977. "Horace's *Navis* of Love Poetry (*C.* 1.14)." *Classical World* 71, 249–54.

General Index

Achilles: as foil to lyrist, 91; as paradigm of lover, 20–21; as symposiast, 11–16
Alcaeus: diction of, imitated, 151, 175; elevated manner of, 139; light manner of, 140; as model for convivial poetry, 159, 237, 267n.52; as representative of lyric, 85–86, 246. *See also* Lyric: Lesbian, as model for Horatian
Alternation in nature. *See* Nature, alternation in
Amator exclusus. See Lover, excluded
Amor. See Desire, erotic
Anacreon. *See* Lyric speaker: Anacreon as model for
Archilochus: erotic diction of, imitated, 73, 264n.11; as paradigm of iambic poet, 76, 255n.76; as prototype of lyrist, 48, 91–94, 169, 246, 257nn.16,19, 263n.9, 264n.12
Aristotle: and doctrine of mean, 167, 170–71, 261n.17; and *ethos* of speaker, 5; and poetic unity, 9; and universal values in poetry, 1
Augustus. See *Laudandus:* Augustus as
Autobiography. See *Mythos*

Bacchus. *See* Muses: Bacchus in role of
Brevity, of life. *See* Mortality
Bucolic poetry. *See* Lyric: bucolic motifs in

Callimachus, poetic doctrine of, 120–22, 185–86, 191–93, 214–15, 263n.4
Carpe diem poetry: basic motifs of, 146–60, 163–72; binary structure of, 12, 148; defined, 145–46; ethical values in, 179–81; insight as element of, 146–47, 159, 177–79, 197; prescription as element of, 146, 151, 160–63, 187–88; *reprise* as element of, 148, 153; rhetorical schema of, 149–50; scene as element of, 146 (*see also* Nature, alternation in). *See also* Mortality; Symposium
Change. *See* Nature, alternation in; Vicissitude, human
Citation. *See* Lyric: direct speech in
Cleopatra. See *Detractandus:* Cleopatra as; *Laudandus:* Cleopatra as
Complementary: as rhetorical device, 84, 106, 110, 152, 163–67, 182, 197, 207, 210, 253n.45, 261n.6; as technical term in linguistics, 163, 252n.25
Convivium. See Symposium
Corona: as emblem of poem, 114–26, 204–5, 258n.36. *See also* Symposium: roses and

Death. *See* Mortality
Decorum: as principle of symposium, 170–72, 188, 222, 223, 229–30, 235–37, 267n.52; and style, 59, 67
Desire, erotic: as motif of lyric, 73–74, 129, 218–19, 222, 264n.11; renounced by lyrist, 63–65; return of, 65–71; and war, 19–22, 23–28, 64–65, 66, 251n.14 (*see also* Epic: heroes of, remodeled as lovers). *See also* Lover, excluded
Detractandus: Chloris as, 222–23; Cleopatra as, 233–37; Lyce as, 223–24; Lydia as, 216–22; Pyrrha's lover as, 224–33; as technical term in dispraise, 215–16, 265n.36
Disavowal, generic. *See* Genre, disavowal of
Dispraise. See *Detractandus; Iambos*

Elegy: complaint as typical of, 39–60, 184–85, 221–22; excessive mourning in, 40–41, 52–60; portrayal of lover in, 41–43, 45–50, 54–55; subversion by lyrist, 57–60
Encomium. *See* Praise
Epic: assimilation of, 11–39; consolatory topoi in, 56, disavowed speci-

Index of Passages Cited

The index lists only those passages from Greek and Latin authors that are quoted or discussed in the text. Passages cited in the notes as illustrative parallels are mainly excluded, unless they are actually quoted. Italic page numbers denote main discussions. The modern critical editions used as sources for textual quotations are Oxford Classical Texts unless otherwise indicated (in parentheses after the author or work).